JOHN CARTER
THE END

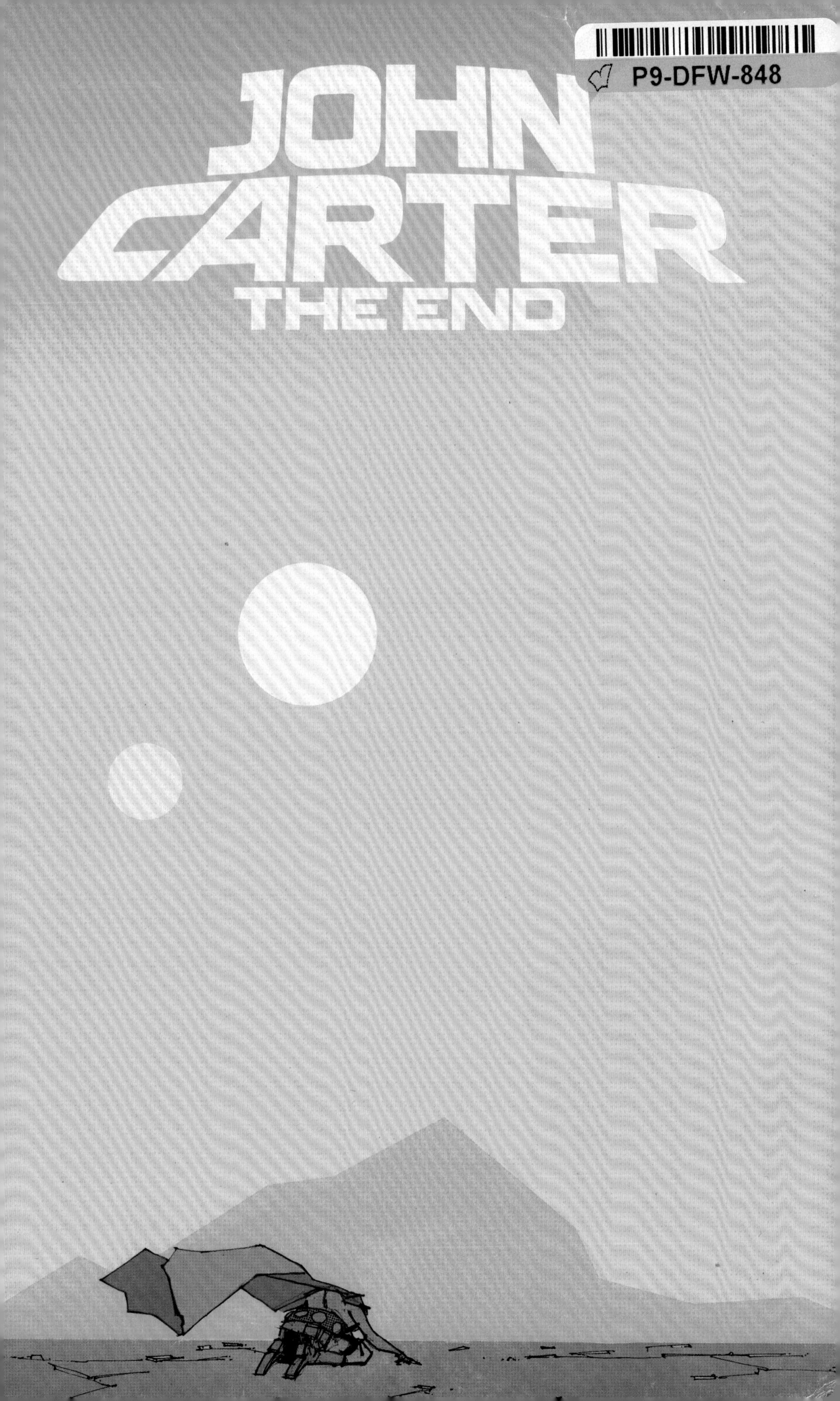

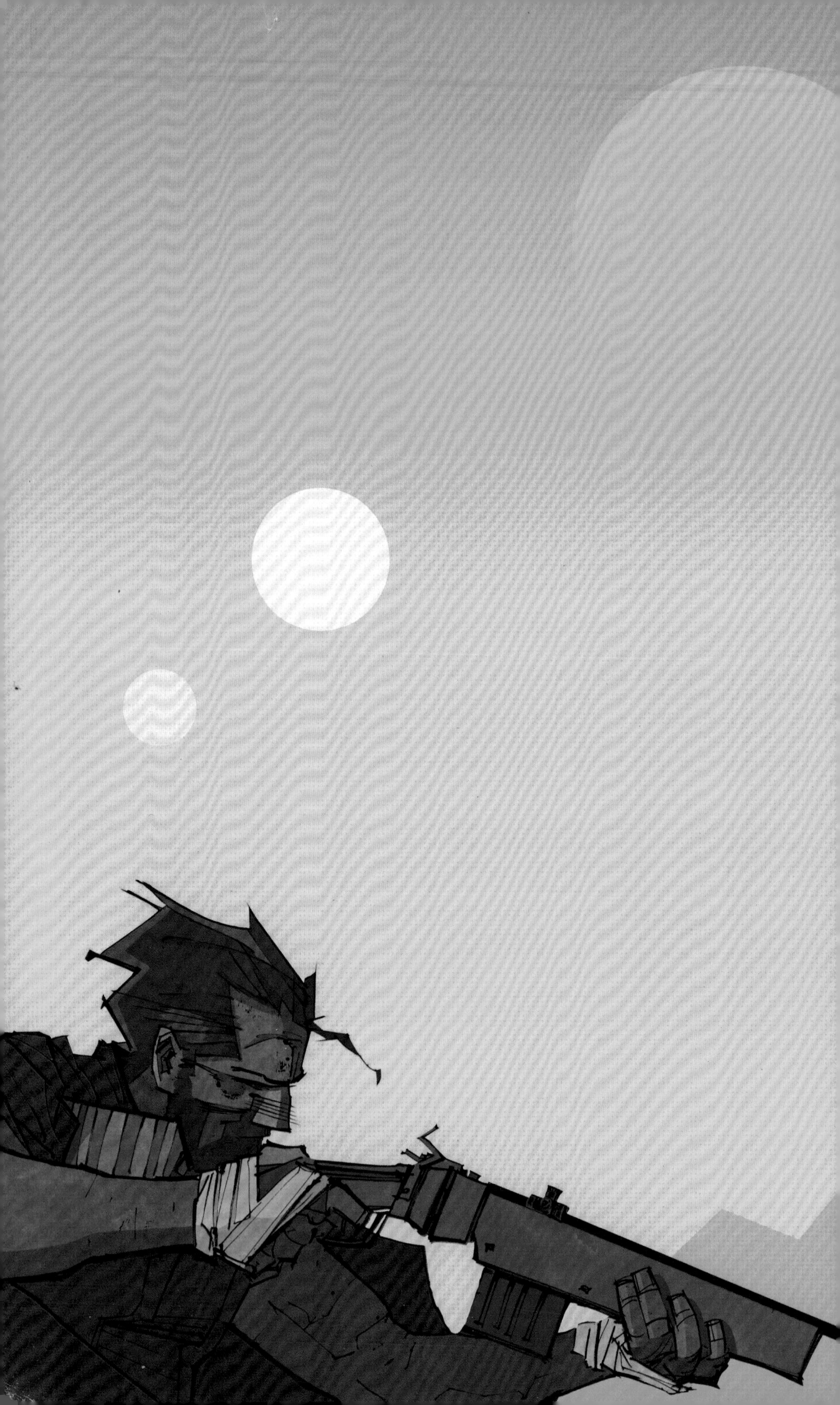

JOHN CARTER
THE END

WRITTEN BY **BRIAN WOOD** AND **ALEX COX**

ART BY **HAYDEN SHERMAN**

COLORS BY **CHRIS O'HALLORAN**

LETTERS BY **THOMAS NAPOLITANO**

COLLECTION COVER BY **JUAN DOE**

EDITS BY **ANTHONY MARQUES** AND **JOSEPH RYBANDT**

COLLECTION DESIGN BY **GEOFF HARKINS**

BASED ON THE STORIES AND CHARACTERS BY **EDGAR RICE BURROUGHS**

DYNAMITE.

Nick Barrucci, CEO / Publisher
Juan Collado, President / COO

Joe Rybandt, Executive Editor
Matt Idelson, Senior Editor
Anthony Marques, Associate Editor
Matt Humphreys, Assistant Editor
Kevin Ketner, Assistant Editor

Jason Ullmeyer, Art Director
Geoff Harkins, Senior Graphic Designer
Cathleen Heard, Graphic Designer
Alexis Persson, Production Artist
Chris Caniano, Digital Associate
Rachel Kilbury, Digital Assistant

Brandon Dante Primavera, V.P. of IT and Operations
Rich Young, Director of Business Development

Alan Payne, V.P. of Sales and Marketing
Keith Davidsen, Marketing Director
Pat O'Connell, Sales Manager

ISBN-13: 978-1-5241-0438-2
First Printing 10 9 8 7 6 5 4 3 2 1

Online at www.DYNAMITE.com | On Facebook /Dynamitecomics
On Instagram /Dynamitecomics | On Tumblr dynamitecomics.tumblr.com
On Twitter @dynamitecomics | On YouTube /Dynamitecomics

THE DEATH OF MARS!

CENTURIES HAVE PASSED AND TIME HAS TAKEN ITS TOLL. CONFLICT BURNS ACROSS THE LANDSCAPE OF BARSOOM. A WAR OF SUPREMACY AND GENOCIDE AT THE HANDS OF A BRUTAL DESPOT HAS BROUGHT THE PLANET TO THE EDGE OF COLLAPSE.

A SEARCH PARTY HAS FINALLY LOCATED AN AGED JOHN CARTER AND DEJAH THORIS, LIVING IN QUIET SECLUSION ON A DESERT MOON, IN PERPETUAL MOURNING FOR A LOST SON.
HOW COULD THEY BE MARS' LAST HOPE?

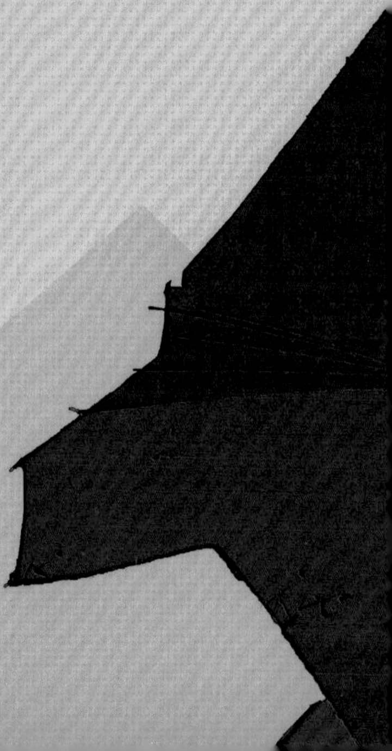

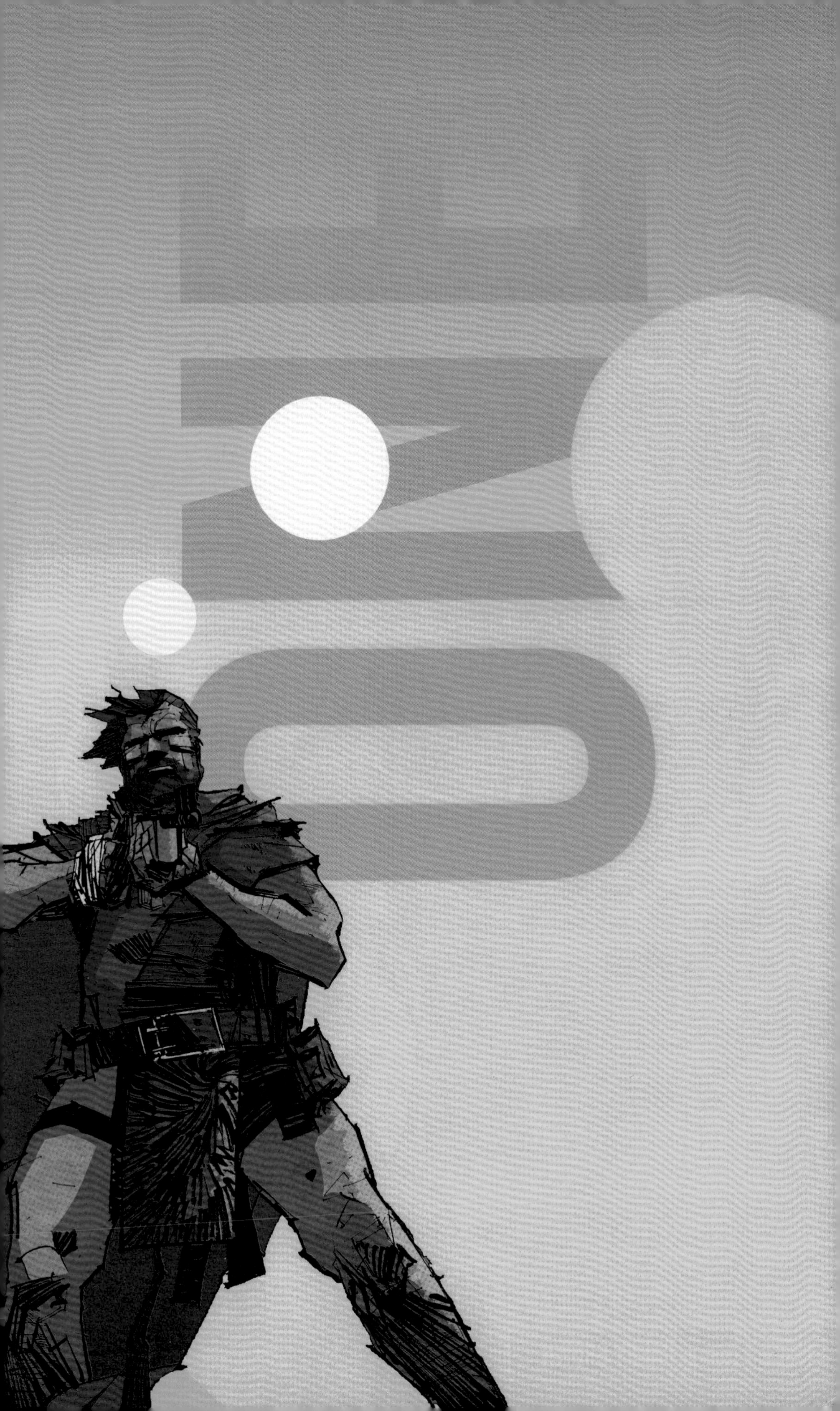

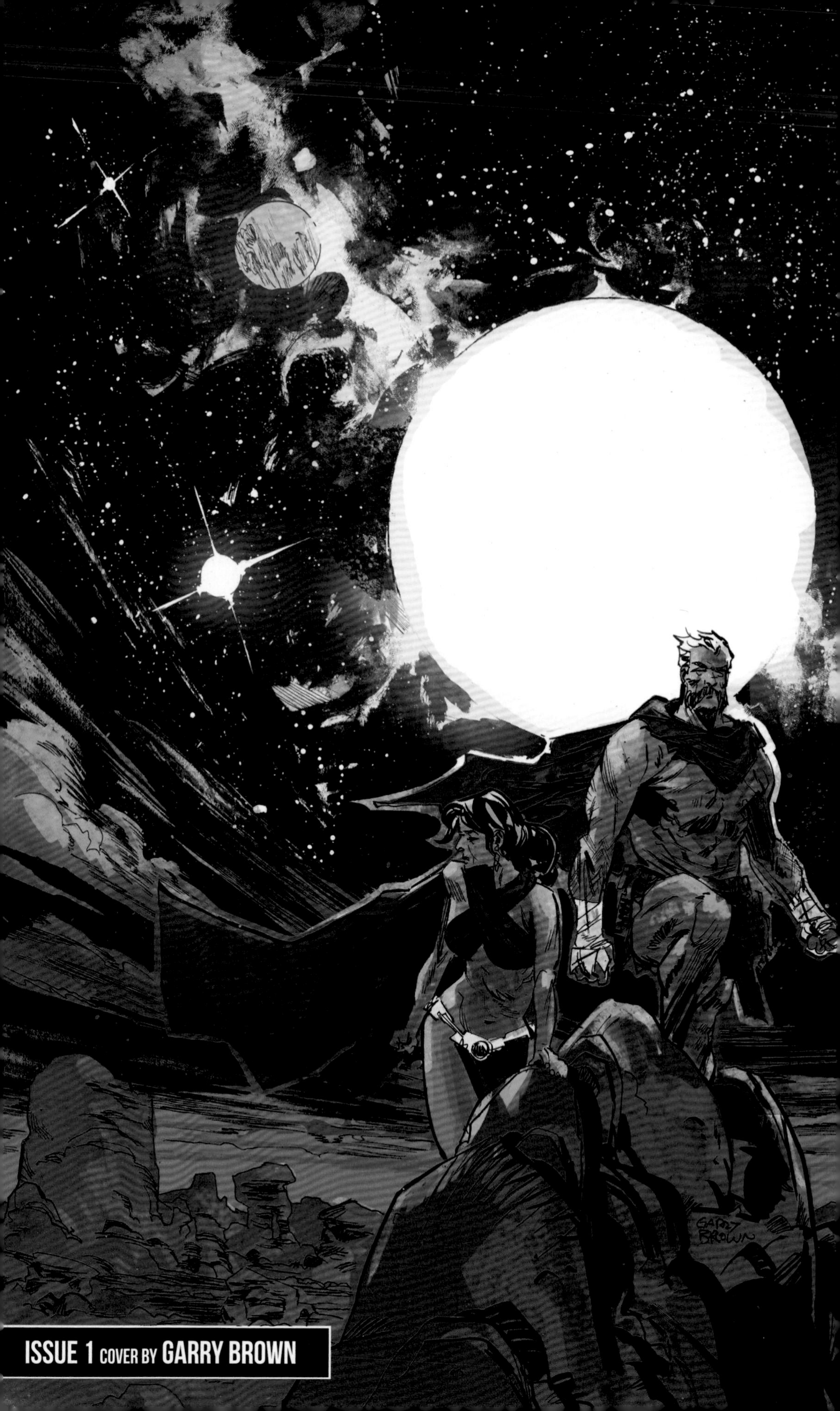

ISSUE 1 COVER BY GARRY BROWN

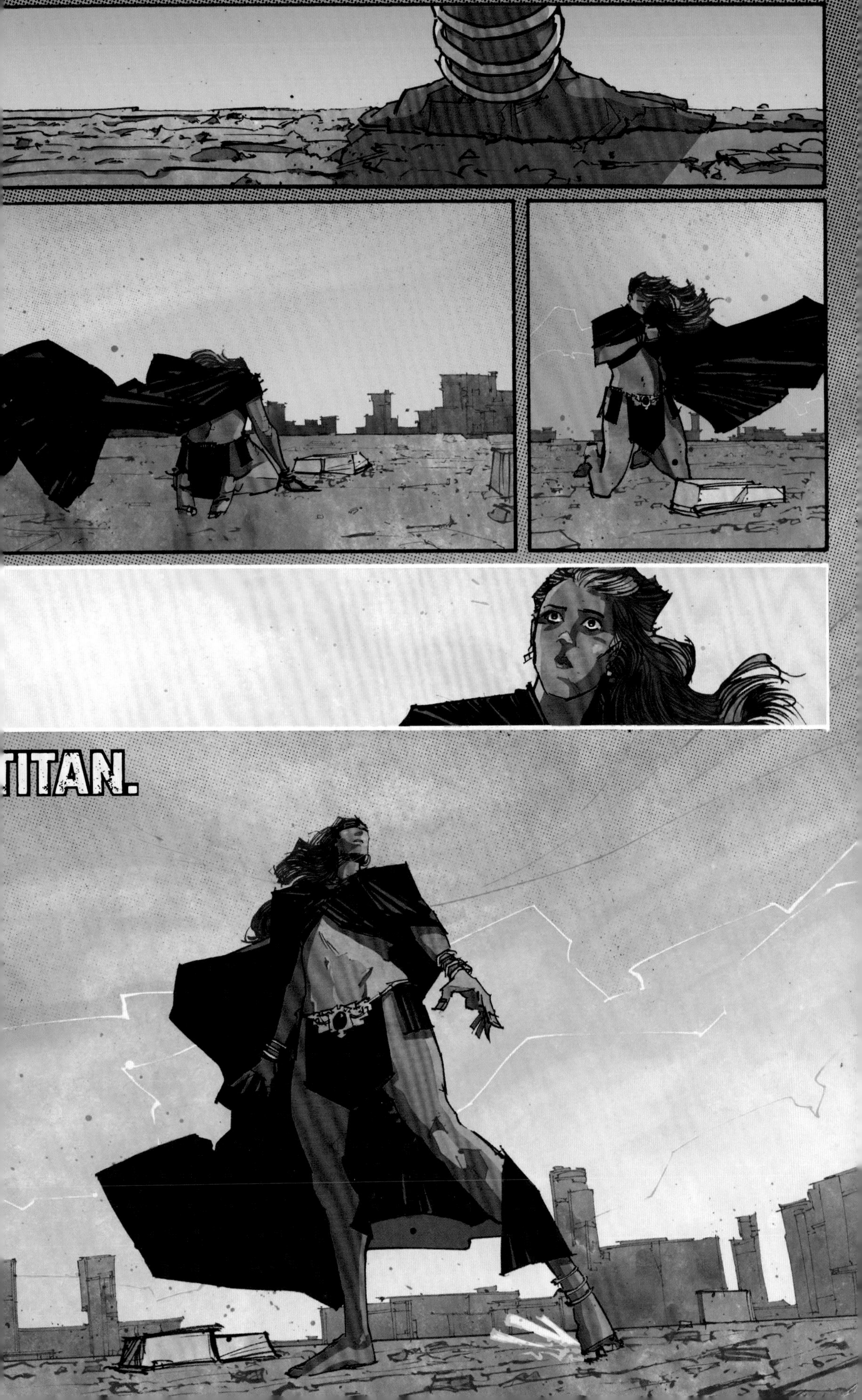
TITAN.

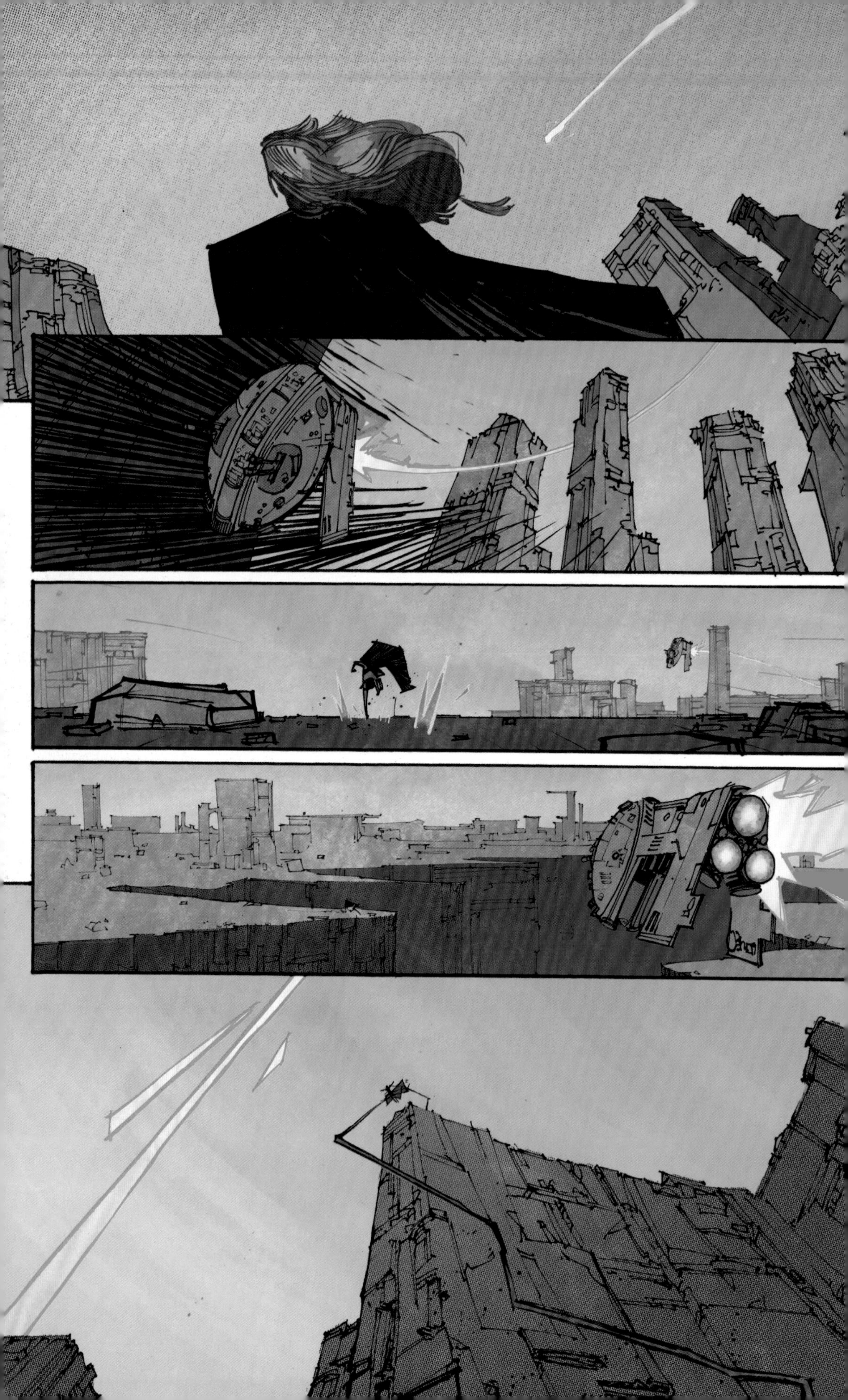

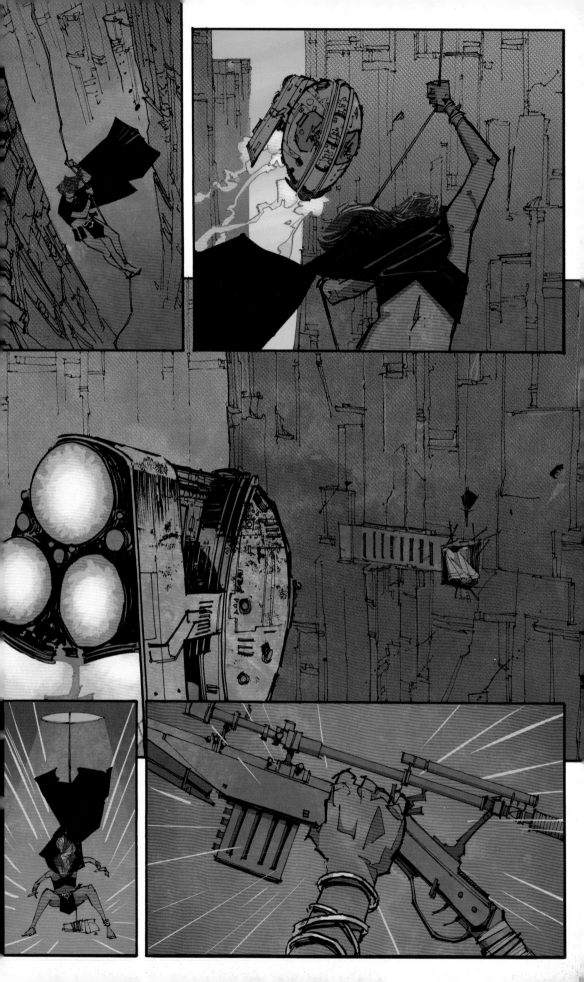

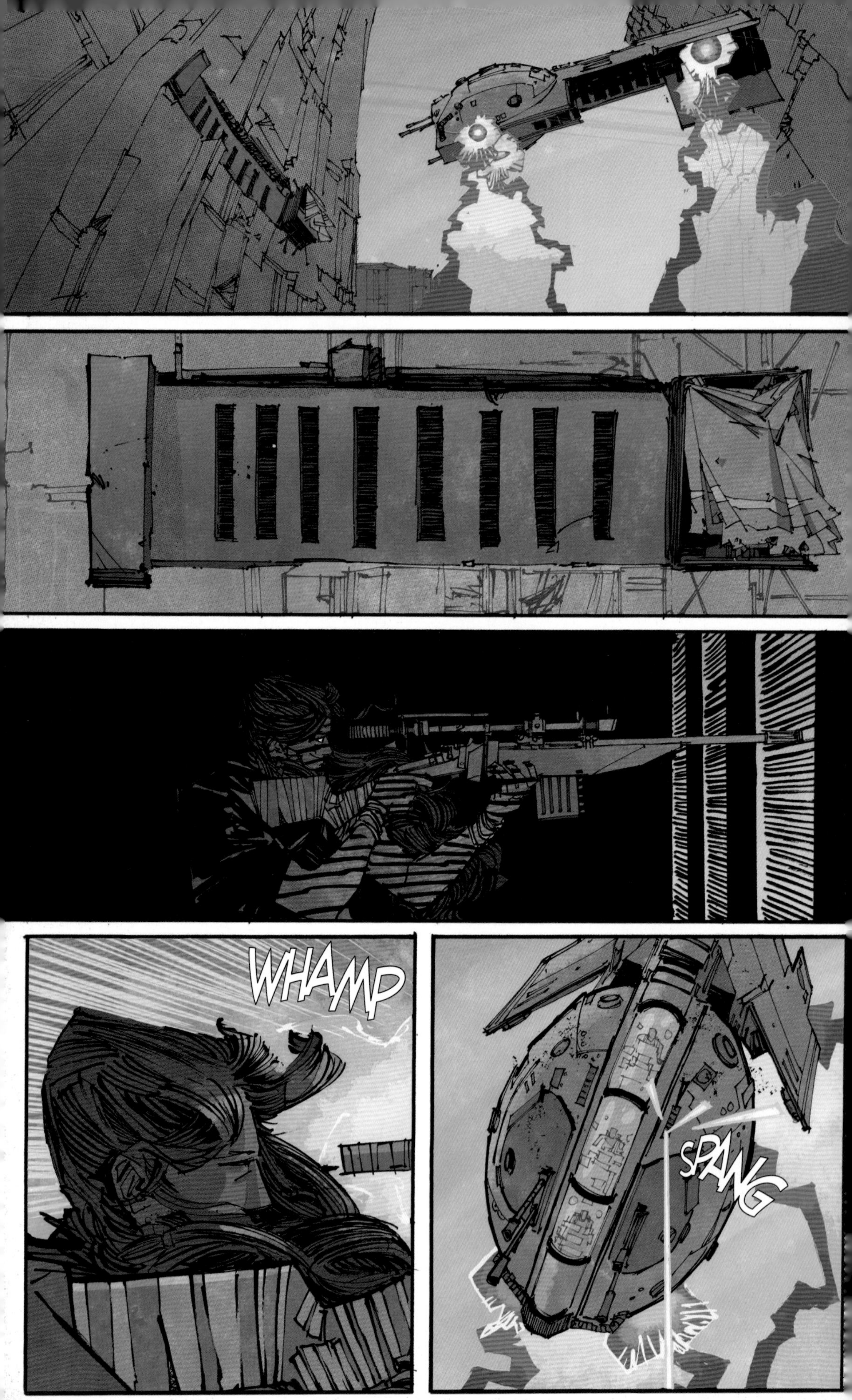
WHAMP
SPANG

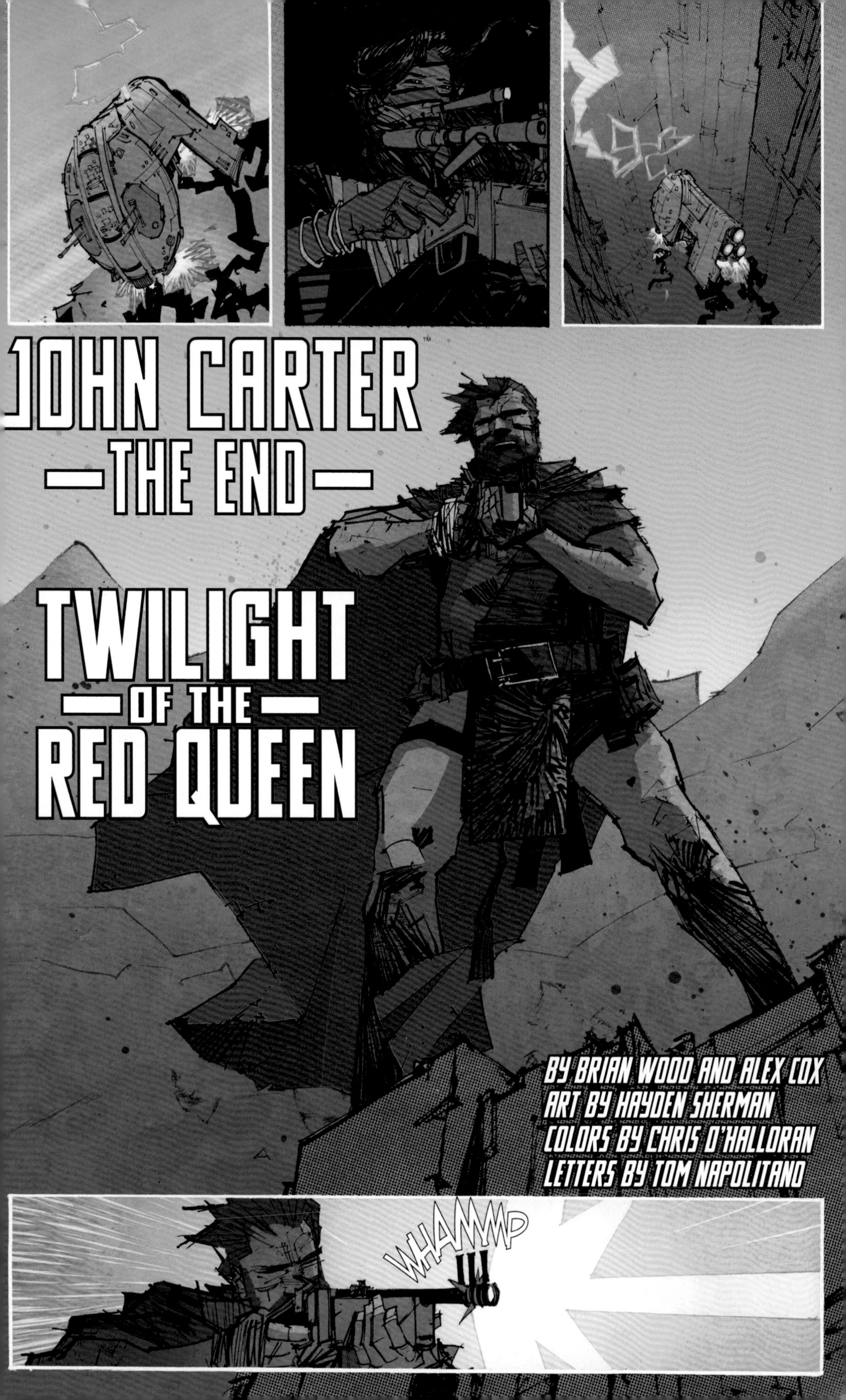
JOHN CARTER™
—THE END—
TWILIGHT
—OF THE—
RED QUEEN
BY BRIAN WOOD AND ALEX COX
ART BY HAYDEN SHERMAN
COLORS BY CHRIS O'HALLORAN
LETTERS BY TOM NAPOLITANO
WHAMMP

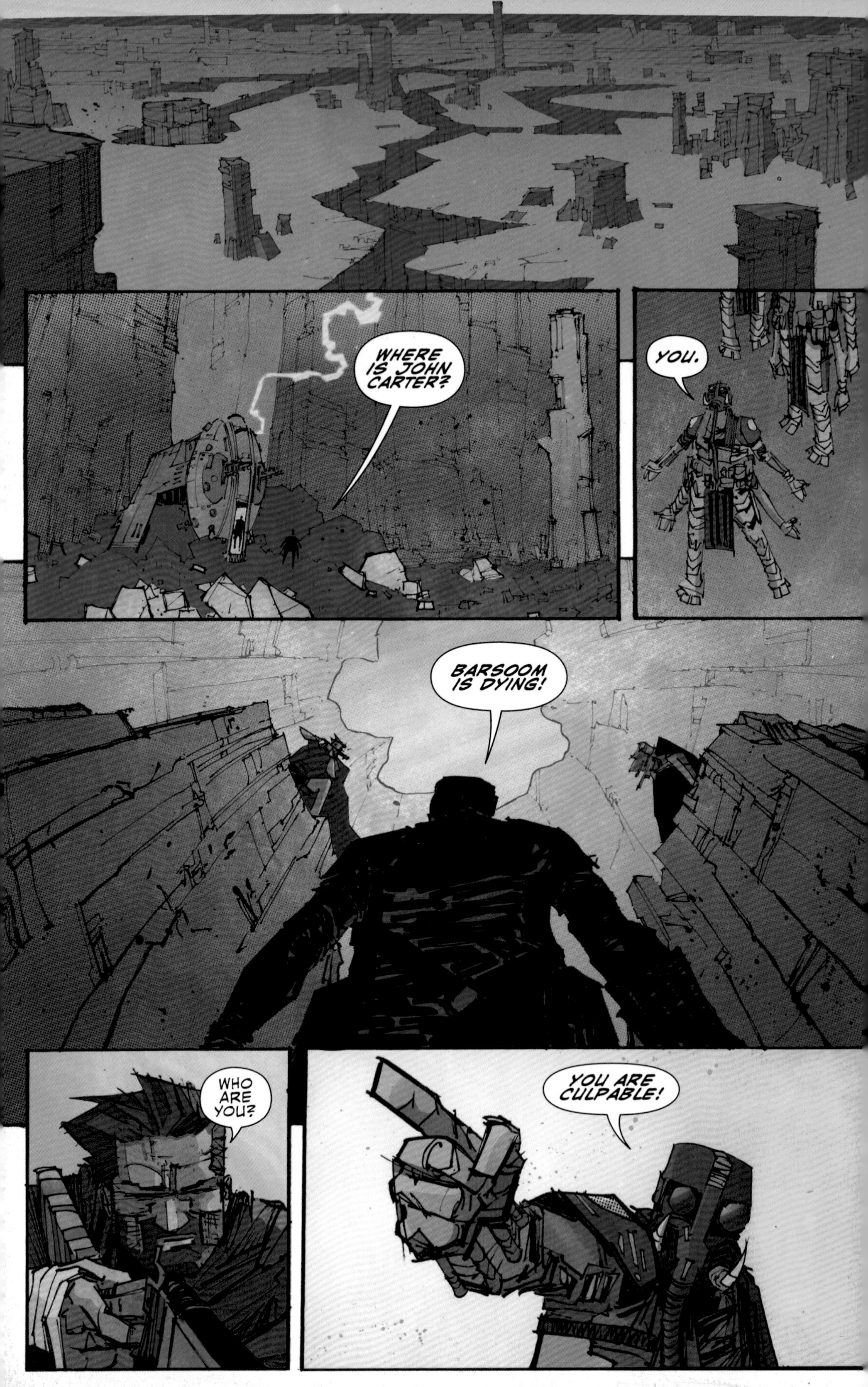
WHERE IS JOHN CARTER?
YOU.
BARSOOM IS DYING!
WHO ARE YOU?
YOU ARE CULPABLE!

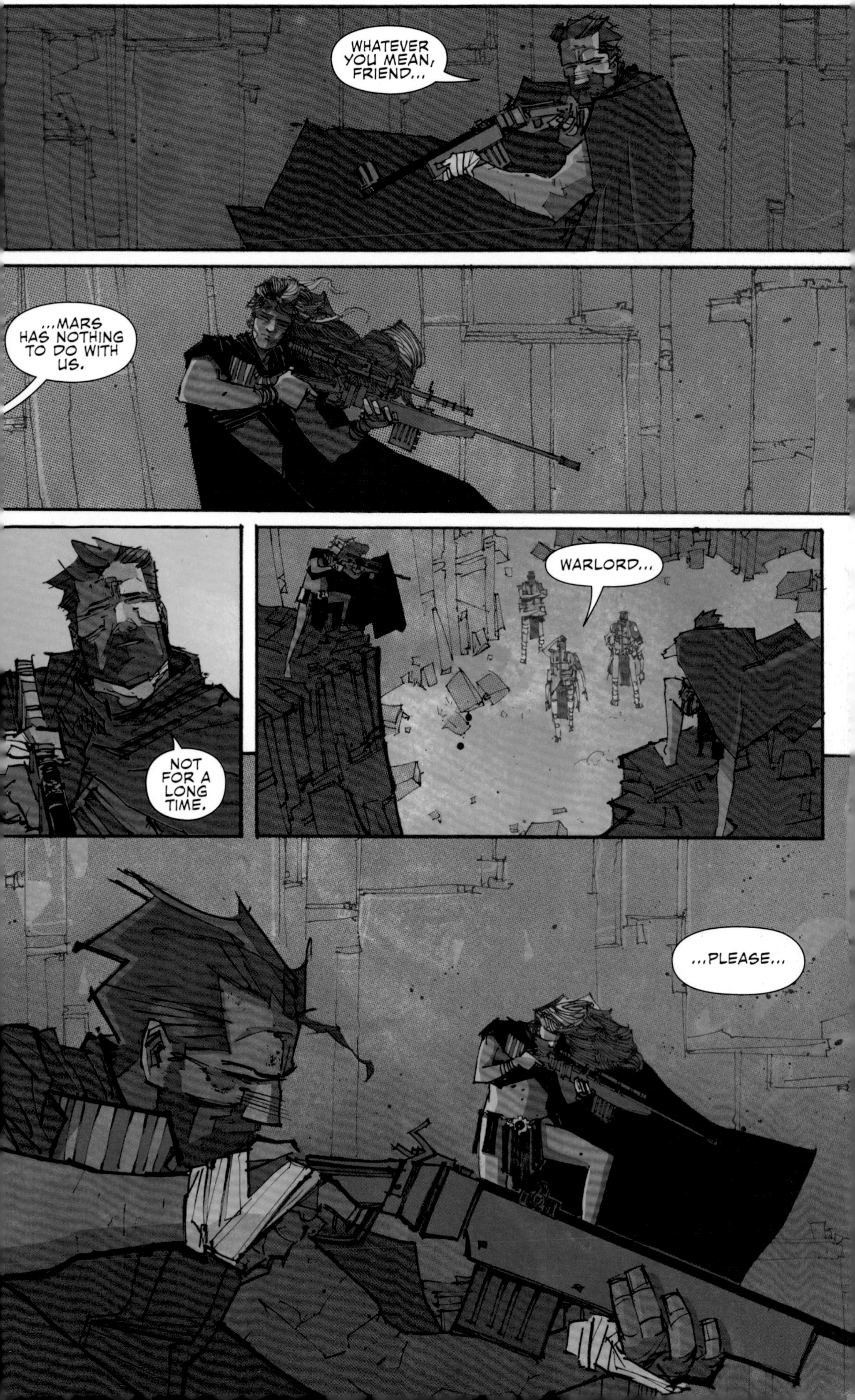
WHATEVER YOU MEAN, FRIEND...
...MARS HAS NOTHING TO DO WITH US.
NOT FOR A LONG TIME.
WARLORD...
...PLEASE...

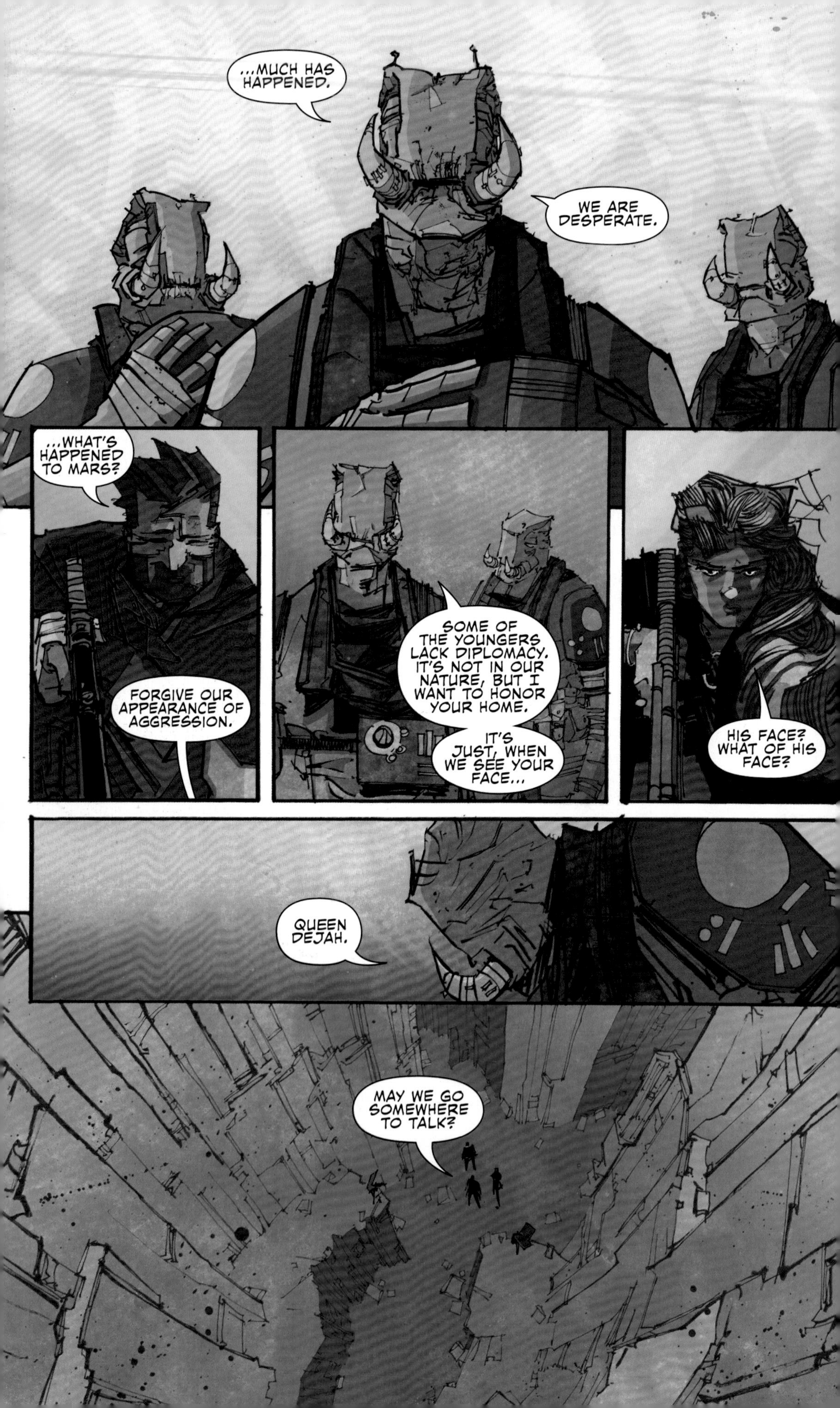
...MUCH HAS HAPPENED.
WE ARE DESPERATE.
...WHAT'S HAPPENED TO MARS?
FORGIVE OUR APPEARANCE OF AGGRESSION.
SOME OF THE YOUNGERS LACK DIPLOMACY. IT'S NOT IN OUR NATURE, BUT I WANT TO HONOR YOUR HOME.
IT'S JUST, WHEN WE SEE YOUR FACE...
HIS FACE? WHAT OF HIS FACE?
QUEEN DEJAH.
MAY WE GO SOMEWHERE TO TALK?

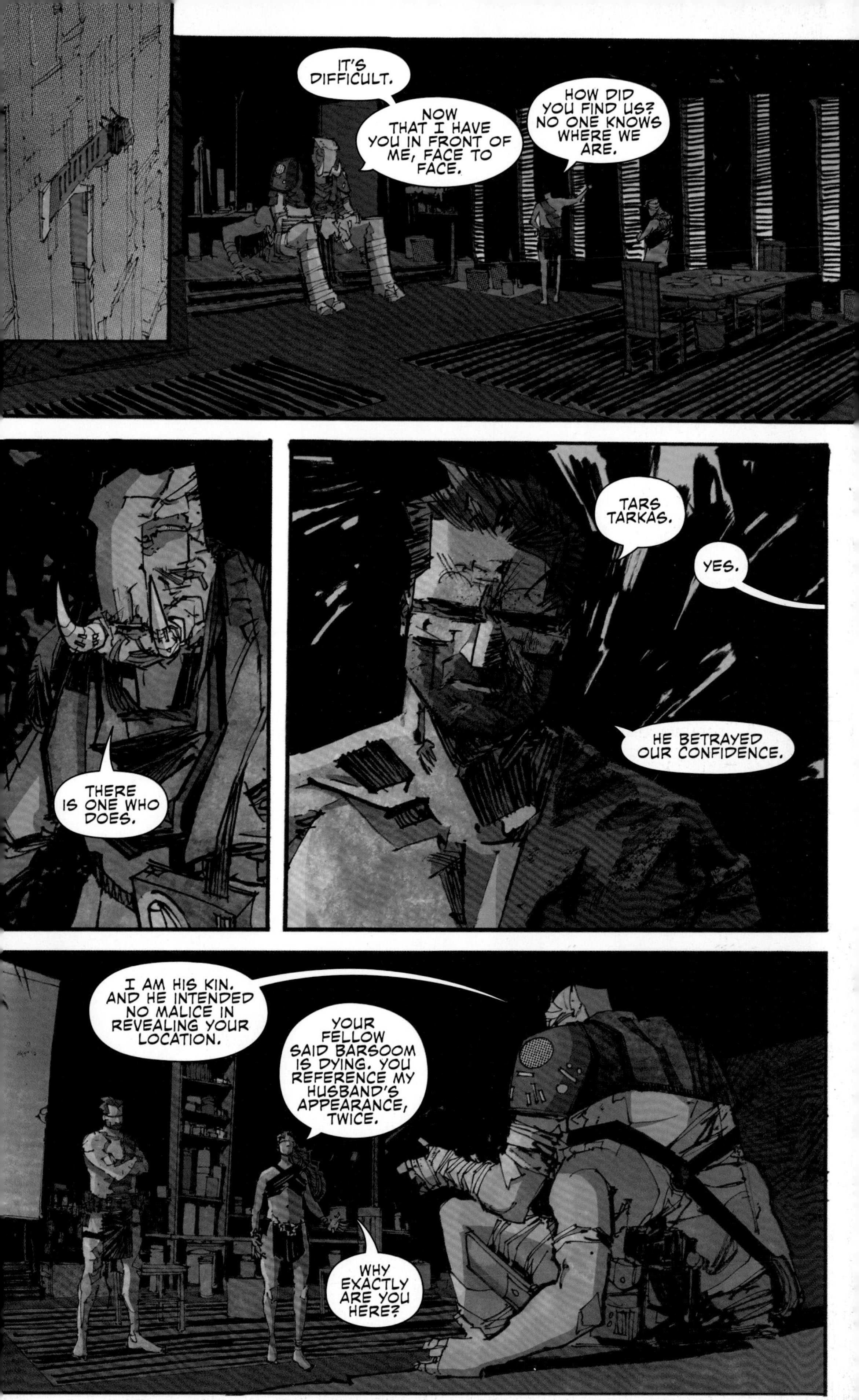

IT'S DIFFICULT.
NOW THAT I HAVE YOU IN FRONT OF ME, FACE TO FACE.
HOW DID YOU FIND US? NO ONE KNOWS WHERE WE ARE.
THERE IS ONE WHO DOES.
TARS TARKAS.
YES.
HE BETRAYED OUR CONFIDENCE.
I AM HIS KIN. AND HE INTENDED NO MALICE IN REVEALING YOUR LOCATION.
YOUR FELLOW SAID BARSOOM IS DYING. YOU REFERENCE MY HUSBAND'S APPEARANCE, TWICE.
WHY EXACTLY ARE YOU HERE?

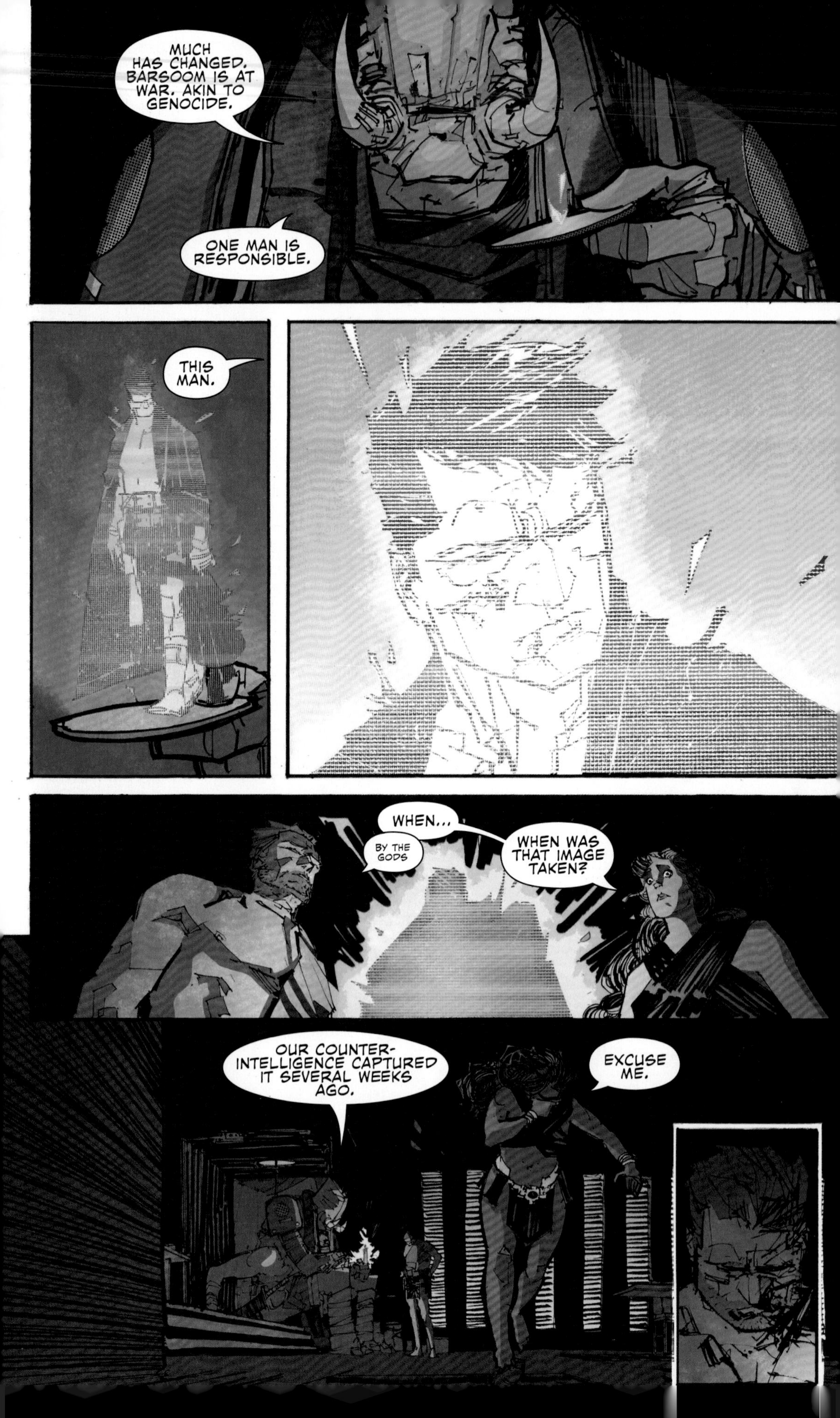
MUCH HAS CHANGED. BARSOOM IS AT WAR. AKIN TO GENOCIDE.
ONE MAN IS RESPONSIBLE.
THIS MAN.
WHEN...
BY THE GODS
WHEN WAS THAT IMAGE TAKEN?
OUR COUNTER-INTELLIGENCE CAPTURED IT SEVERAL WEEKS AGO.
EXCUSE ME.

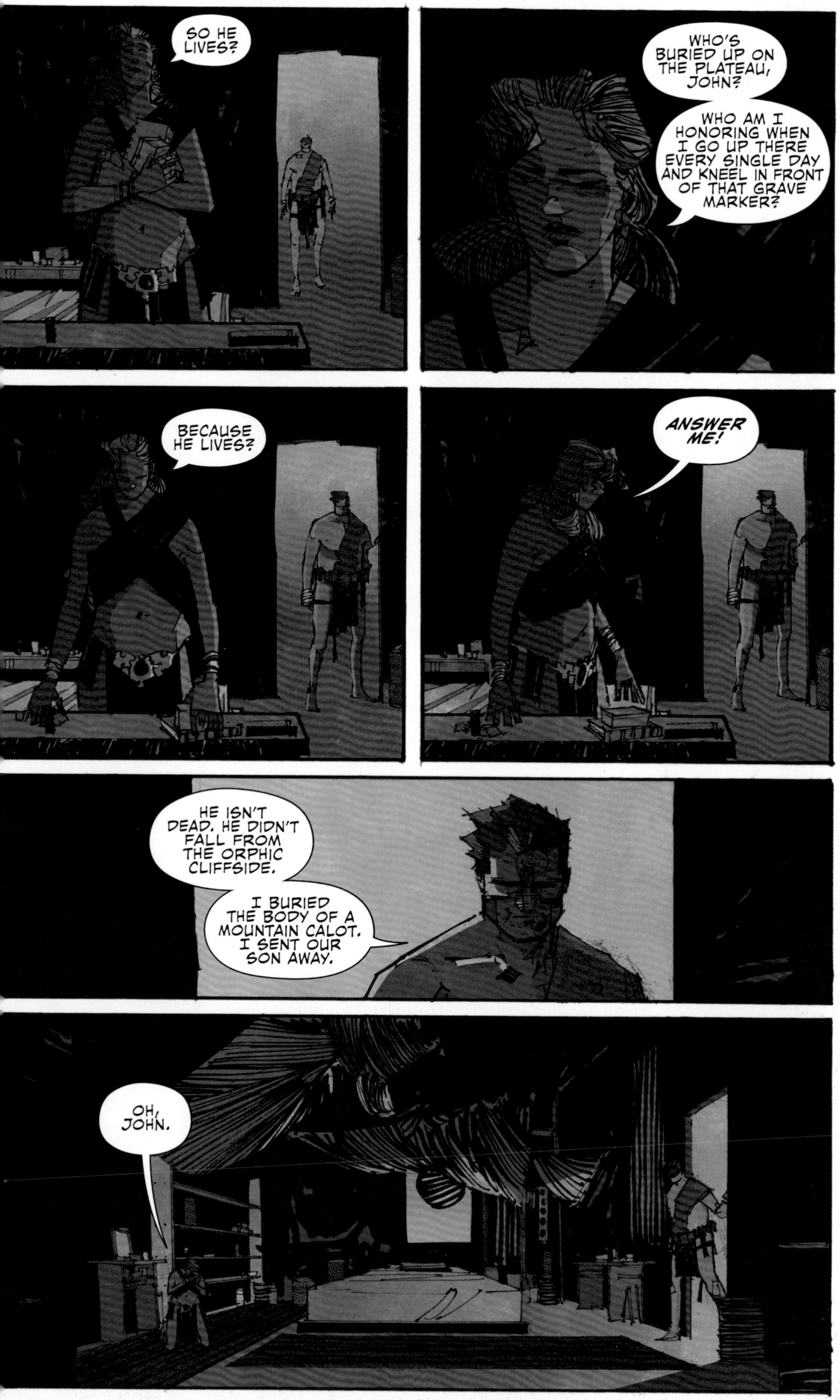
SO HE LIVES?
WHO'S BURIED UP ON THE PLATEAU, JOHN?
WHO AM I HONORING WHEN I GO UP THERE EVERY SINGLE DAY AND KNEEL IN FRONT OF THAT GRAVE MARKER?
BECAUSE HE LIVES?
ANSWER ME!
HE ISN'T DEAD. HE DIDN'T FALL FROM THE ORPHIC CLIFFSIDE.
I BURIED THE BODY OF A MOUNTAIN CALOT. I SENT OUR SON AWAY.
OH, JOHN.

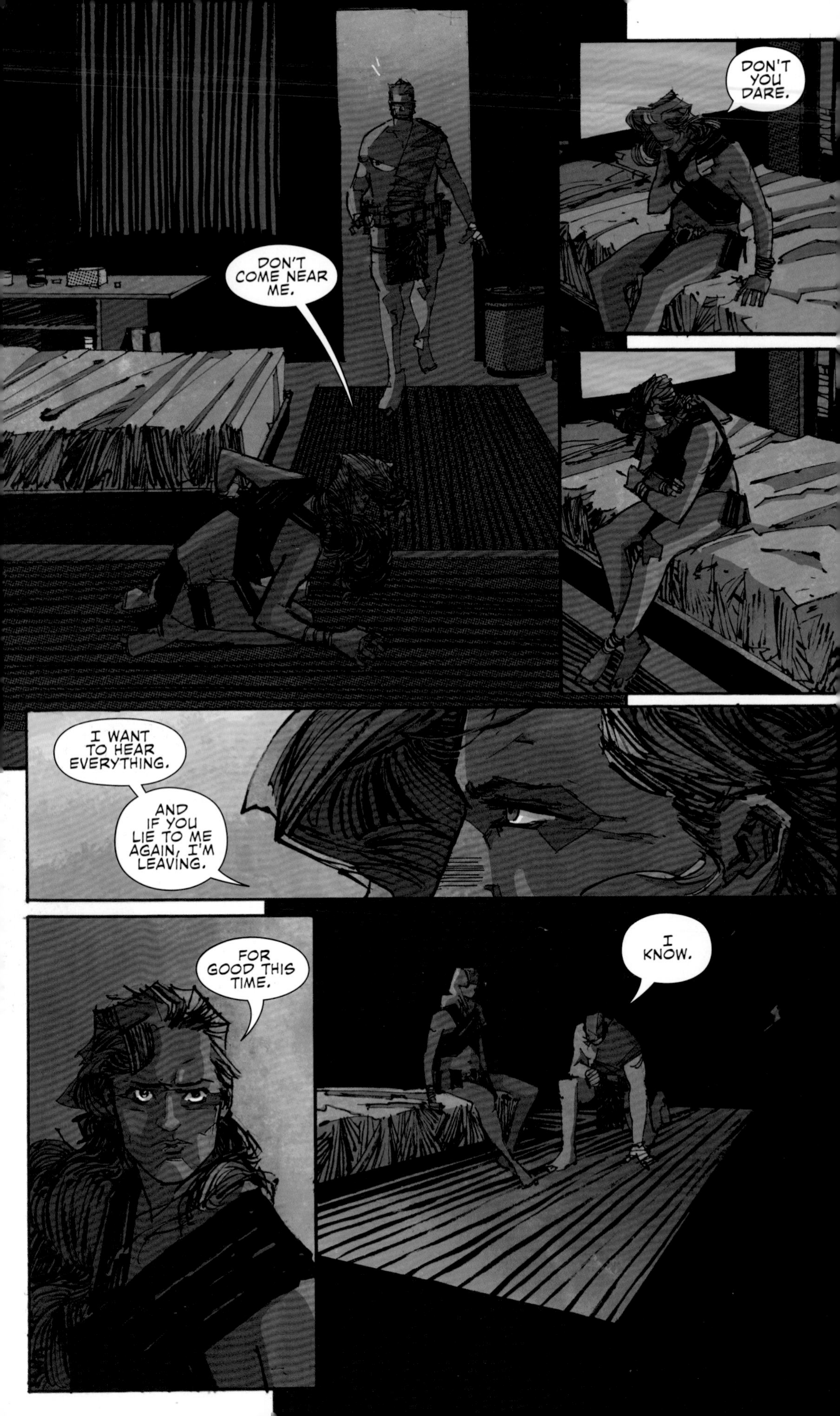
DON'T COME NEAR ME.
DON'T YOU DARE.
I WANT TO HEAR EVERYTHING.
AND IF YOU LIE TO ME AGAIN, I'M LEAVING.
FOR GOOD THIS TIME.
I KNOW.

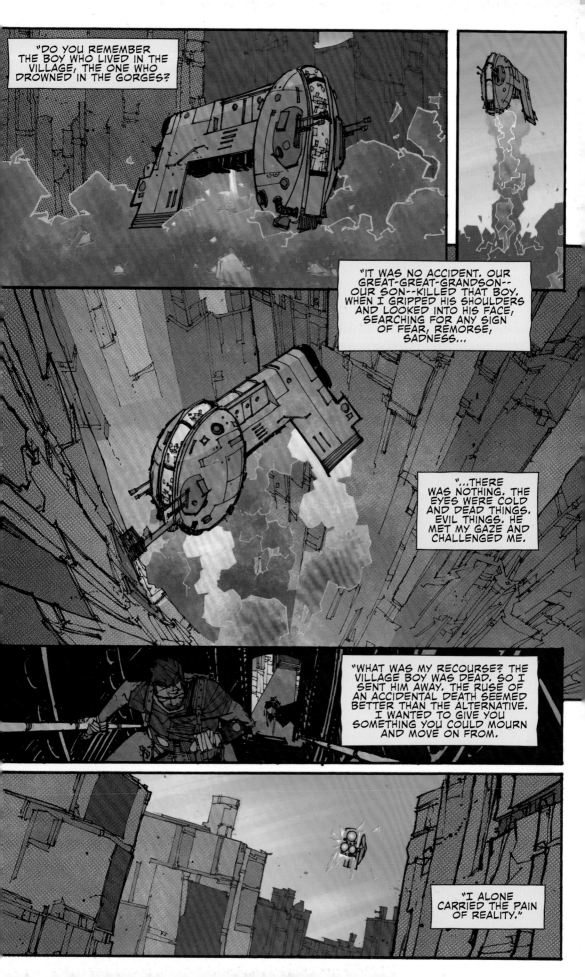

"DO YOU REMEMBER THE BOY WHO LIVED IN THE VILLAGE, THE ONE WHO DROWNED IN THE GORGES?

"IT WAS NO ACCIDENT. OUR GREAT-GREAT-GRANDSON-- OUR SON--KILLED THAT BOY. WHEN I GRIPPED HIS SHOULDERS AND LOOKED INTO HIS FACE, SEARCHING FOR ANY SIGN OF FEAR, REMORSE, SADNESS...

"...THERE WAS NOTHING. THE EYES WERE COLD AND DEAD THINGS. EVIL THINGS. HE MET MY GAZE AND CHALLENGED ME.

"WHAT WAS MY RECOURSE? THE VILLAGE BOY WAS DEAD. SO I SENT HIM AWAY. THE RUSE OF AN ACCIDENTAL DEATH SEEMED BETTER THAN THE ALTERNATIVE. I WANTED TO GIVE YOU SOMETHING YOU COULD MOURN AND MOVE ON FROM.

"I ALONE CARRIED THE PAIN OF REALITY."

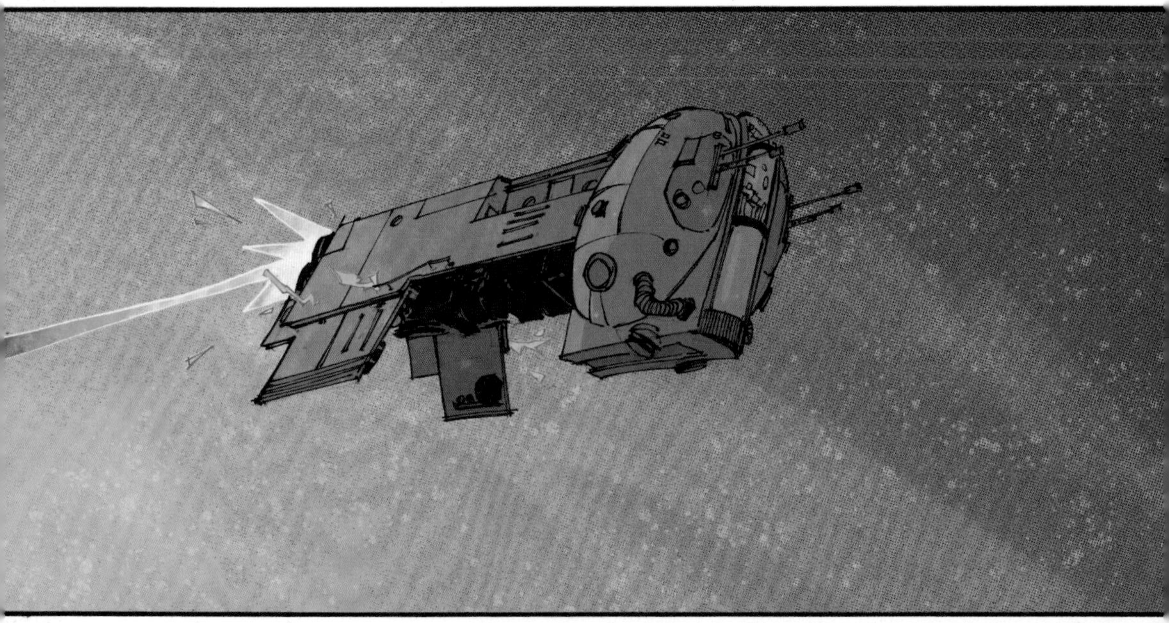

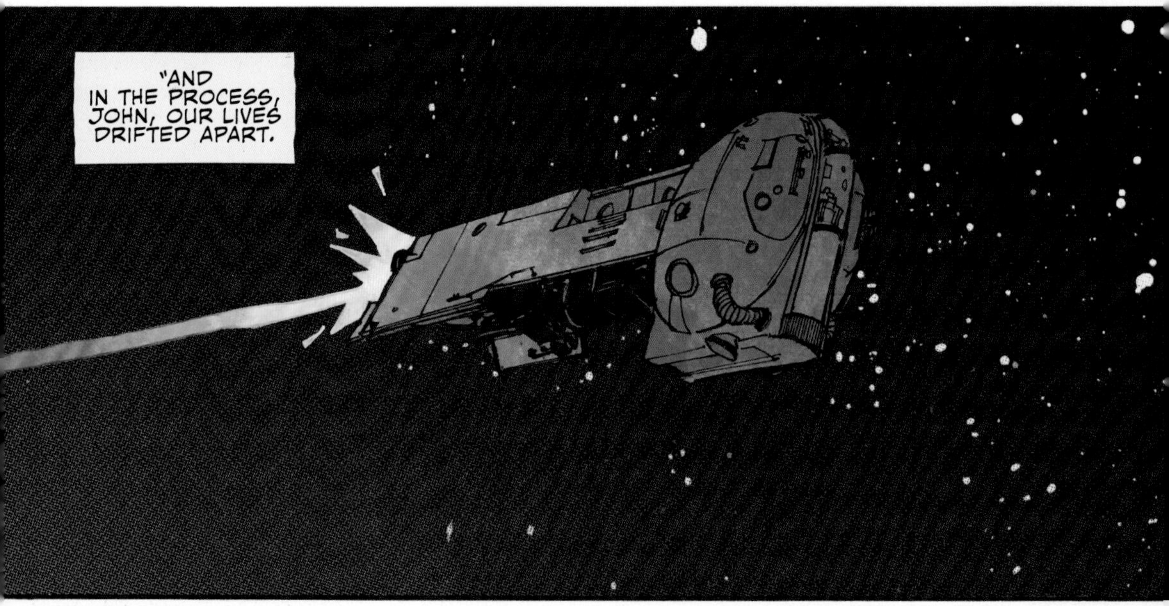
"AND IN THE PROCESS, JOHN, OUR LIVES DRIFTED APART.

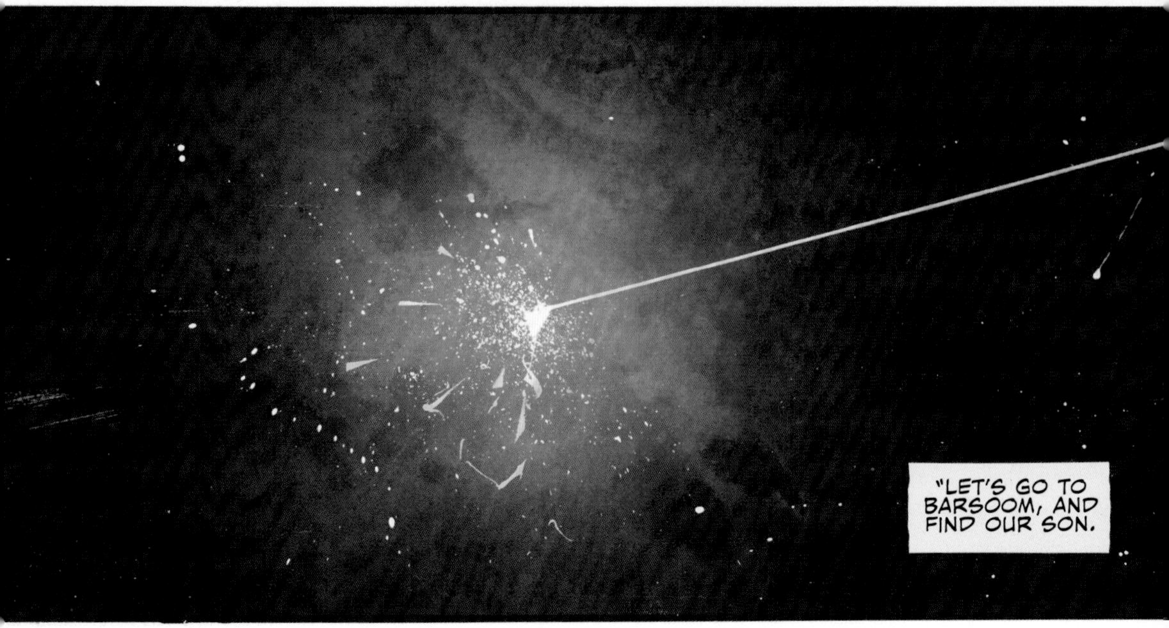
"LET'S GO TO BARSOOM, AND FIND OUR SON.

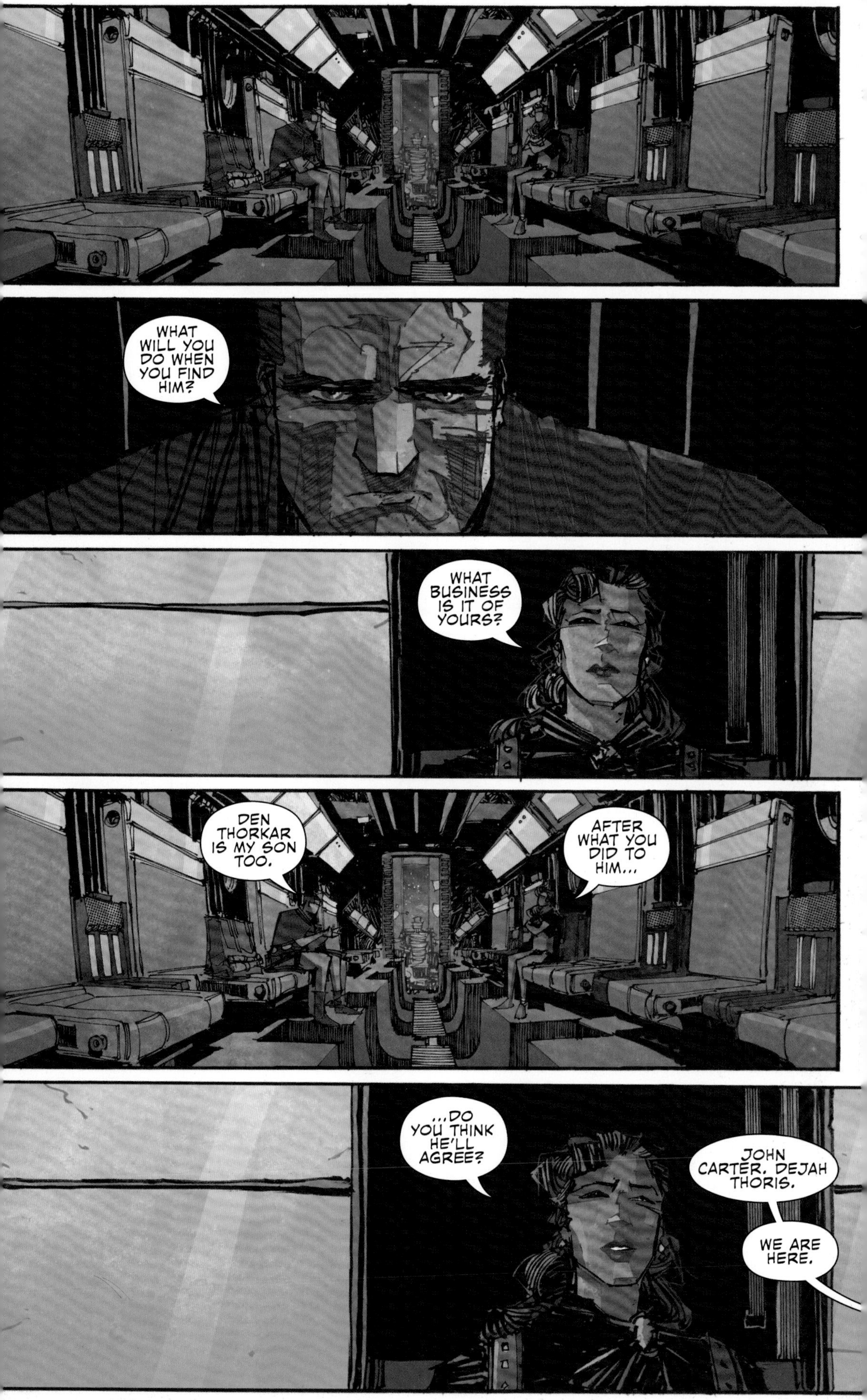

WHAT WILL YOU DO WHEN YOU FIND HIM?
WHAT BUSINESS IS IT OF YOURS?
DEN THORKAR IS MY SON TOO.
AFTER WHAT YOU DID TO HIM...
...DO YOU THINK HE'LL AGREE?
JOHN CARTER. DEJAH THORIS.
WE ARE HERE.

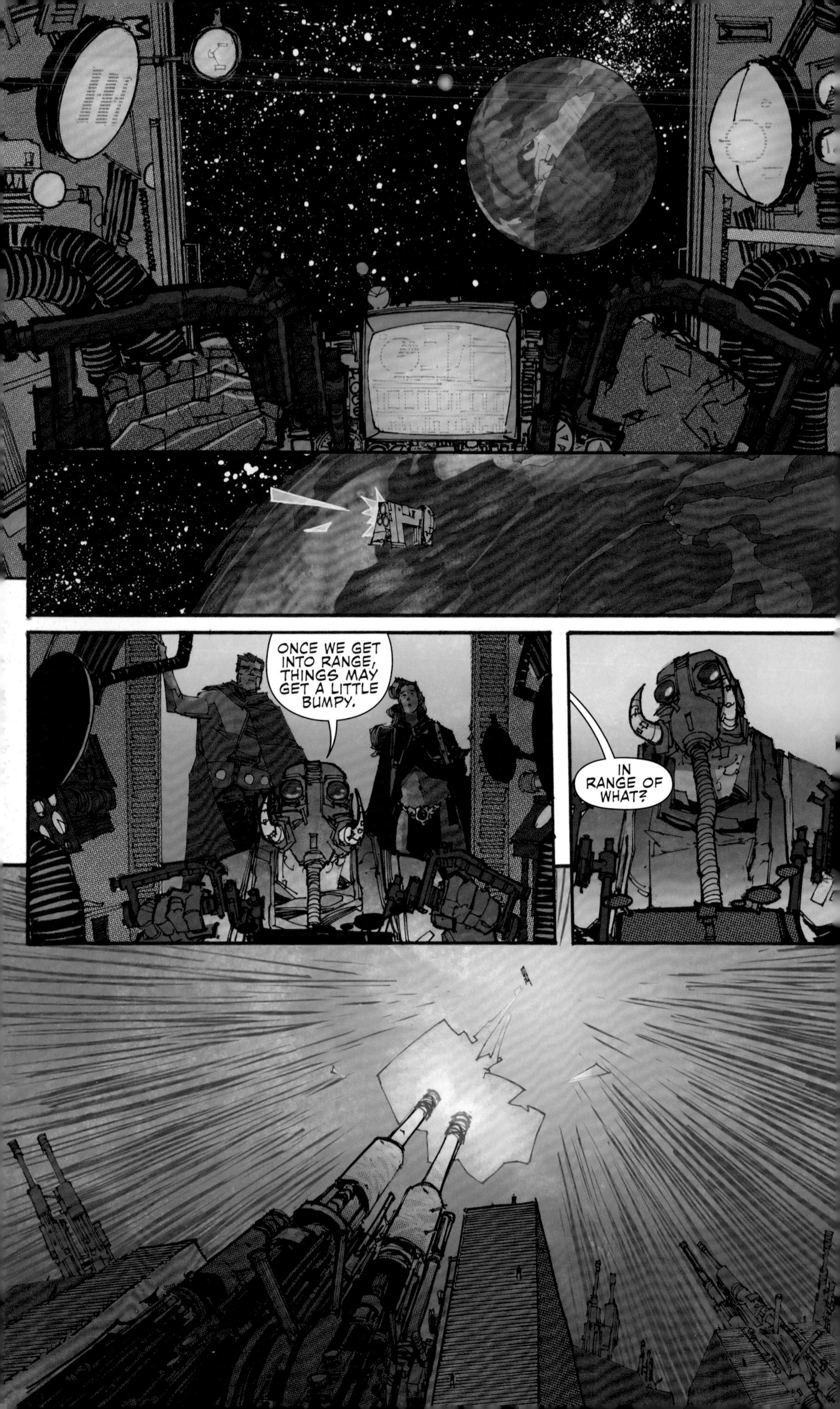
ONCE WE GET INTO RANGE, THINGS MAY GET A LITTLE BUMPY.
IN RANGE OF WHAT?

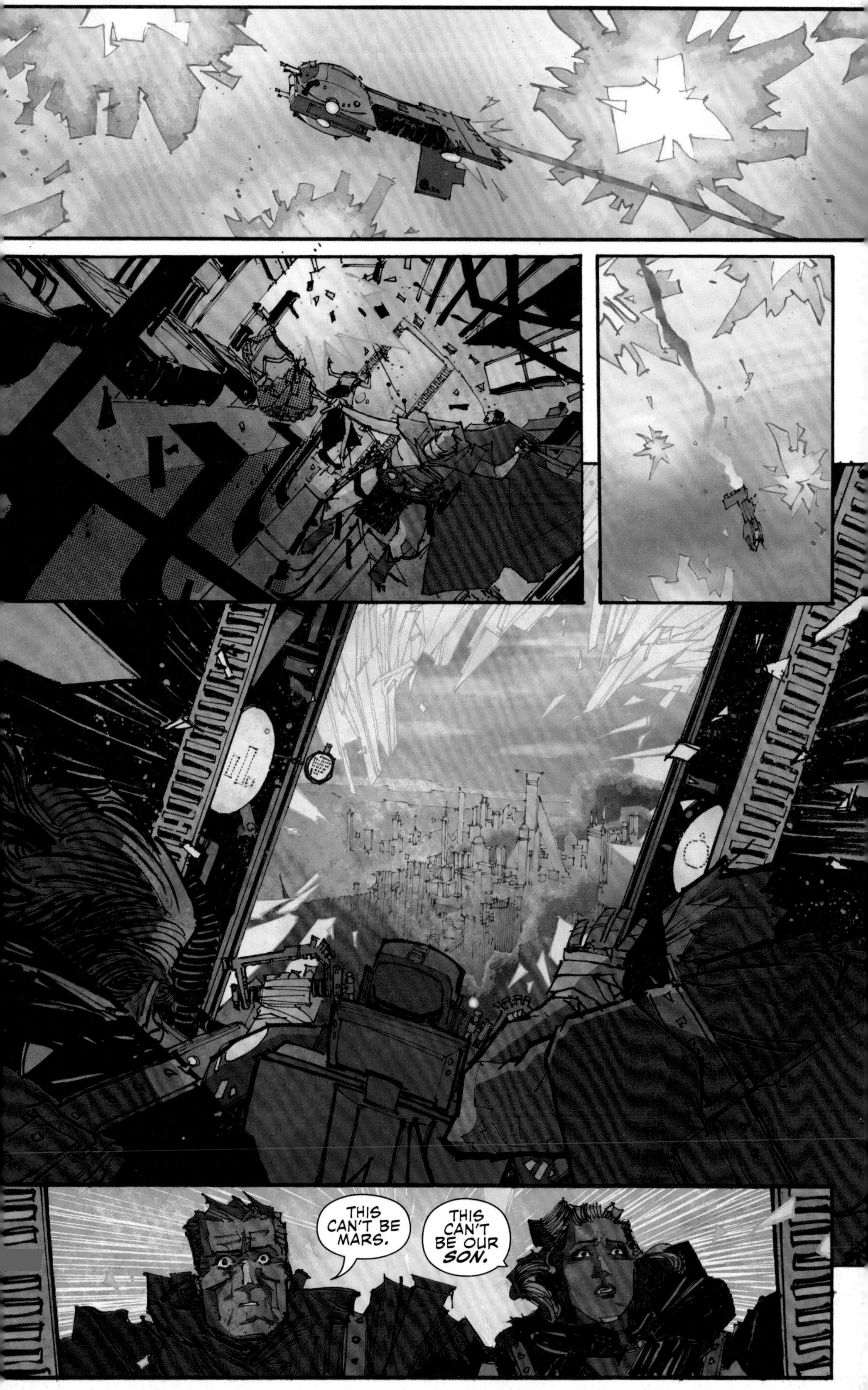

THIS CAN'T BE MARS.
THIS CAN'T BE OUR *SON.*

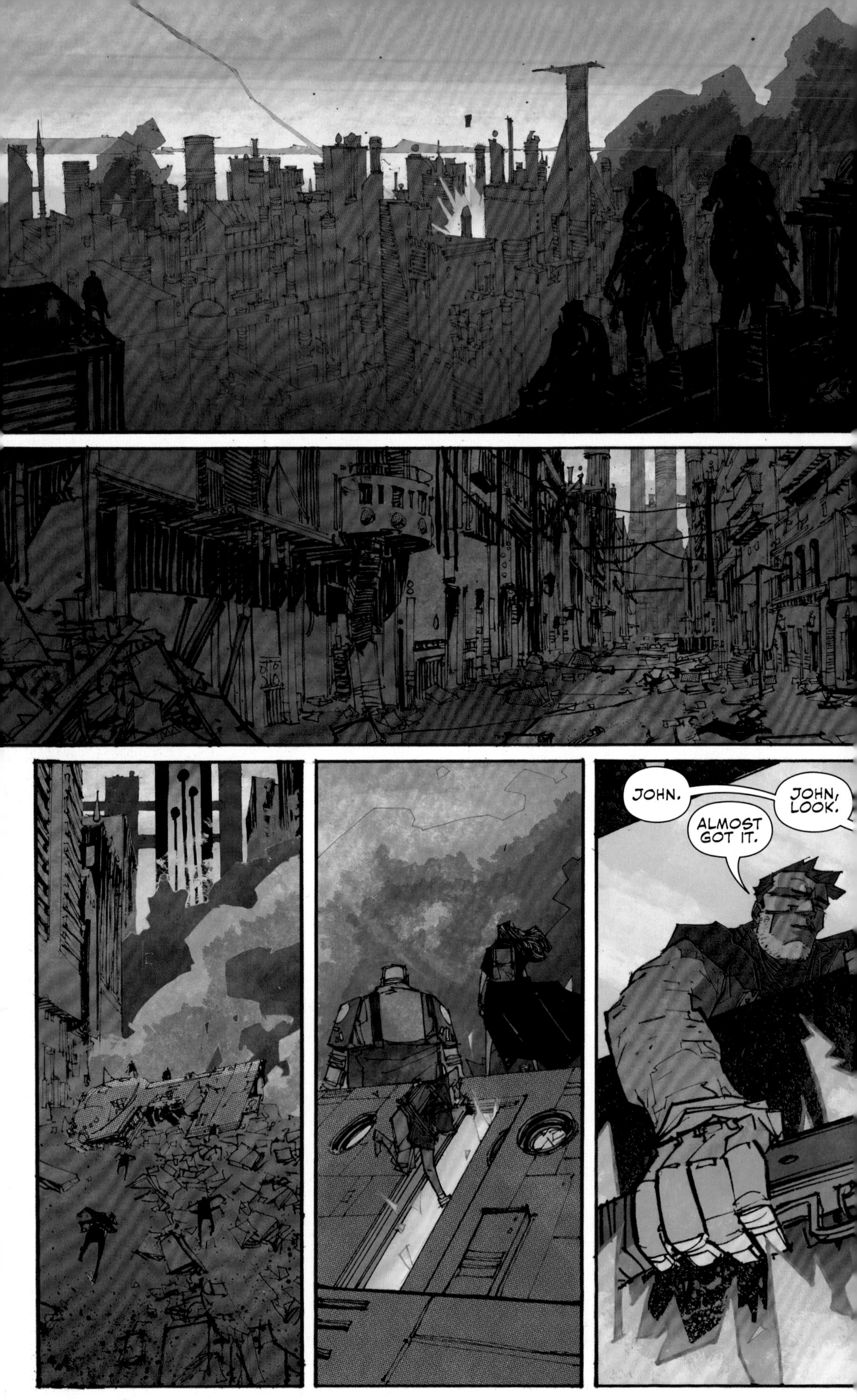
JOHN.
JOHN, LOOK.
ALMOST GOT IT.

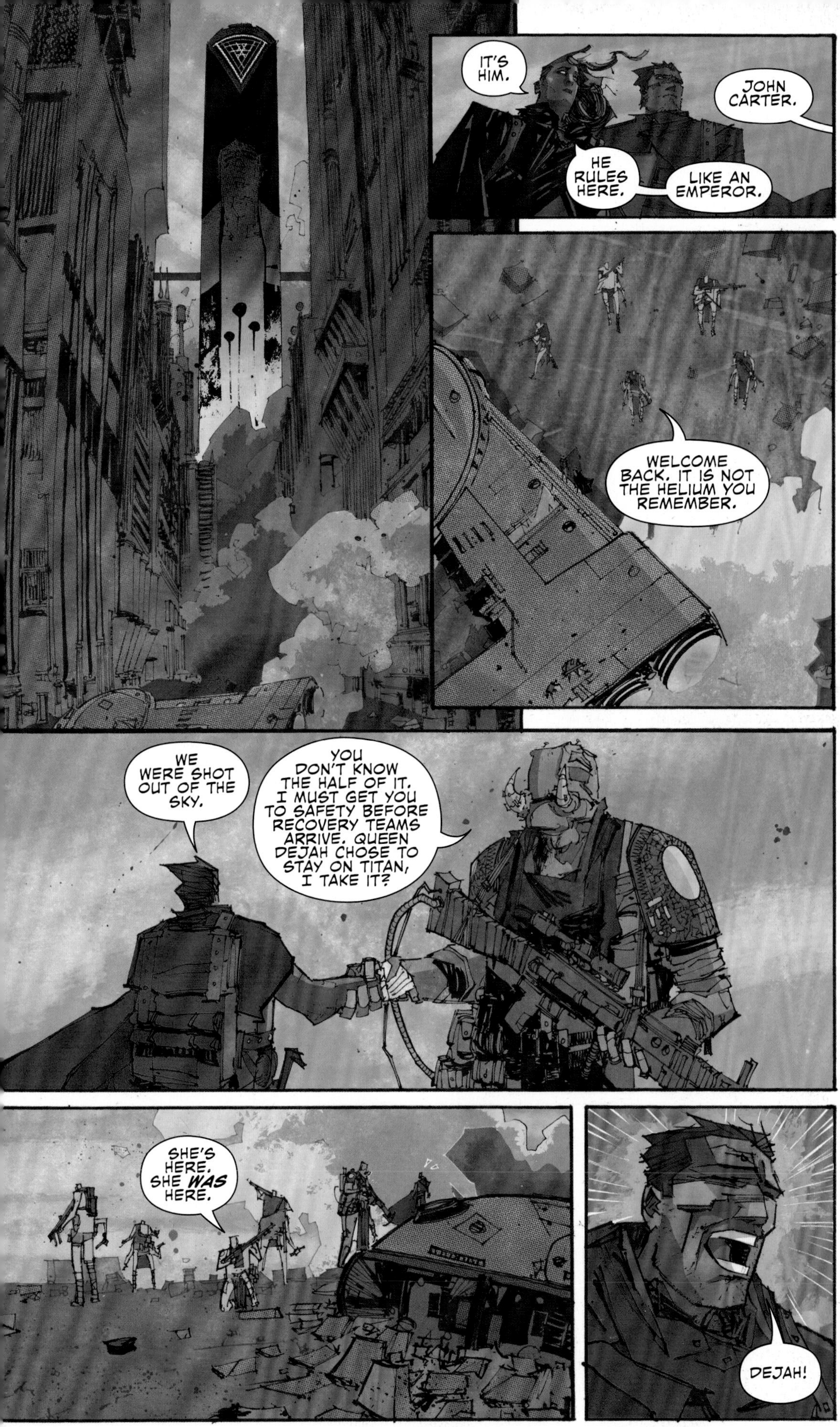
IT'S HIM.
JOHN CARTER.
HE RULES HERE.
LIKE AN EMPEROR.
WELCOME BACK. IT IS NOT THE HELIUM YOU REMEMBER.
WE WERE SHOT OUT OF THE SKY.
YOU DON'T KNOW THE HALF OF IT. I MUST GET YOU TO SAFETY BEFORE RECOVERY TEAMS ARRIVE. QUEEN DEJAH CHOSE TO STAY ON TITAN, I TAKE IT?
SHE'S HERE. SHE *WAS* HERE.
DEJAH!

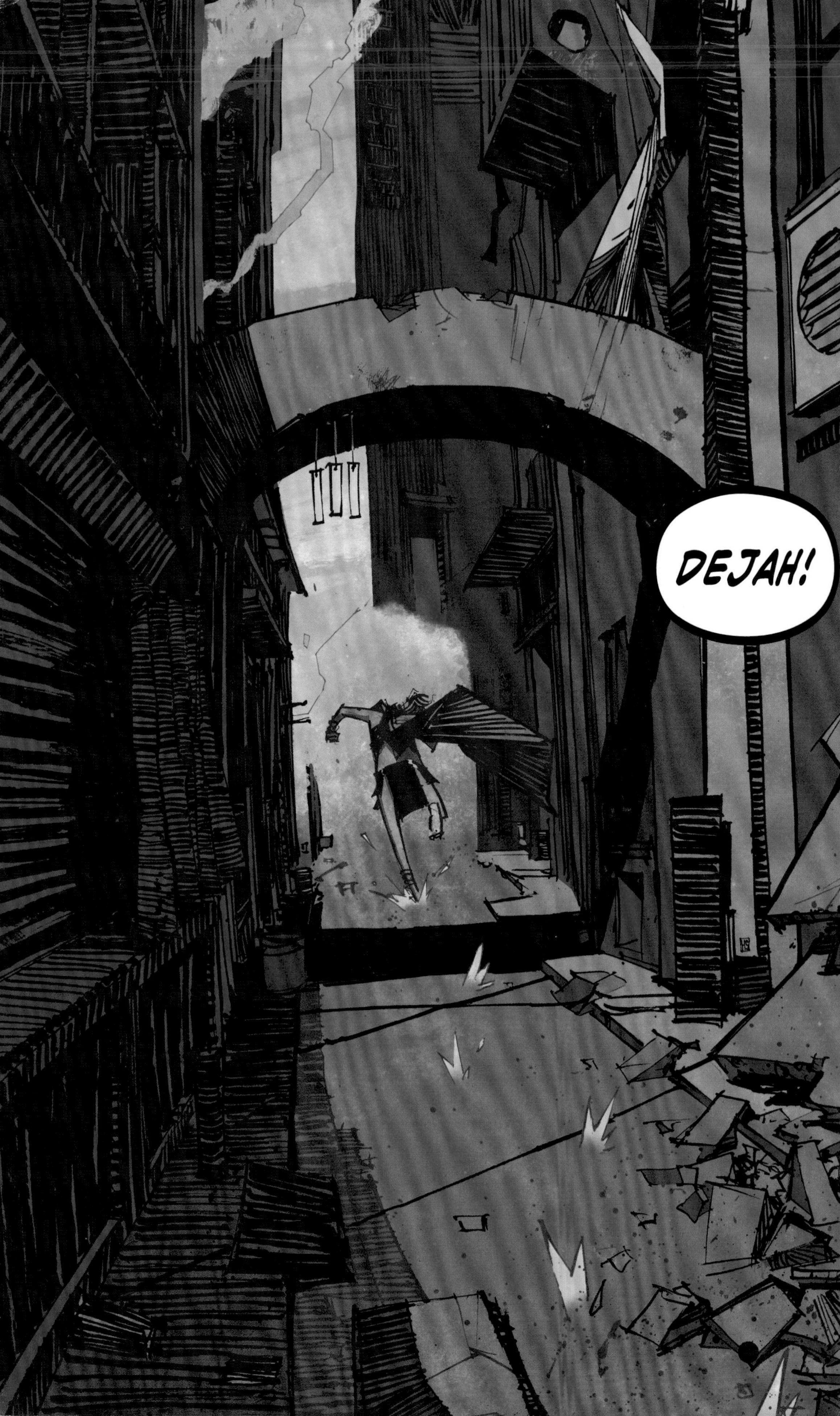
DEJAH!

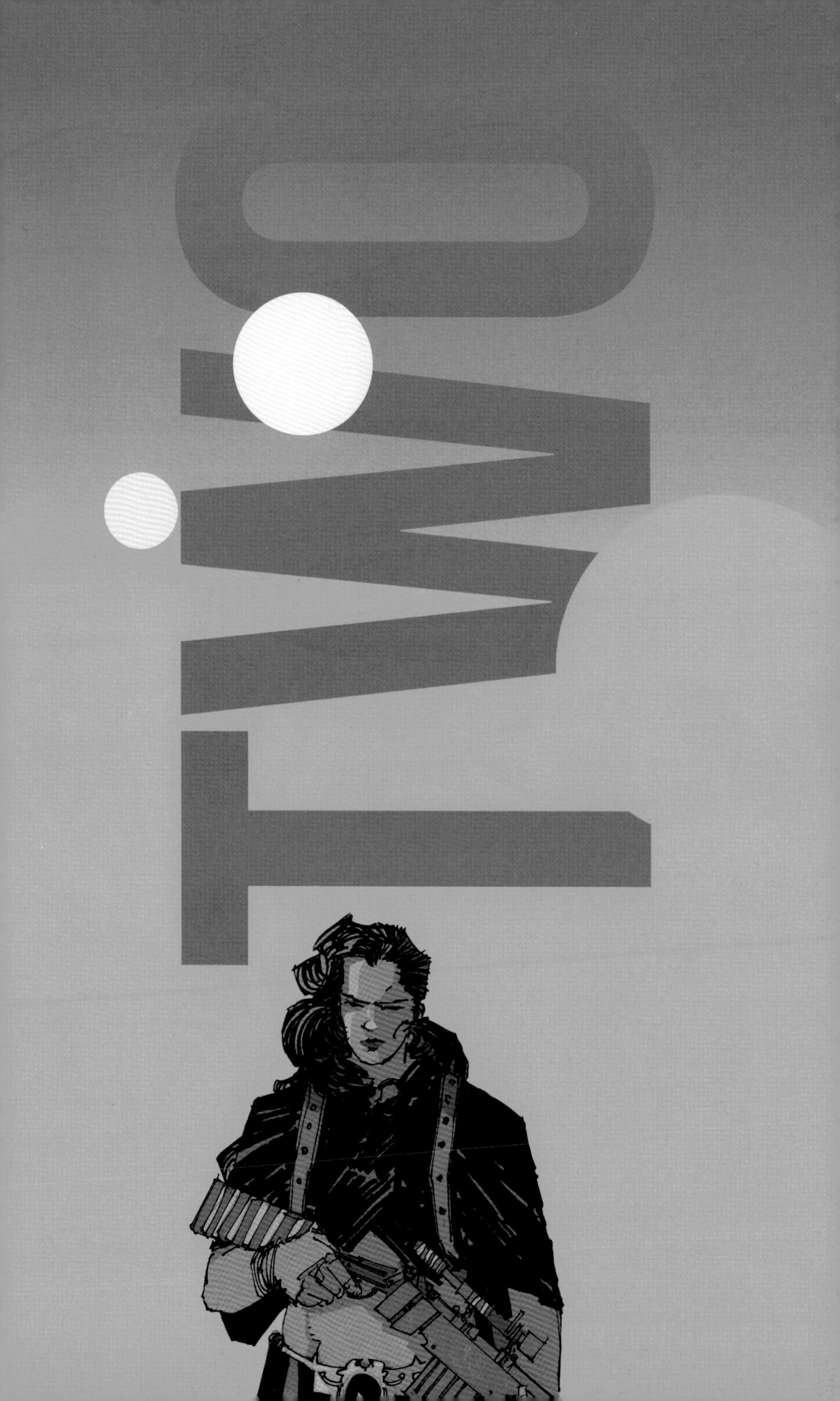
TWO

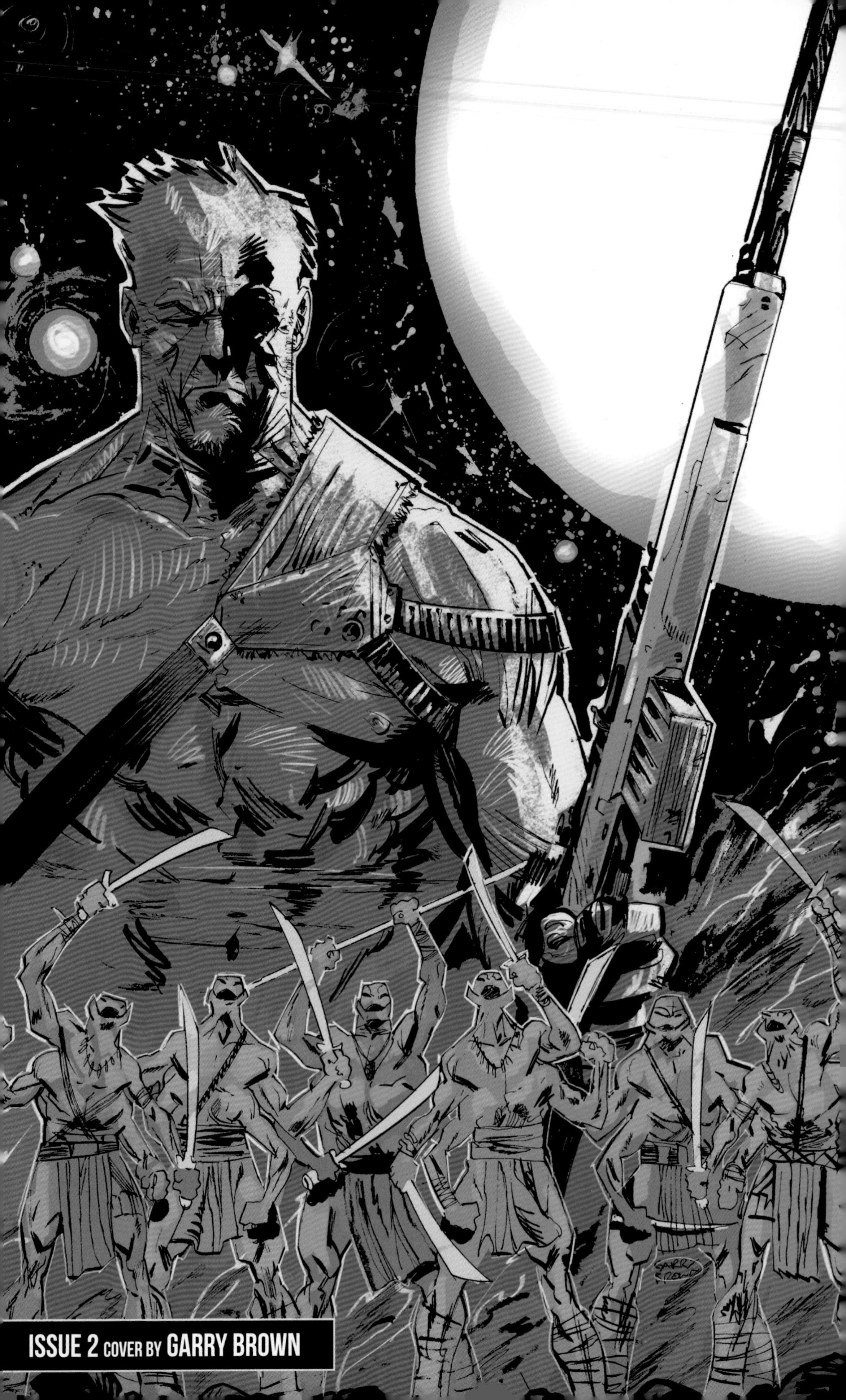

ISSUE 2 COVER BY GARRY BROWN

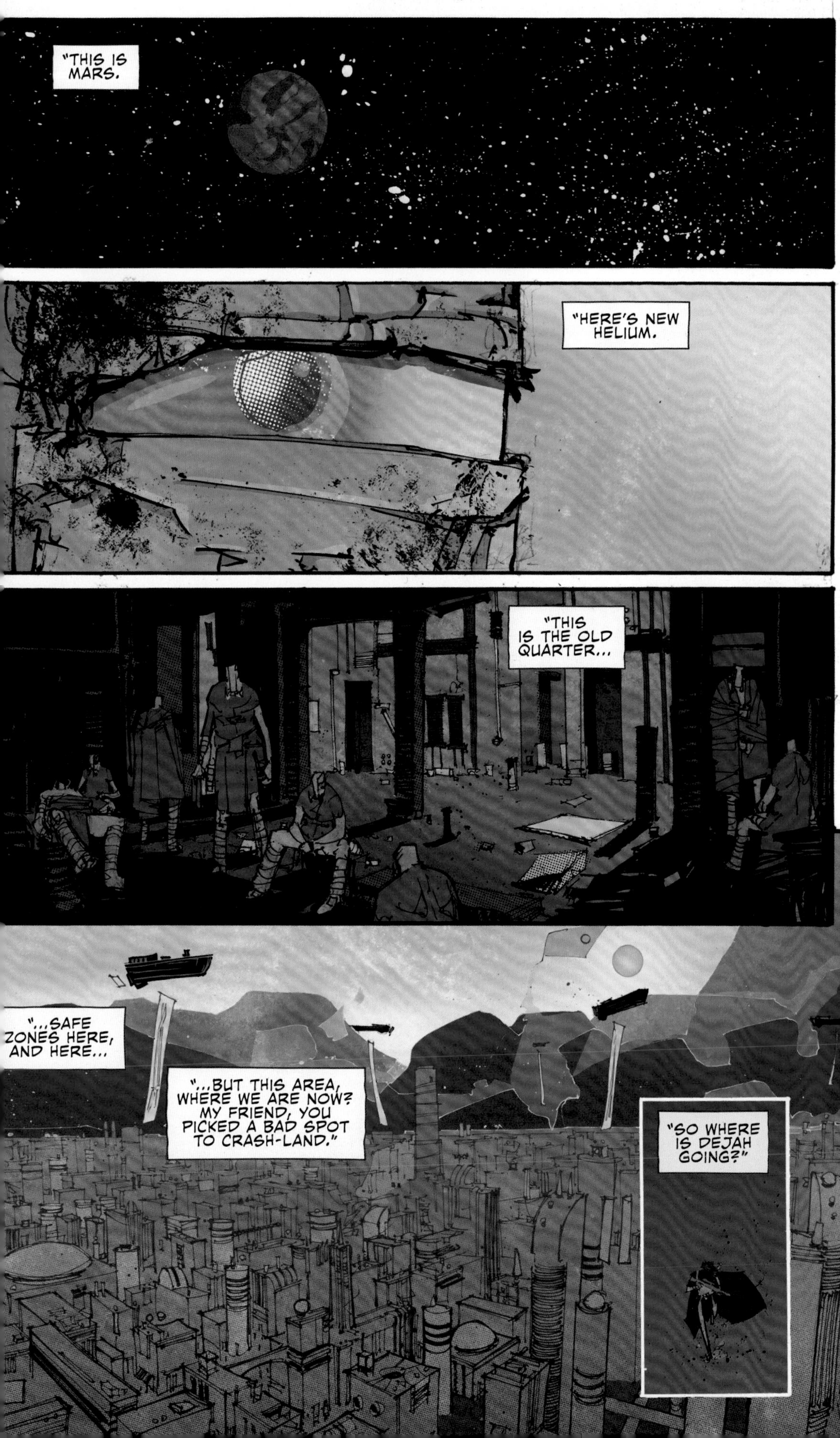

"THIS IS MARS.
"HERE'S NEW HELIUM.
"THIS IS THE OLD QUARTER...
"...SAFE ZONES HERE, AND HERE...
"...BUT THIS AREA, WHERE WE ARE NOW? MY FRIEND, YOU PICKED A BAD SPOT TO CRASH-LAND."
"SO WHERE IS DEJAH GOING?"

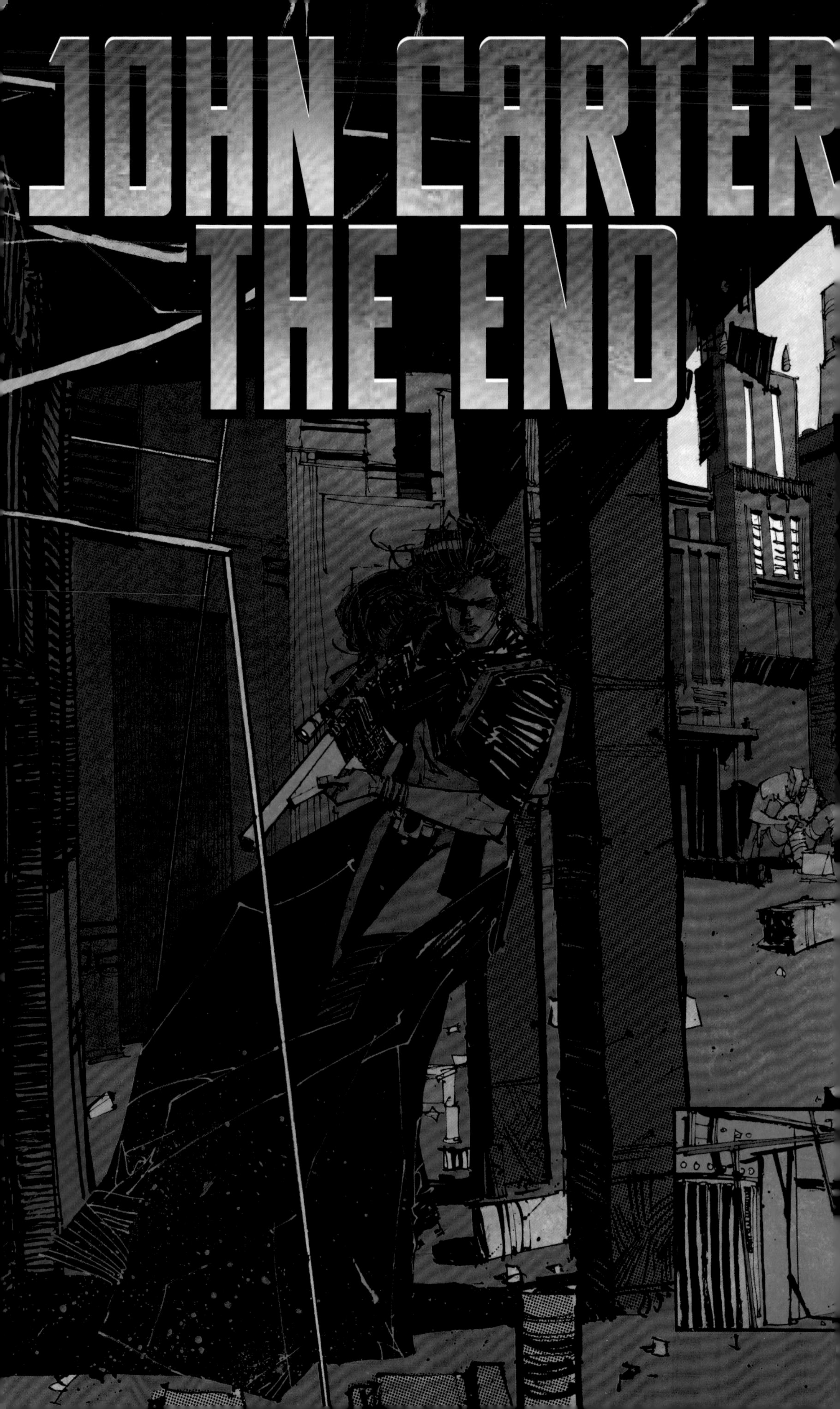
JOHN CARTER
THE END

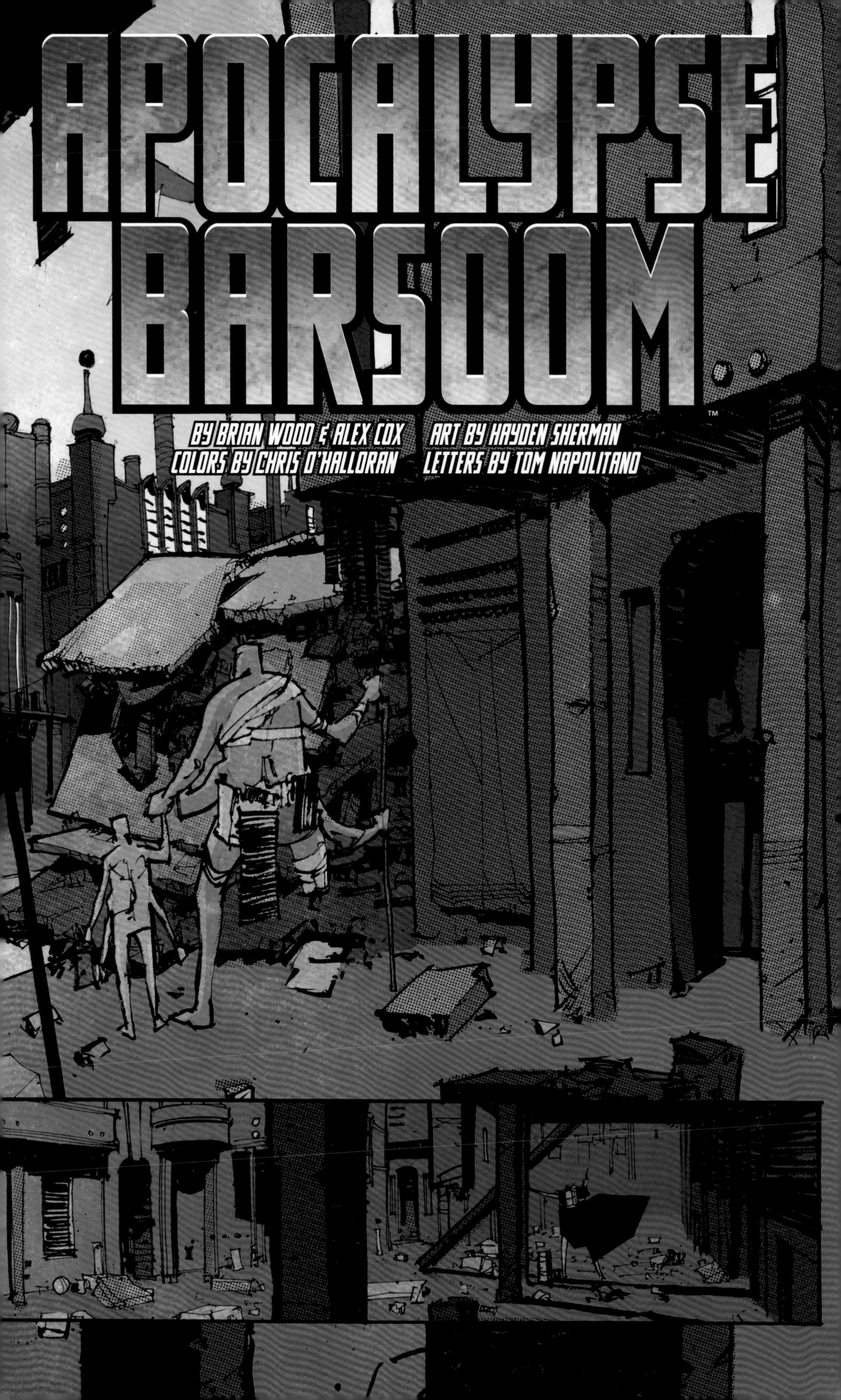

APOCALYPSE BARSOOM™
BY BRIAN WOOD & ALEX COX
ART BY HAYDEN SHERMAN
COLORS BY CHRIS O'HALLORAN
LETTERS BY TOM NAPOLITANO

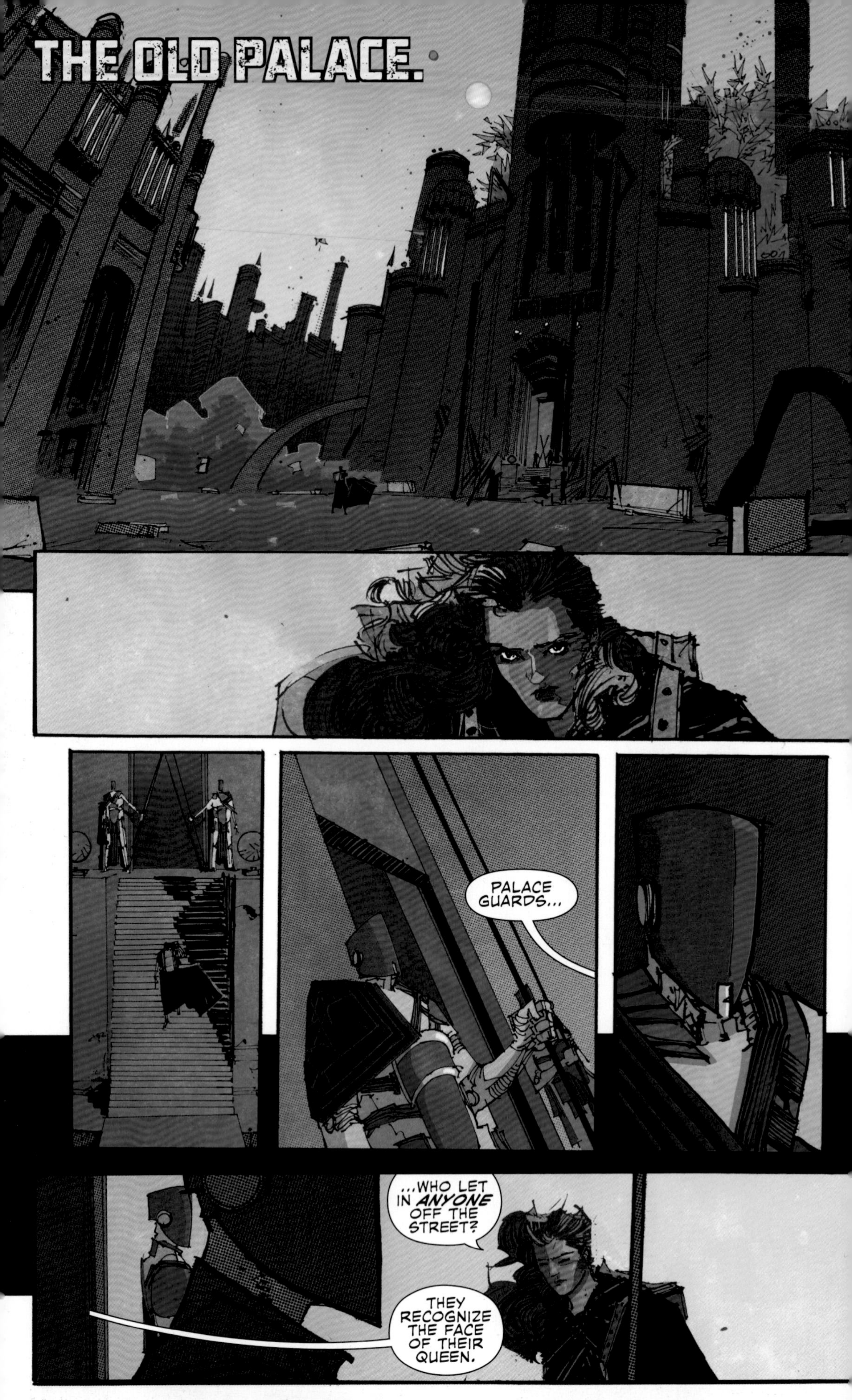
THE OLD PALACE.
PALACE GUARDS...
...WHO LET IN ANYONE OFF THE STREET?
THEY RECOGNIZE THE FACE OF THEIR QUEEN.

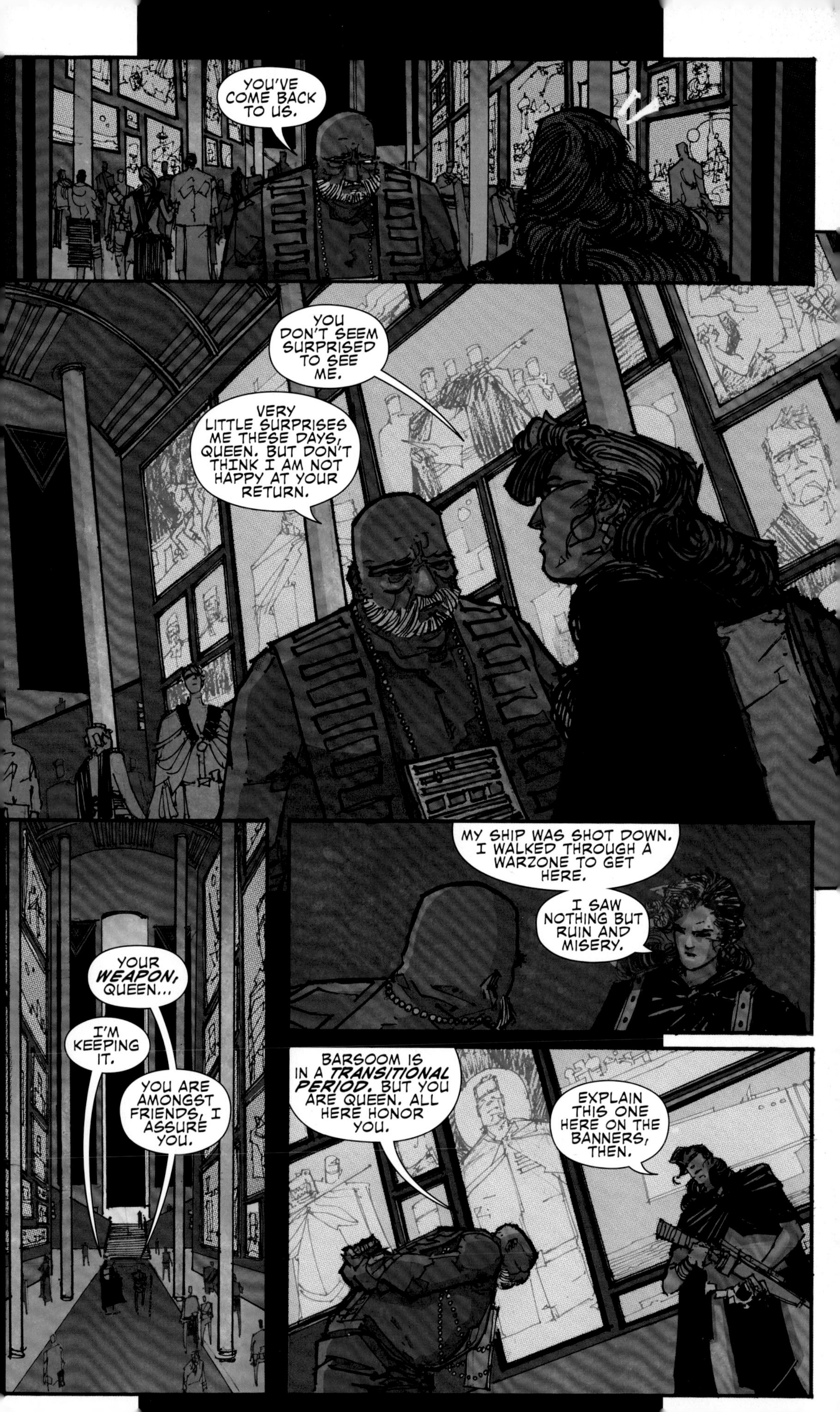
YOU'VE COME BACK TO US.
YOU DON'T SEEM SURPRISED TO SEE ME.
VERY LITTLE SURPRISES ME THESE DAYS, QUEEN. BUT DON'T THINK I AM NOT HAPPY AT YOUR RETURN.
YOUR *WEAPON,* QUEEN...
I'M KEEPING IT.
YOU ARE AMONGST FRIENDS, I ASSURE YOU.
MY SHIP WAS SHOT DOWN. I WALKED THROUGH A WARZONE TO GET HERE.
I SAW NOTHING BUT RUIN AND MISERY.
BARSOOM IS IN A *TRANSITIONAL PERIOD.* BUT YOU ARE QUEEN. ALL HERE HONOR YOU.
EXPLAIN THIS ONE HERE ON THE BANNERS, THEN.

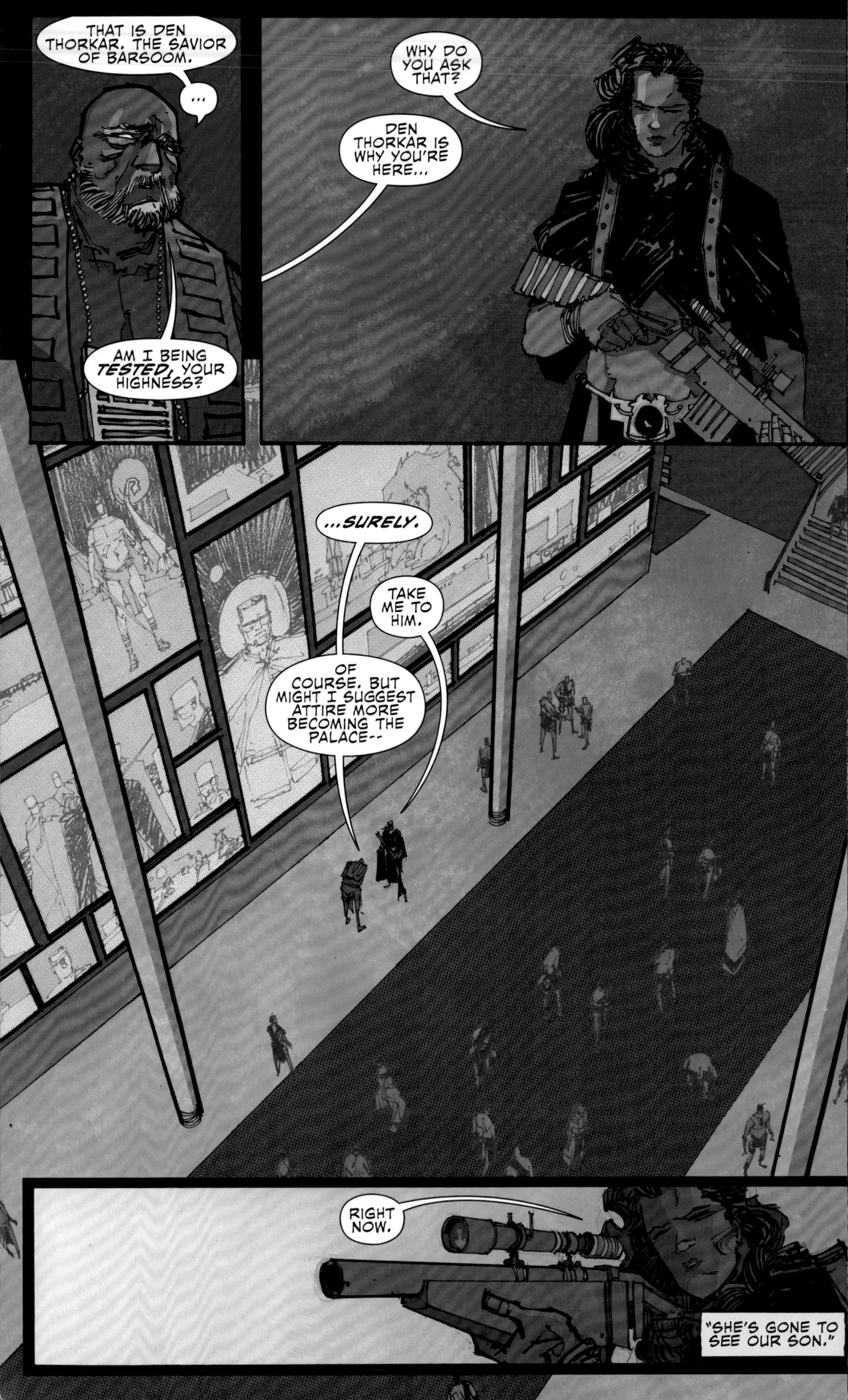
THAT IS DEN THORKAR. THE SAVIOR OF BARSOOM.
...
WHY DO YOU ASK THAT?
DEN THORKAR IS WHY YOU'RE HERE...
AM I BEING *TESTED*, YOUR HIGHNESS?
...SURELY.
TAKE ME TO HIM.
OF COURSE. BUT MIGHT I SUGGEST ATTIRE MORE BECOMING THE PALACE--
RIGHT NOW.
"SHE'S GONE TO SEE OUR SON."

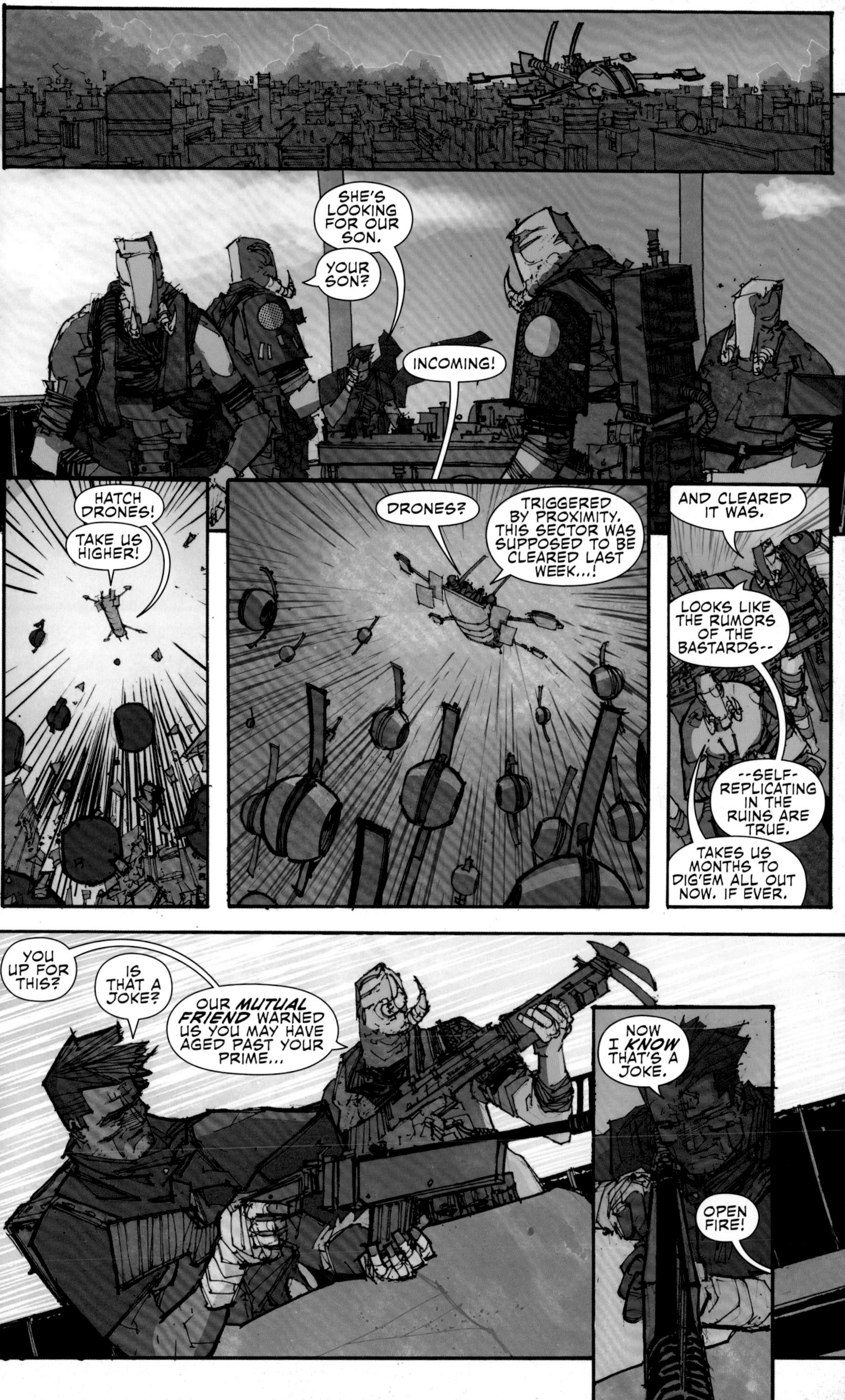
SHE'S LOOKING FOR OUR SON.
YOUR SON?
INCOMING!
HATCH DRONES!
TAKE US HIGHER!
DRONES?
TRIGGERED BY PROXIMITY. THIS SECTOR WAS SUPPOSED TO BE CLEARED LAST WEEK...!
AND CLEARED IT WAS.
LOOKS LIKE THE RUMORS OF THE BASTARDS--
--SELF-REPLICATING IN THE RUINS ARE TRUE.
TAKES US MONTHS TO DIG'EM ALL OUT NOW. IF EVER.
YOU UP FOR THIS?
IS THAT A JOKE?
OUR *MUTUAL FRIEND* WARNED US YOU MAY HAVE AGED PAST YOUR PRIME...
NOW I *KNOW* THAT'S A JOKE.
OPEN FIRE!

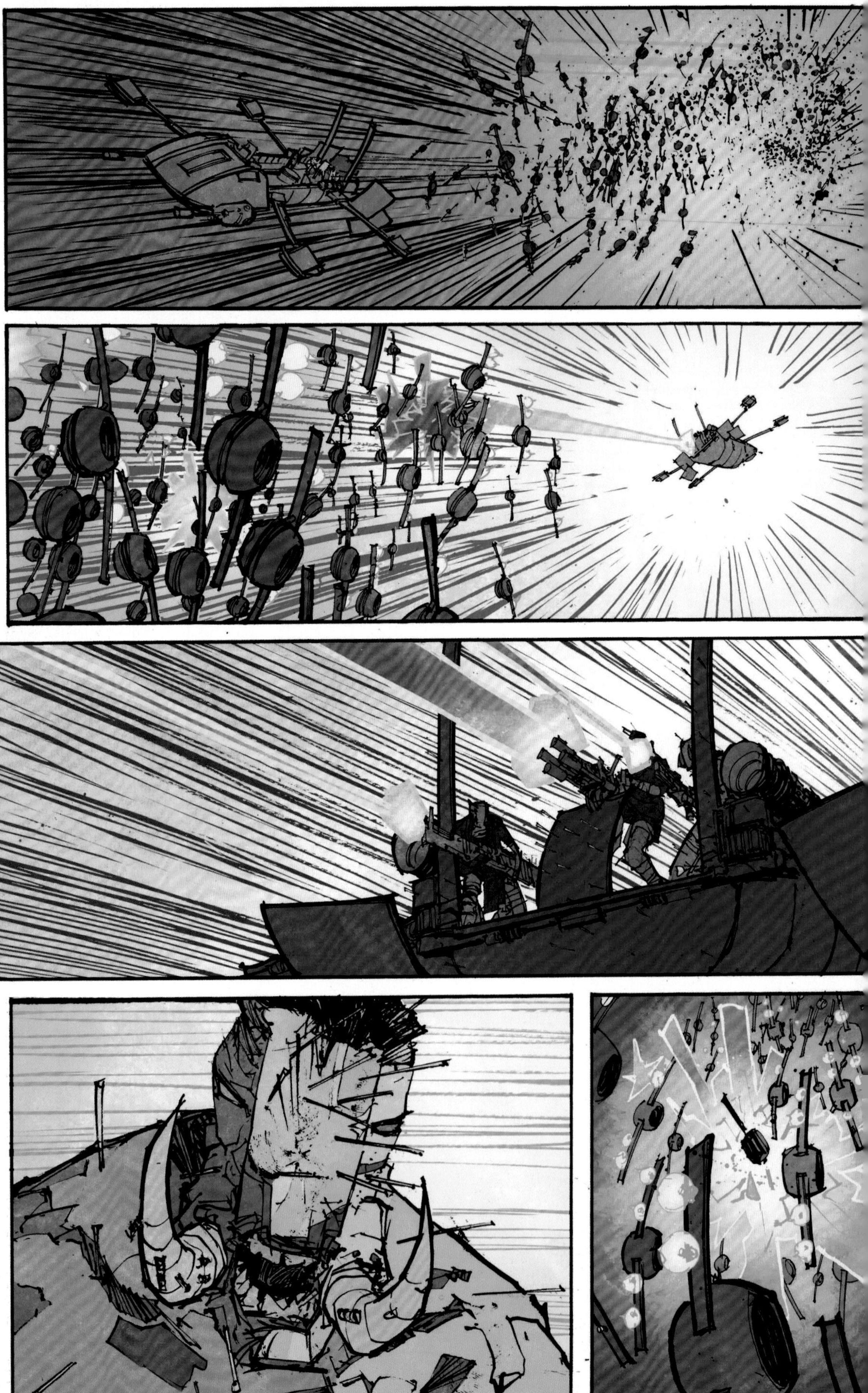

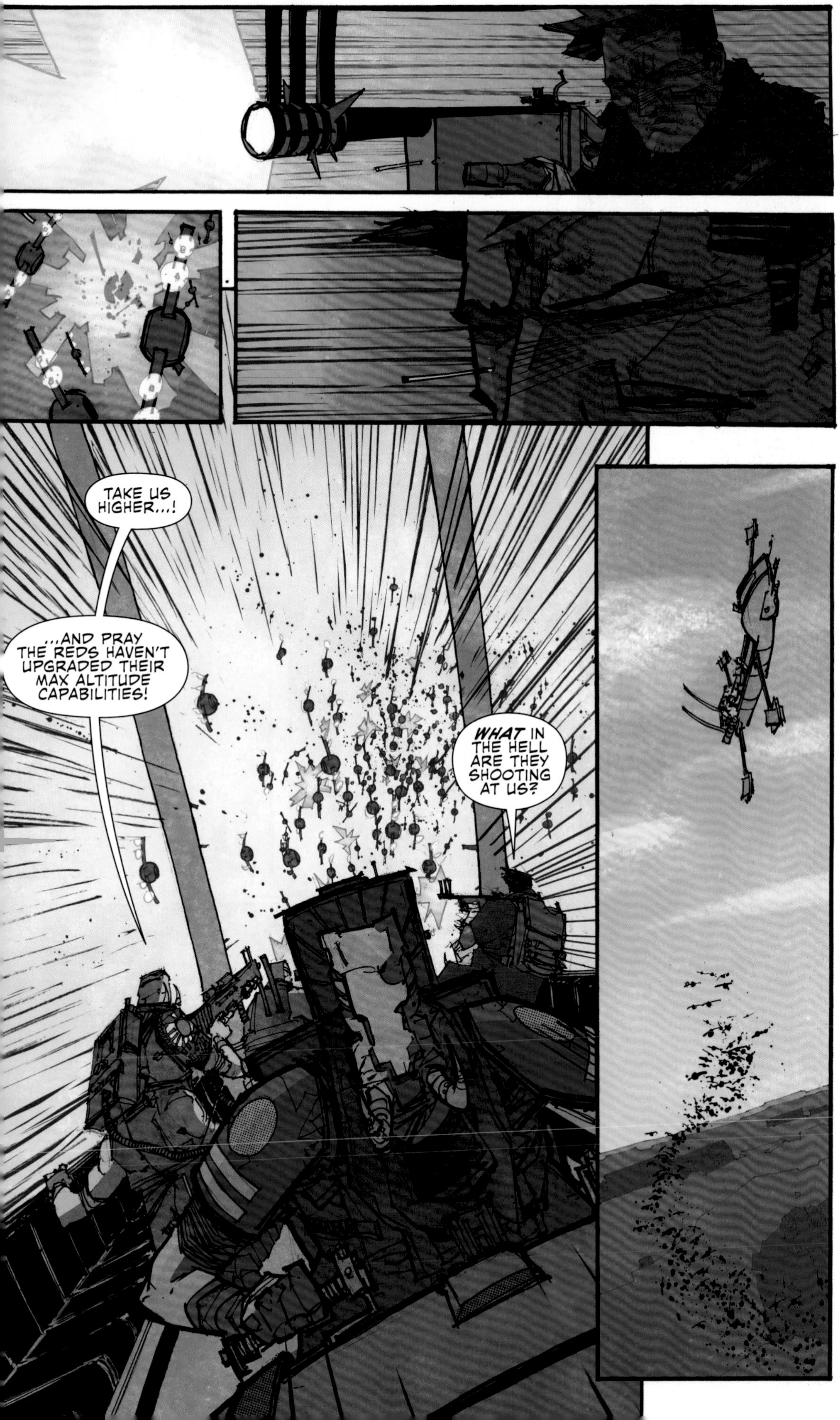
TAKE US HIGHER...!
...AND PRAY THE REDS HAVEN'T UPGRADED THEIR MAX ALTITUDE CAPABILITIES!
WHAT IN THE HELL ARE THEY SHOOTING AT US?

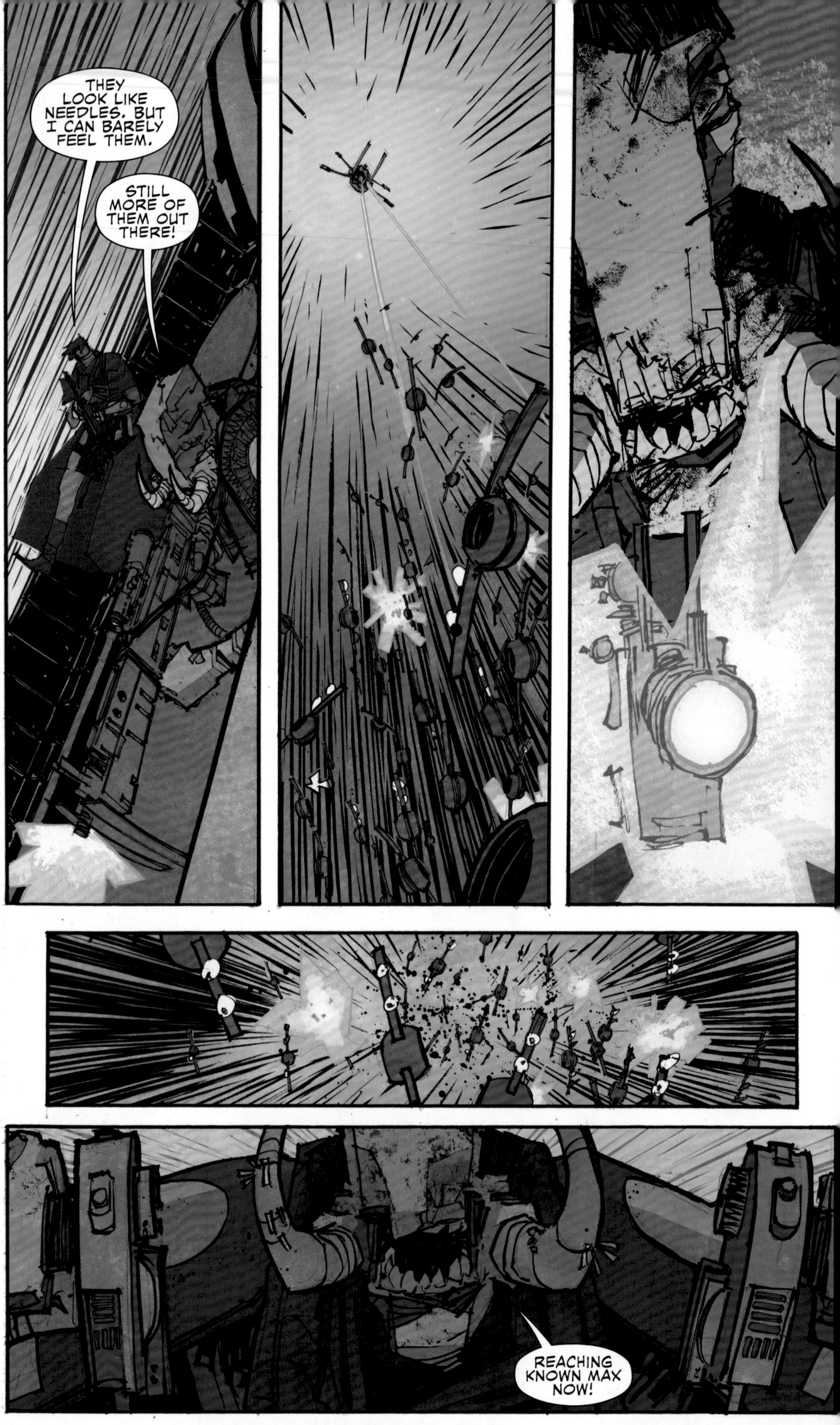
THEY LOOK LIKE NEEDLES. BUT I CAN BARELY FEEL THEM.
STILL MORE OF THEM OUT THERE!
REACHING KNOWN MAX NOW!

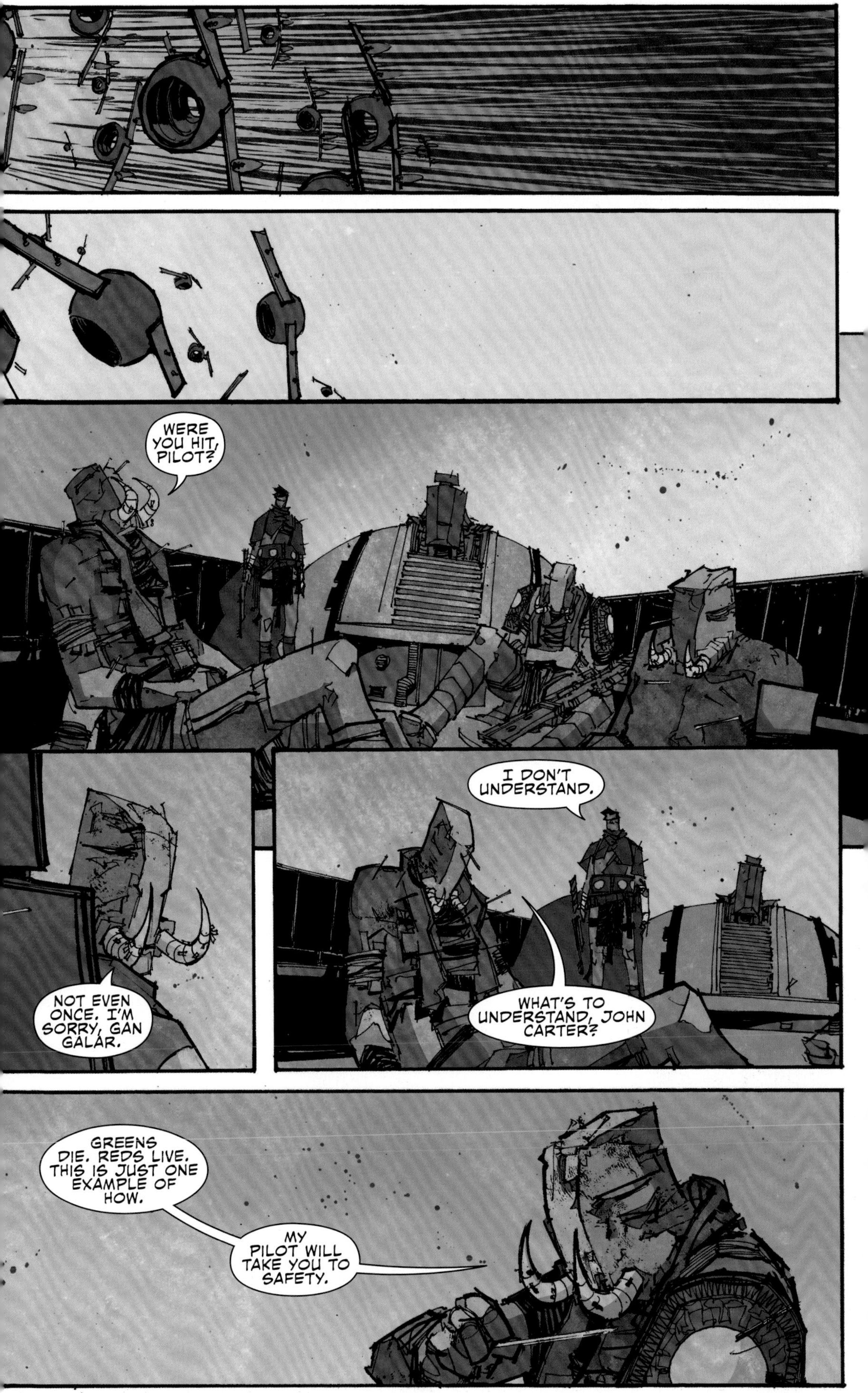
WERE YOU HIT, PILOT?
NOT EVEN ONCE. I'M SORRY, GAN GALAR.
I DON'T UNDERSTAND.
WHAT'S TO UNDERSTAND, JOHN CARTER?
GREENS DIE. REDS LIVE. THIS IS JUST ONE EXAMPLE OF HOW.
MY PILOT WILL TAKE YOU TO SAFETY.

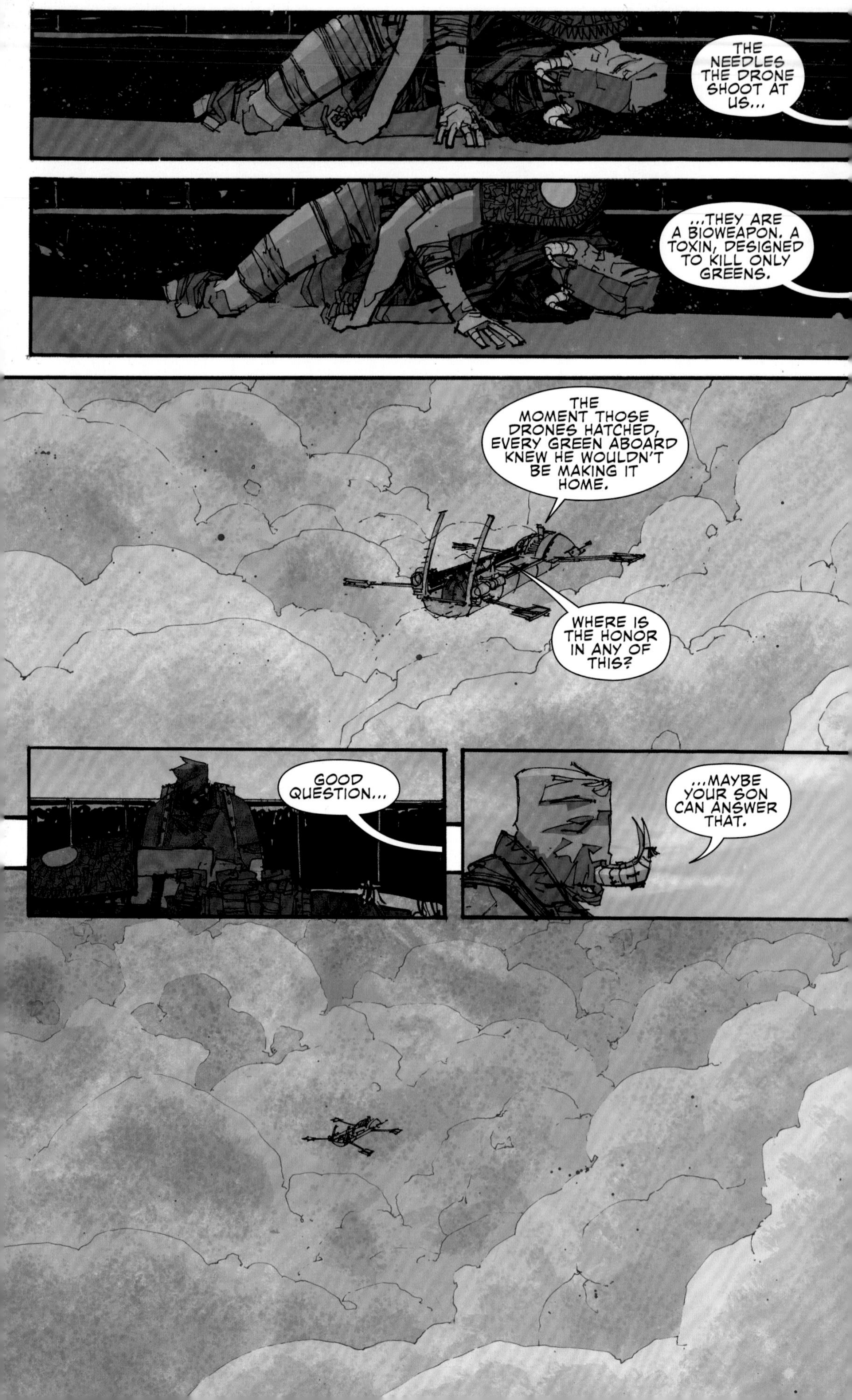
THE NEEDLES THE DRONE SHOOT AT US...
...THEY ARE A BIOWEAPON. A TOXIN, DESIGNED TO KILL ONLY GREENS.
THE MOMENT THOSE DRONES HATCHED, EVERY GREEN ABOARD KNEW HE WOULDN'T BE MAKING IT HOME.
WHERE IS THE HONOR IN ANY OF THIS?
GOOD QUESTION...
...MAYBE YOUR SON CAN ANSWER THAT.

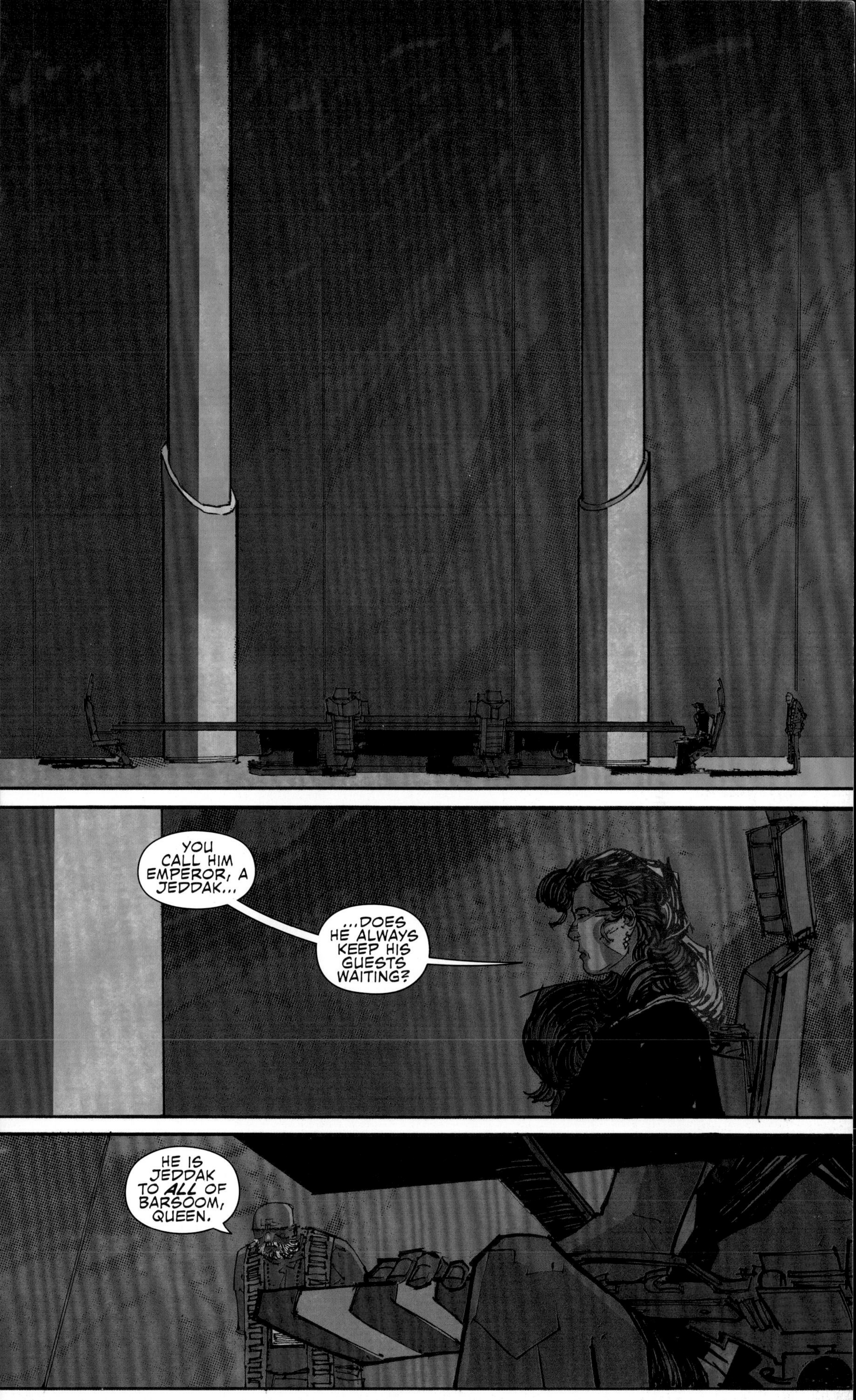
YOU CALL HIM EMPEROR, A JEDDAK...
...DOES HE ALWAYS KEEP HIS GUESTS WAITING?
HE IS JEDDAK TO ALL OF BARSOOM, QUEEN.

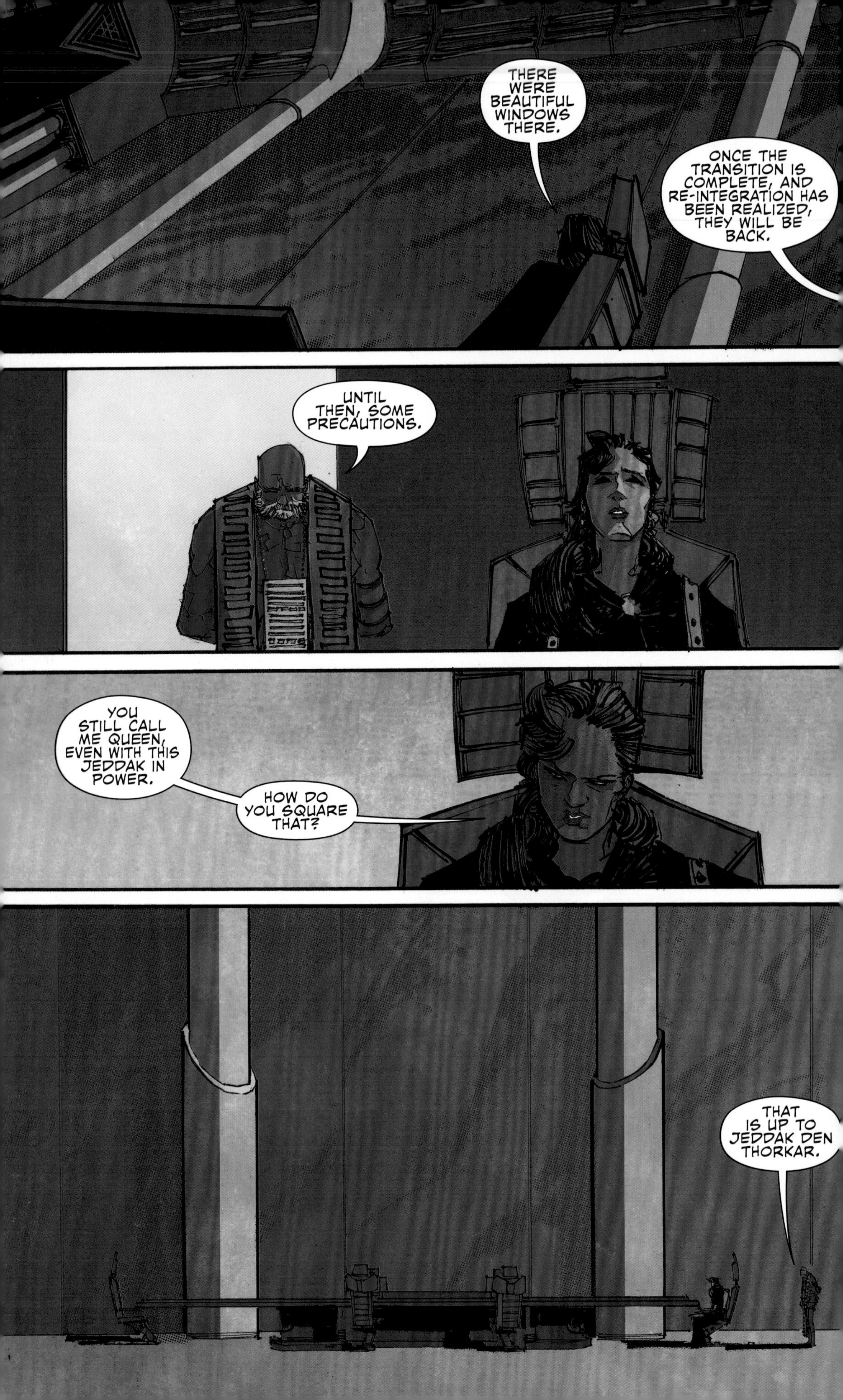
THERE WERE BEAUTIFUL WINDOWS THERE.
ONCE THE TRANSITION IS COMPLETE, AND RE-INTEGRATION HAS BEEN REALIZED, THEY WILL BE BACK.
UNTIL THEN, SOME PRECAUTIONS.
YOU STILL CALL ME QUEEN, EVEN WITH THIS JEDDAK IN POWER.
HOW DO YOU SQUARE THAT?
THAT IS UP TO JEDDAK DEN THORKAR.

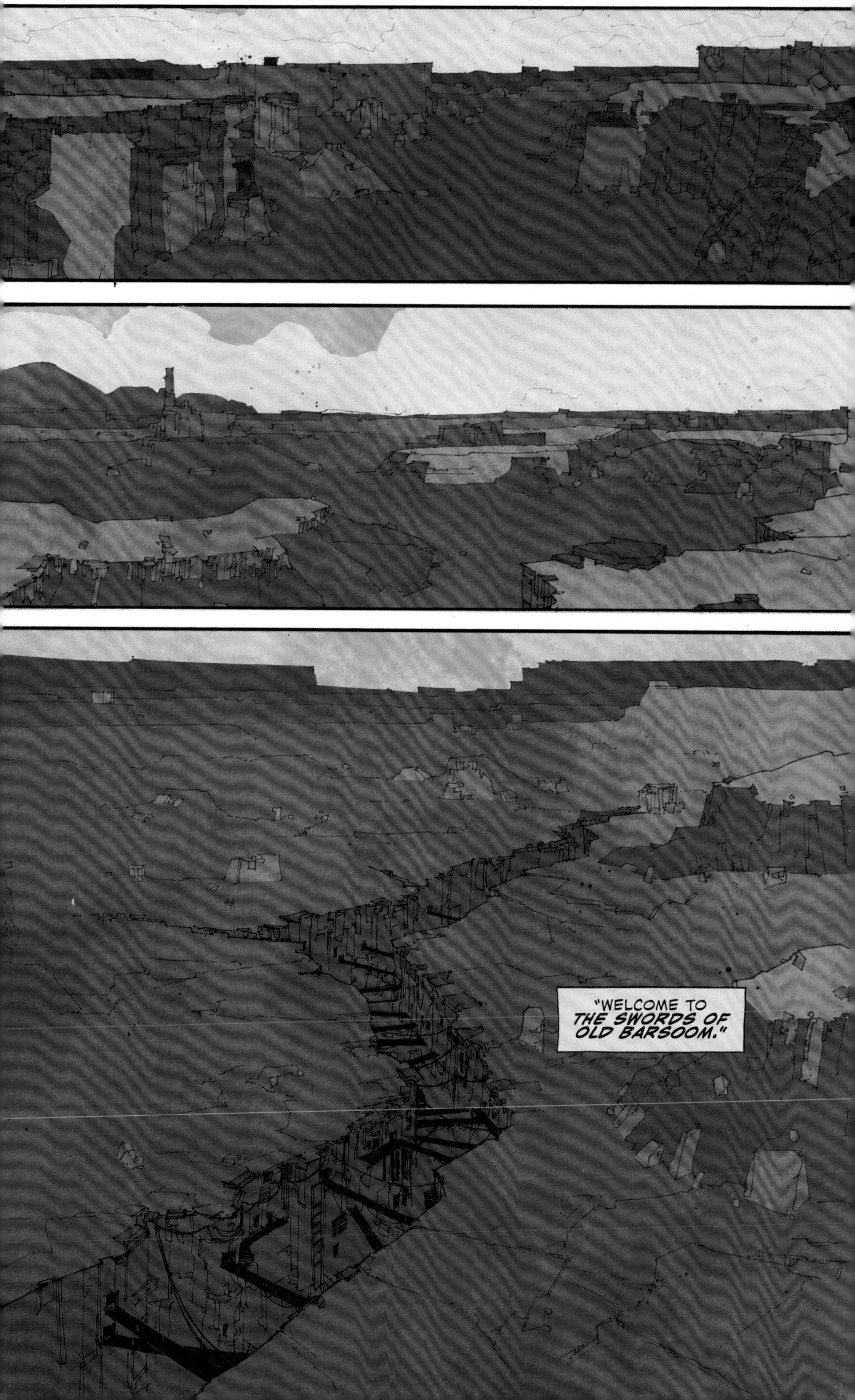
"WELCOME TO THE SWORDS OF OLD BARSOOM."

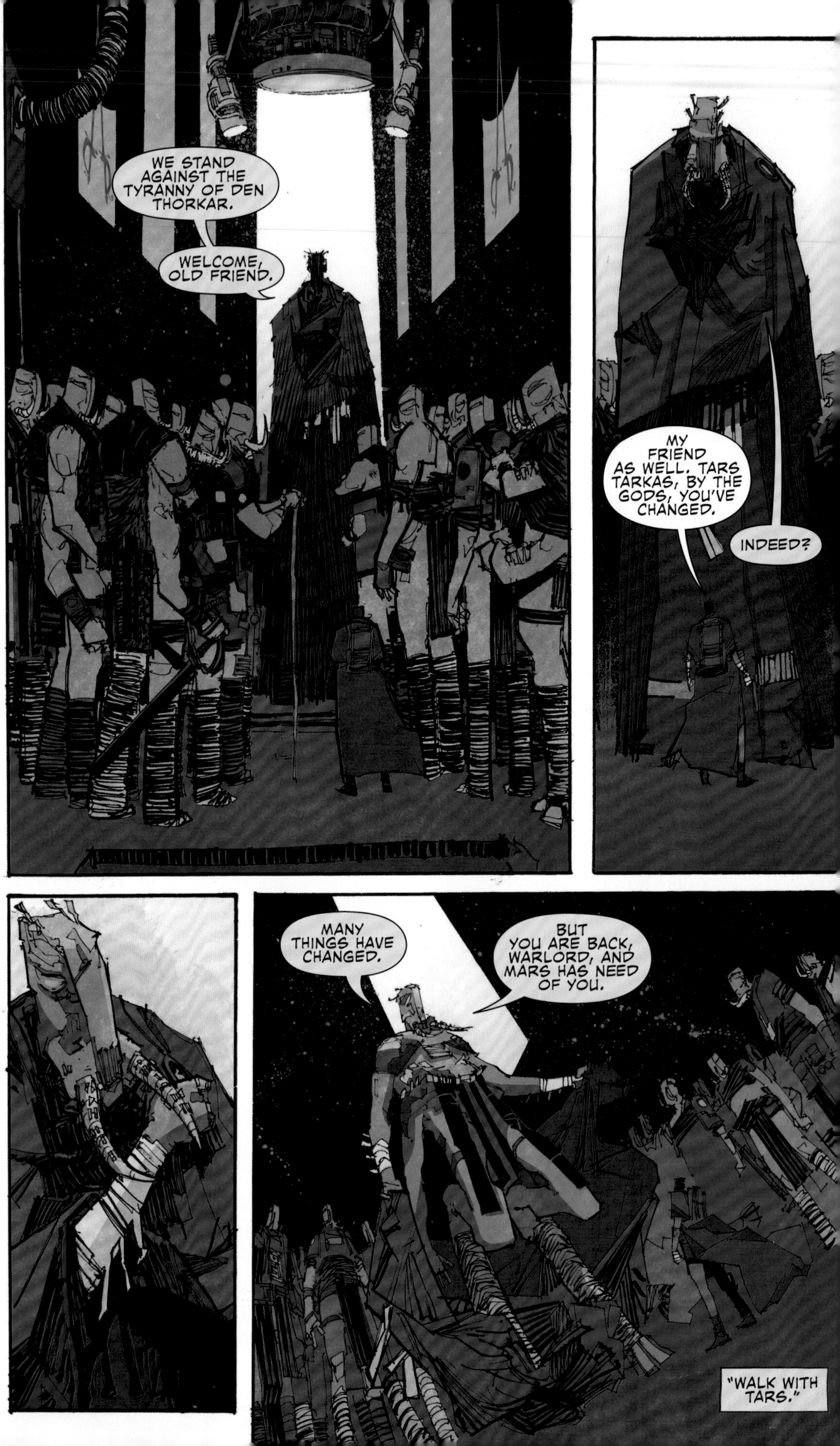
WE STAND AGAINST THE TYRANNY OF DEN THORKAR.
WELCOME, OLD FRIEND.
MY FRIEND AS WELL. TARS TARKAS, BY THE GODS, YOU'VE CHANGED.
INDEED?
MANY THINGS HAVE CHANGED.
BUT YOU ARE BACK, WARLORD, AND MARS HAS NEED OF YOU.
"WALK WITH TARS."

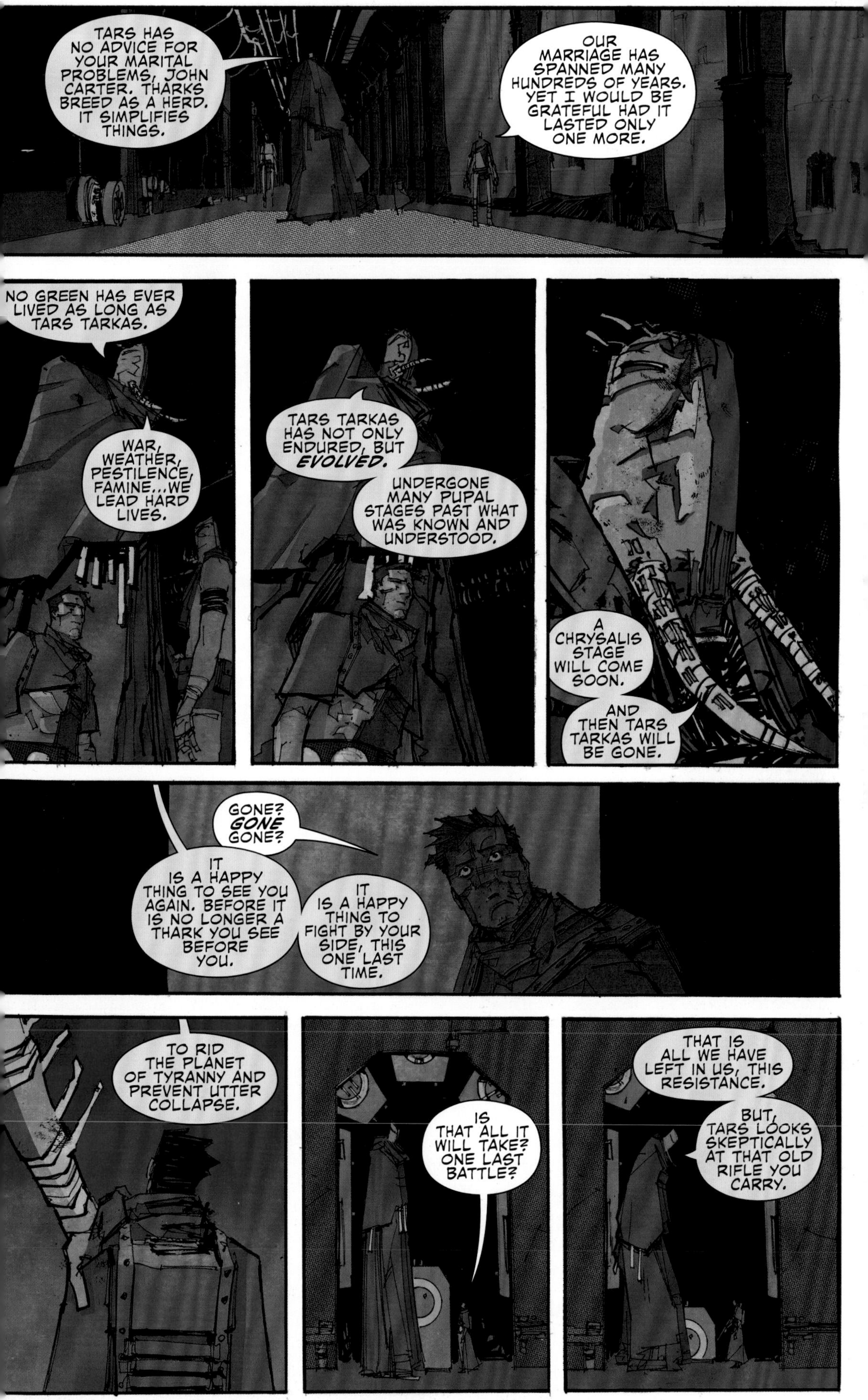
TARS HAS NO ADVICE FOR YOUR MARITAL PROBLEMS, JOHN CARTER. THARKS BREED AS A HERD. IT SIMPLIFIES THINGS.
OUR MARRIAGE HAS SPANNED MANY HUNDREDS OF YEARS. YET I WOULD BE GRATEFUL HAD IT LASTED ONLY ONE MORE.
NO GREEN HAS EVER LIVED AS LONG AS TARS TARKAS.
WAR, WEATHER, PESTILENCE, FAMINE...WE LEAD HARD LIVES.
TARS TARKAS HAS NOT ONLY ENDURED, BUT *EVOLVED.*
UNDERGONE MANY PUPAL STAGES PAST WHAT WAS KNOWN AND UNDERSTOOD.
A CHRYSALIS STAGE WILL COME SOON.
AND THEN TARS TARKAS WILL BE GONE.
GONE? ***GONE*** GONE?
IT IS A HAPPY THING TO SEE YOU AGAIN. BEFORE IT IS NO LONGER A THARK YOU SEE BEFORE YOU.
IT IS A HAPPY THING TO FIGHT BY YOUR SIDE, THIS ONE LAST TIME.
TO RID THE PLANET OF TYRANNY AND PREVENT UTTER COLLAPSE.
IS THAT ALL IT WILL TAKE? ONE LAST BATTLE?
THAT IS ALL WE HAVE LEFT IN US, THIS RESISTANCE.
BUT, TARS LOOKS SKEPTICALLY AT THAT OLD RIFLE YOU CARRY.

THIS RIFLE HAS SERVED ME WELL FOR ALMOST FOUR HUNDRED YEARS.

ON TITAN, PERHAPS, IT IS FINE.

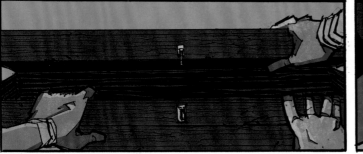

TARS SUGGESTS SOMETHING ELSE FOR THE FIGHT TO COME...

...JOHN CARTER, WARLORD OF MARS.

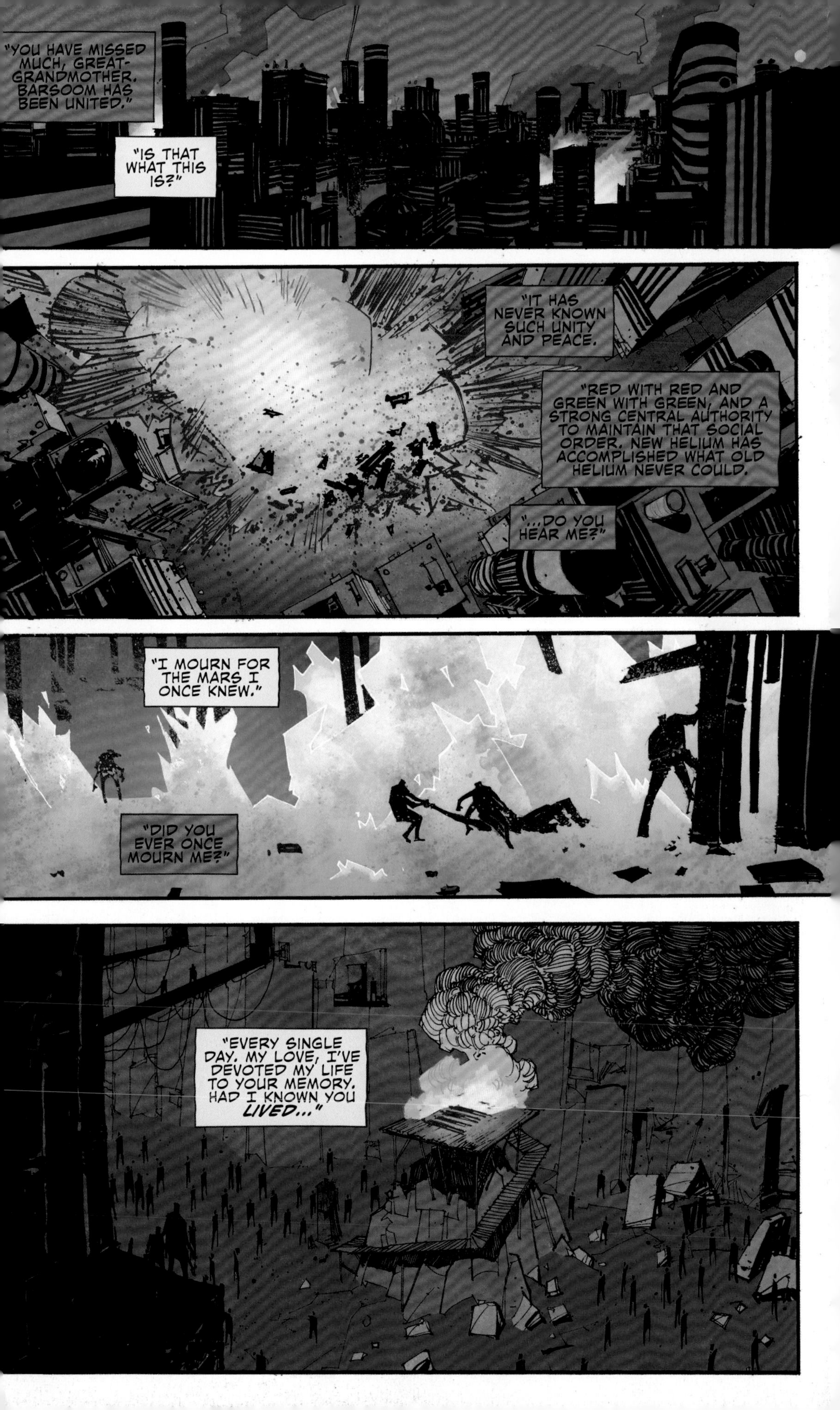
"YOU HAVE MISSED MUCH, GREAT-GRANDMOTHER. BARSOOM HAS BEEN UNITED."
"IS THAT WHAT THIS IS?"
"IT HAS NEVER KNOWN SUCH UNITY AND PEACE.
"RED WITH RED AND GREEN WITH GREEN, AND A STRONG CENTRAL AUTHORITY TO MAINTAIN THAT SOCIAL ORDER. NEW HELIUM HAS ACCOMPLISHED WHAT OLD HELIUM NEVER COULD.
"...DO YOU HEAR ME?"
"I MOURN FOR THE MARS I ONCE KNEW."
"DID YOU EVER ONCE MOURN ME?"
"EVERY SINGLE DAY. MY LOVE, I'VE DEVOTED MY LIFE TO YOUR MEMORY. HAD I KNOWN YOU *LIVED*..."

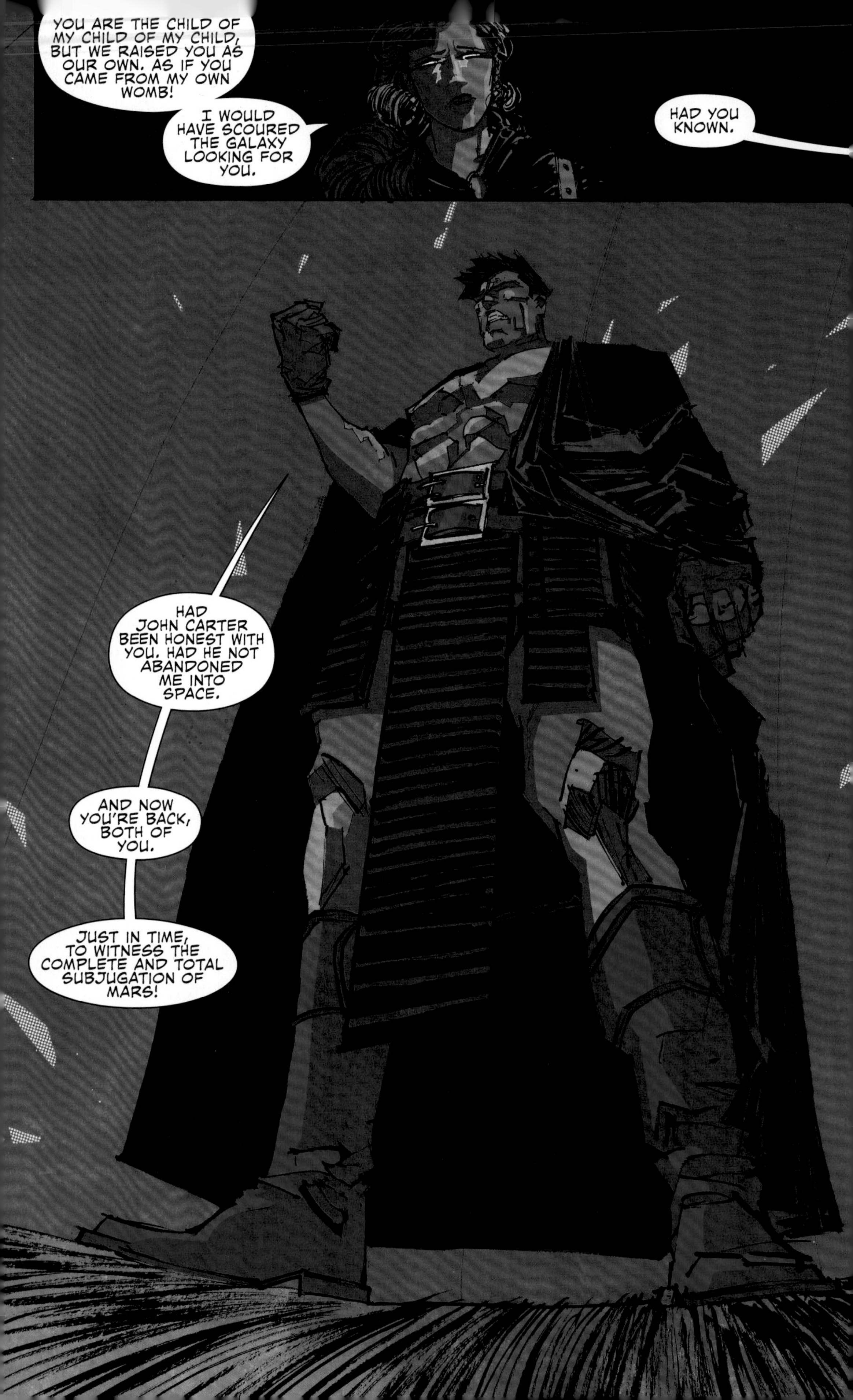
YOU ARE THE CHILD OF MY CHILD OF MY CHILD, BUT WE RAISED YOU AS OUR OWN. AS IF YOU CAME FROM MY OWN WOMB!
I WOULD HAVE SCOURED THE GALAXY LOOKING FOR YOU.
HAD YOU KNOWN.
HAD JOHN CARTER BEEN HONEST WITH YOU. HAD HE NOT ABANDONED ME INTO SPACE.
AND NOW YOU'RE BACK, BOTH OF YOU.
JUST IN TIME, TO WITNESS THE COMPLETE AND TOTAL SUBJUGATION OF MARS!

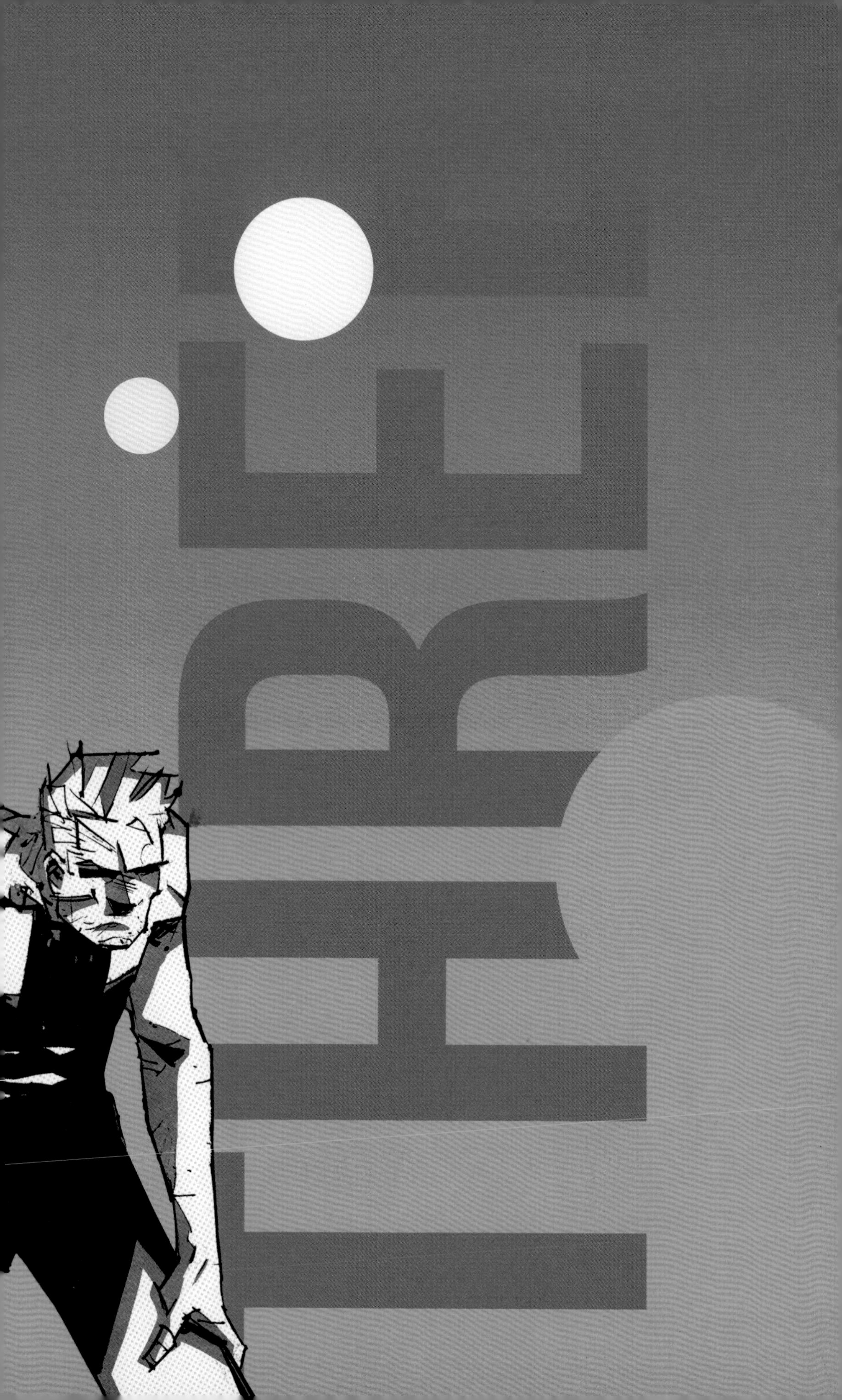

THREE

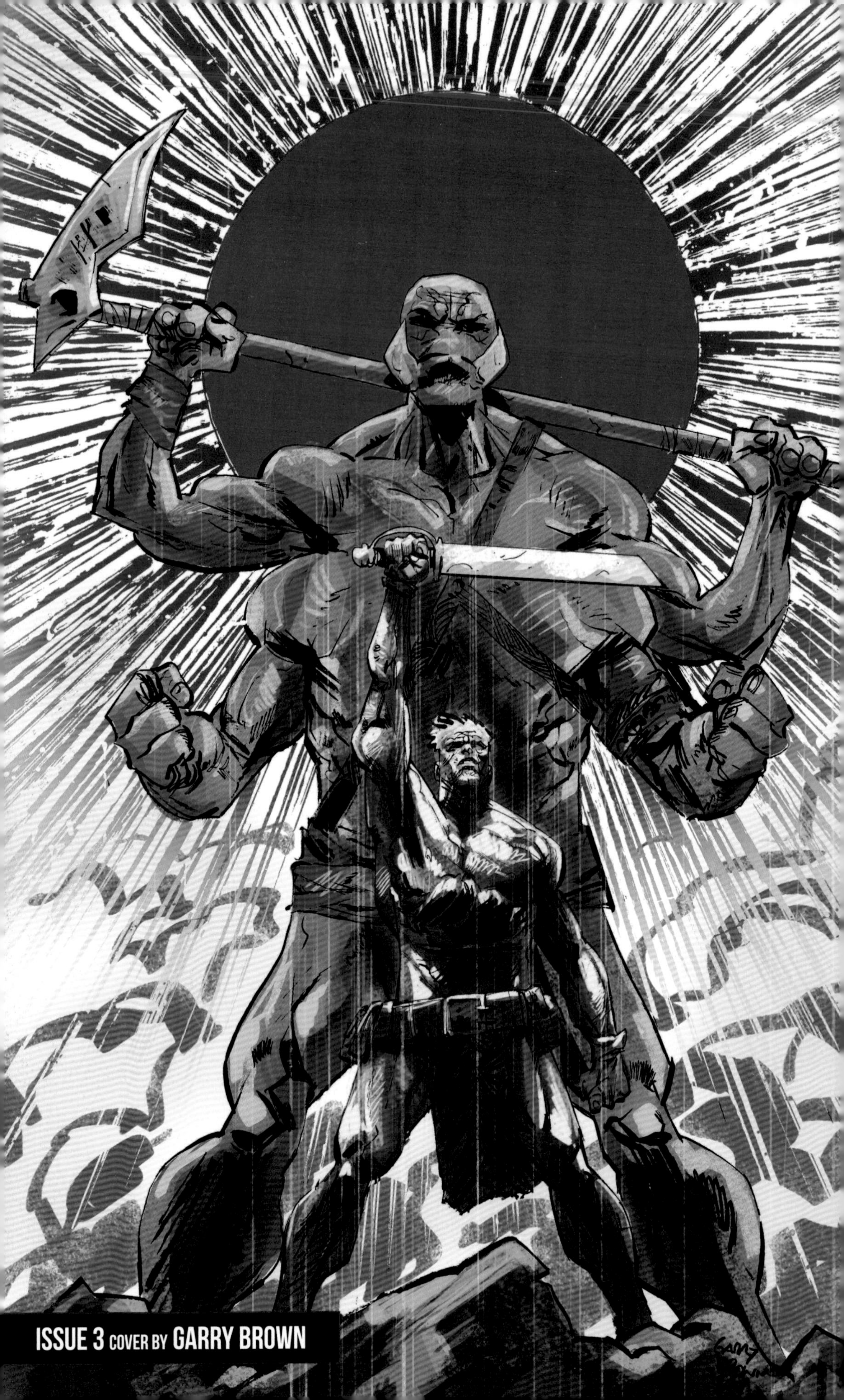

ISSUE 3 COVER BY GARRY BROWN

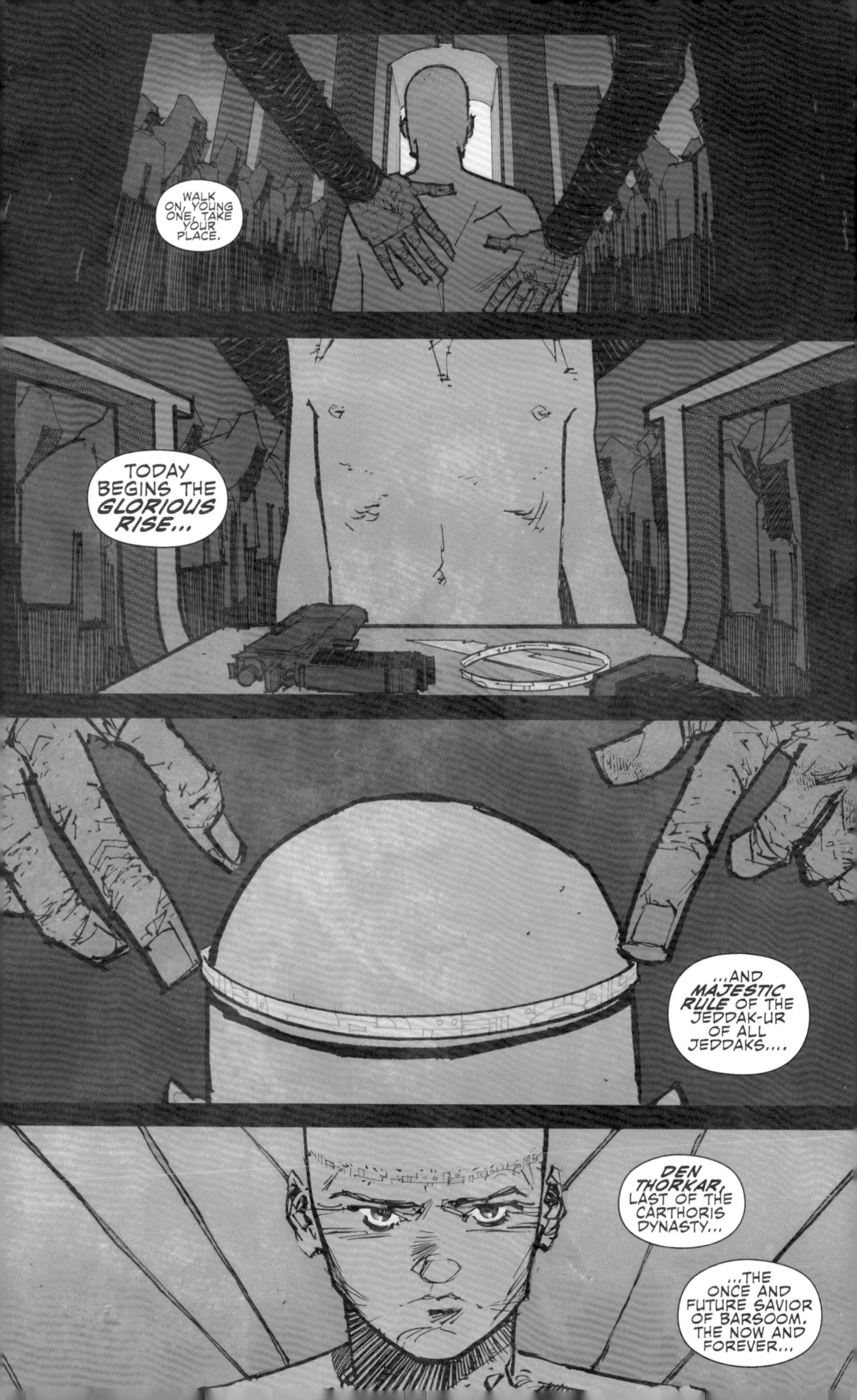
WALK ON, YOUNG ONE, TAKE YOUR PLACE.
TODAY BEGINS THE GLORIOUS RISE...
...AND MAJESTIC RULE OF THE JEDDAK-UR OF ALL JEDDAKS....
DEN THORKAR, LAST OF THE CARTHORIS DYNASTY...
...THE ONCE AND FUTURE SAVIOR OF BARSOOM. THE NOW AND FOREVER...

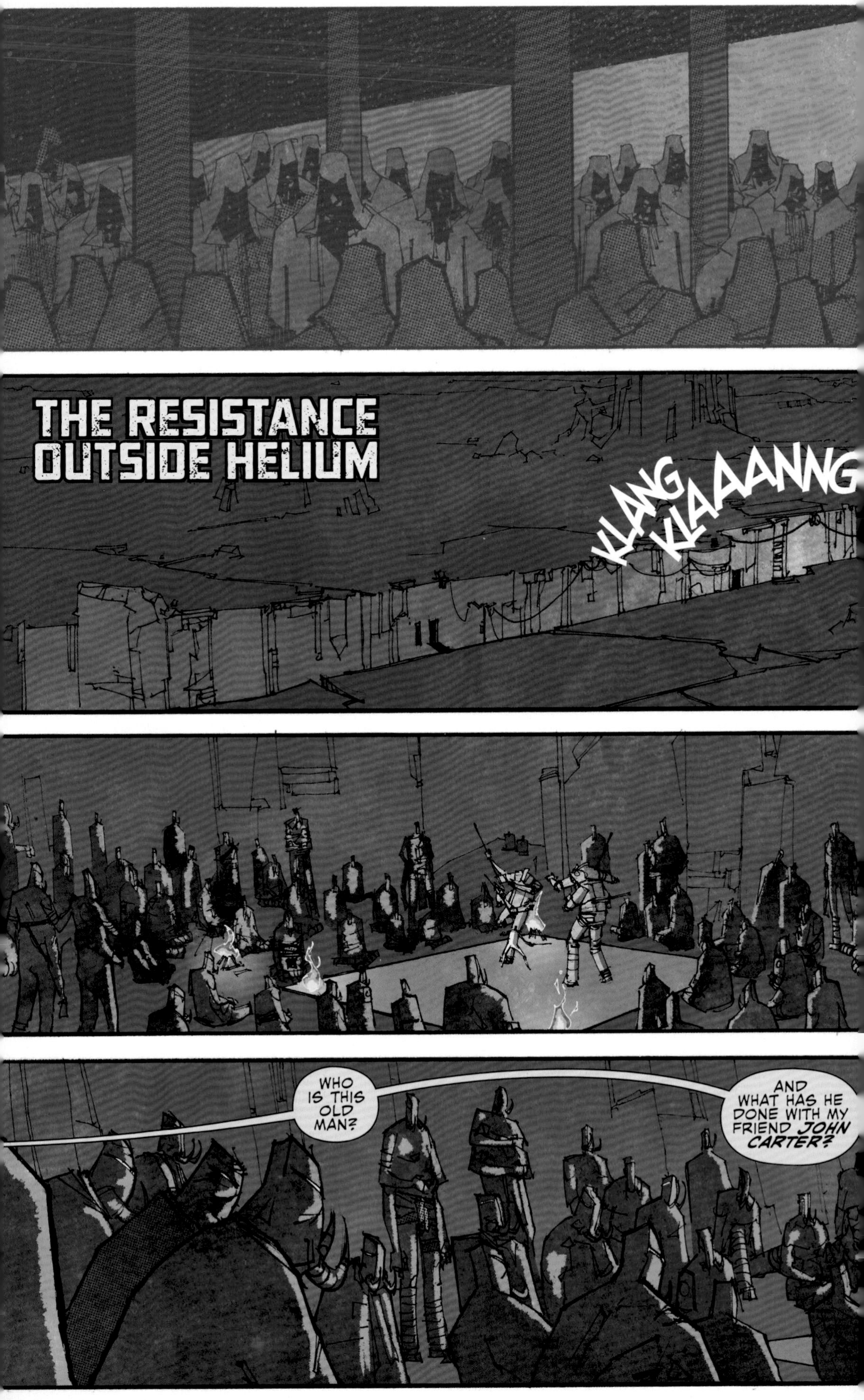
THE RESISTANCE OUTSIDE HELIUM
KLANG KLAAANNG
WHO IS THIS OLD MAN?
AND WHAT HAS HE DONE WITH MY FRIEND JOHN CARTER?

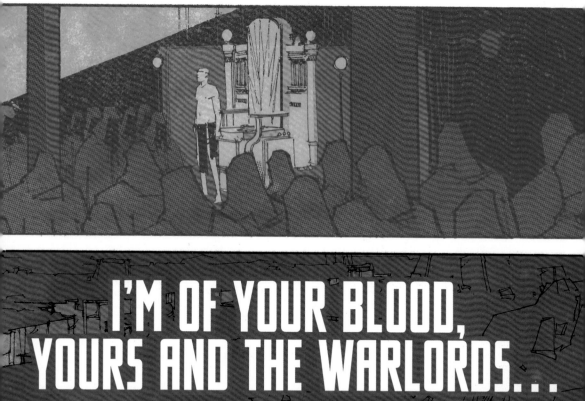

I'M OF YOUR BLOOD, YOURS AND THE WARLORDS....

BY BRIAN WOOD AND ALEX COX   ART BY HAYDEN SHERMAN
COLORS BY CHRIS O'HALLORAN   LETTERS BY TOM NAPOLITANO

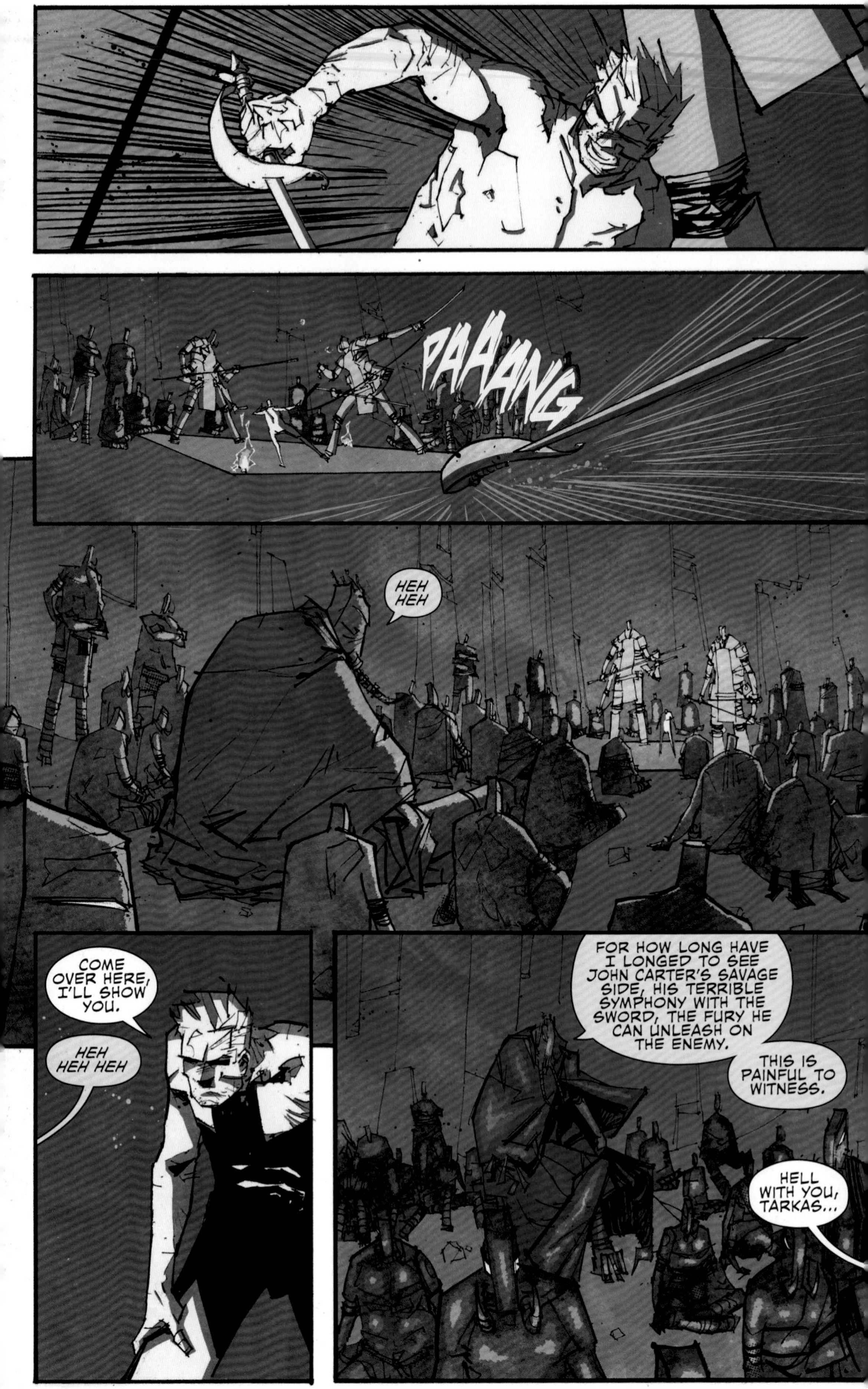
PAAANG
HEH HEH
COME OVER HERE, I'LL SHOW YOU.
HEH HEH HEH
FOR HOW LONG HAVE I LONGED TO SEE JOHN CARTER'S SAVAGE SIDE, HIS TERRIBLE SYMPHONY WITH THE SWORD, THE FURY HE CAN UNLEASH ON THE ENEMY.
THIS IS PAINFUL TO WITNESS.
HELL WITH YOU, TARKAS...

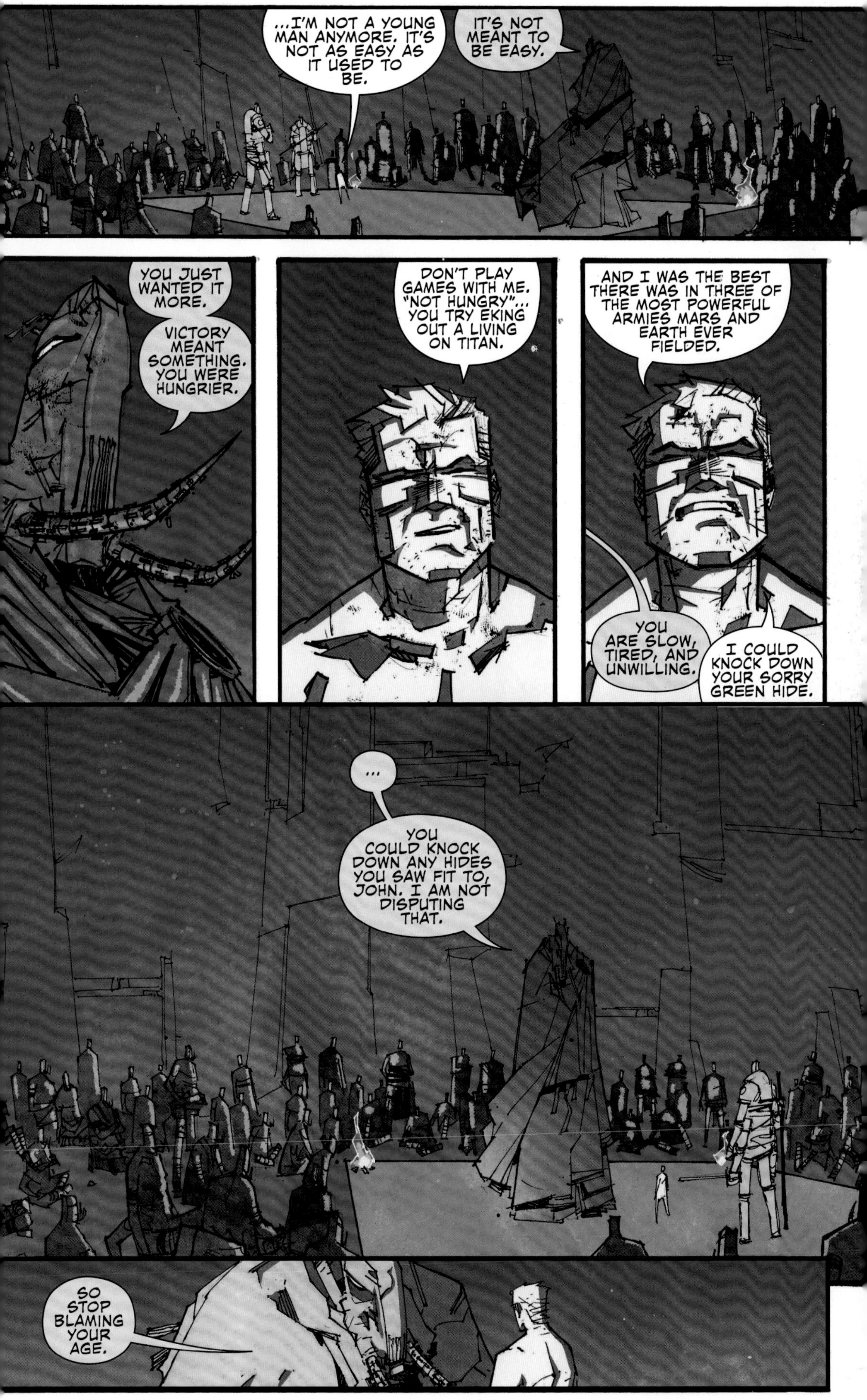
...I'M NOT A YOUNG MAN ANYMORE. IT'S NOT AS EASY AS IT USED TO BE.
IT'S NOT MEANT TO BE EASY.
YOU JUST WANTED IT MORE.
VICTORY MEANT SOMETHING. YOU WERE HUNGRIER.
DON'T PLAY GAMES WITH ME. "NOT HUNGRY"... YOU TRY EKING OUT A LIVING ON TITAN.
AND I WAS THE BEST THERE WAS IN THREE OF THE MOST POWERFUL ARMIES MARS AND EARTH EVER FIELDED.
YOU ARE SLOW, TIRED, AND UNWILLING.
I COULD KNOCK DOWN YOUR SORRY GREEN HIDE.
...
YOU COULD KNOCK DOWN ANY HIDES YOU SAW FIT TO, JOHN. I AM NOT DISPUTING THAT.
SO STOP BLAMING YOUR AGE.

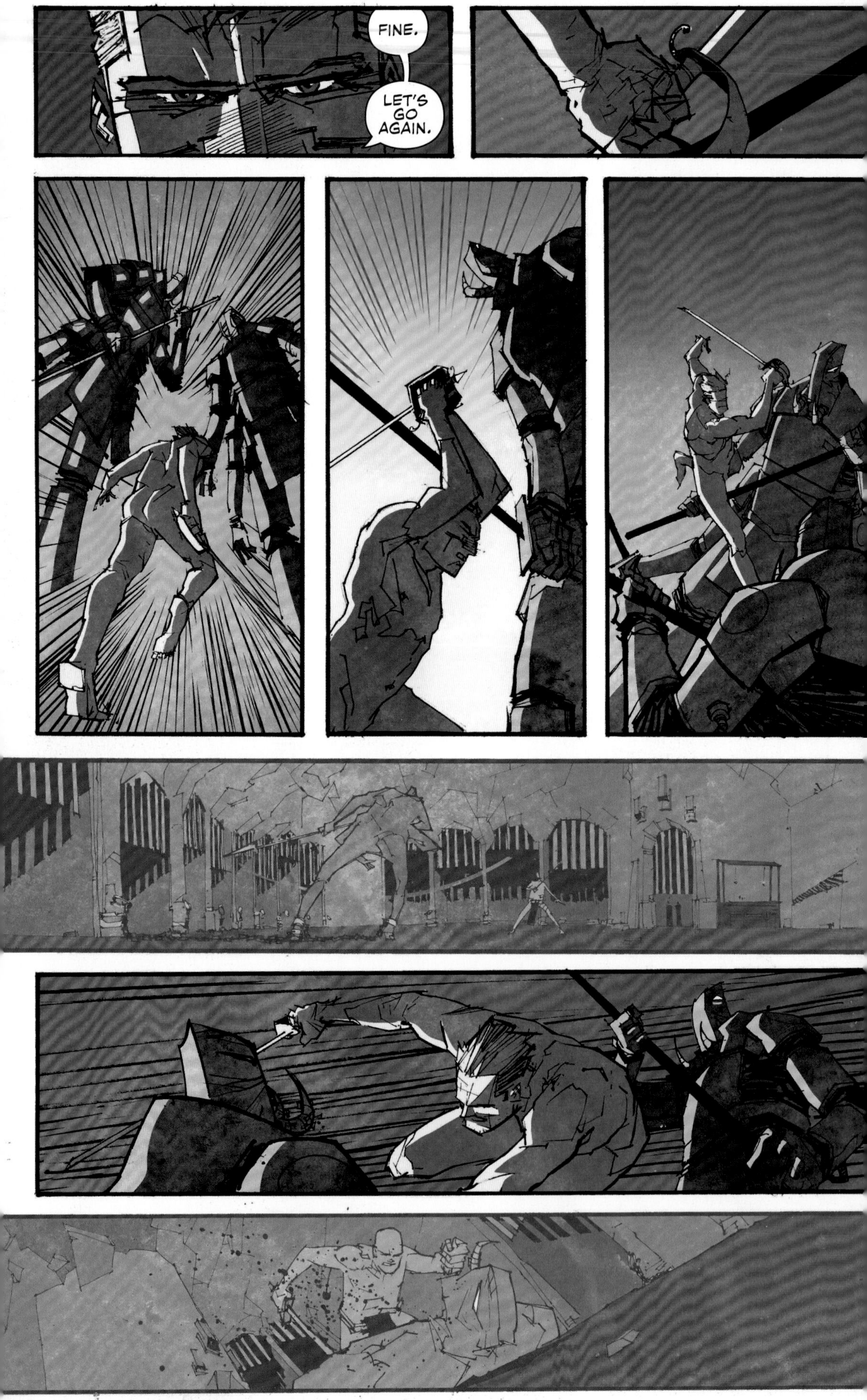
FINE.
LET'S GO AGAIN.

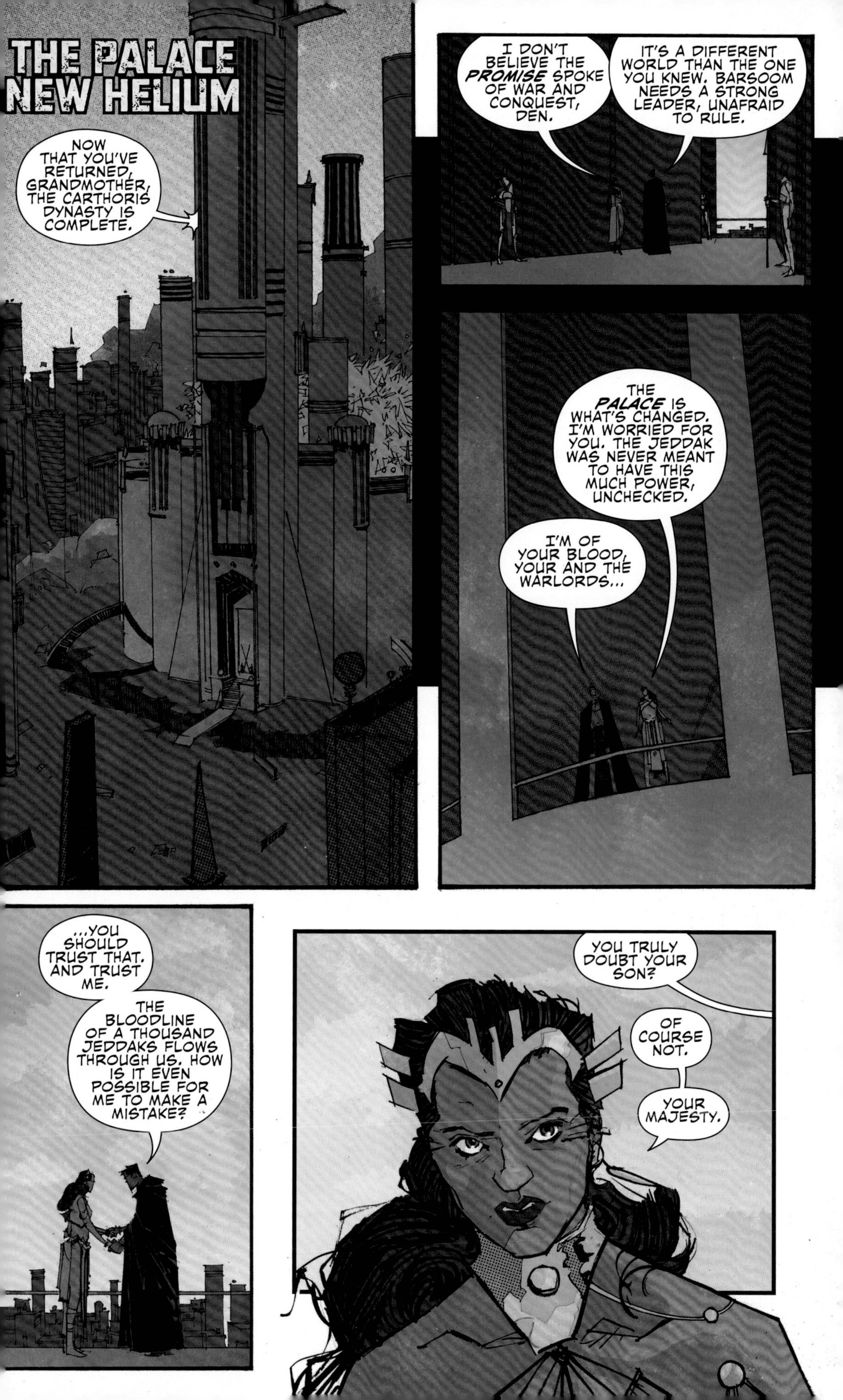
THE PALACE
NEW HELIUM
NOW THAT YOU'VE RETURNED, GRANDMOTHER, THE CARTHORIS DYNASTY IS COMPLETE.
I DON'T BELIEVE THE PROMISE SPOKE OF WAR AND CONQUEST, DEN.
IT'S A DIFFERENT WORLD THAN THE ONE YOU KNEW. BARSOOM NEEDS A STRONG LEADER, UNAFRAID TO RULE.
THE PALACE IS WHAT'S CHANGED. I'M WORRIED FOR YOU. THE JEDDAK WAS NEVER MEANT TO HAVE THIS MUCH POWER, UNCHECKED.
I'M OF YOUR BLOOD, YOUR AND THE WARLORDS...
...YOU SHOULD TRUST THAT. AND TRUST ME.
THE BLOODLINE OF A THOUSAND JEDDAKS FLOWS THROUGH US. HOW IS IT EVEN POSSIBLE FOR ME TO MAKE A MISTAKE?
YOU TRULY DOUBT YOUR SON?
OF COURSE NOT.
YOUR MAJESTY.

OUR YOUNG JEDDAK-UR IS INFALLIABLE. HE'S SURVIVED COUNTLESS MILITARY CAMPAIGNS. NEITHER A DROP OF SWEAT NOR BLOOD.

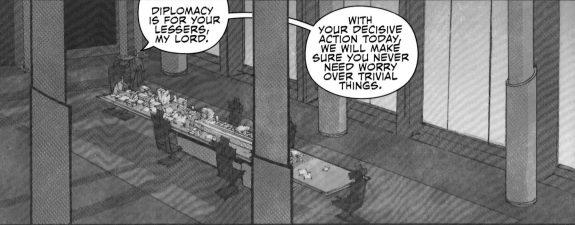

DIPLOMACY IS FOR YOUR LESSERS, MY LORD.

WITH YOUR DECISIVE ACTION TODAY, WE WILL MAKE SURE YOU NEVER NEED WORRY OVER TRIVIAL THINGS.

HE IS WITHOUT EQUAL. THE PALACE ITSELF BENDS TO HIS WILL, AS DOES HIS PEOPLE.

BUT HE DOES NOT ABUSE THAT TRUST. HE REWARDS IT, AND IS LOVED BY ALL.

YOU ARE IMMORTAL, DEN THORKAR, AS IS OUR CAUSE. WIELD YOUR SWORD WITH PRIDE...

AND BARSOOM WILL RETURN YOU TO US.

ABSOLUTE POWER IS DANGEROUS.

IN THE HANDS OF ANYONE BUT DEN THORKAR.

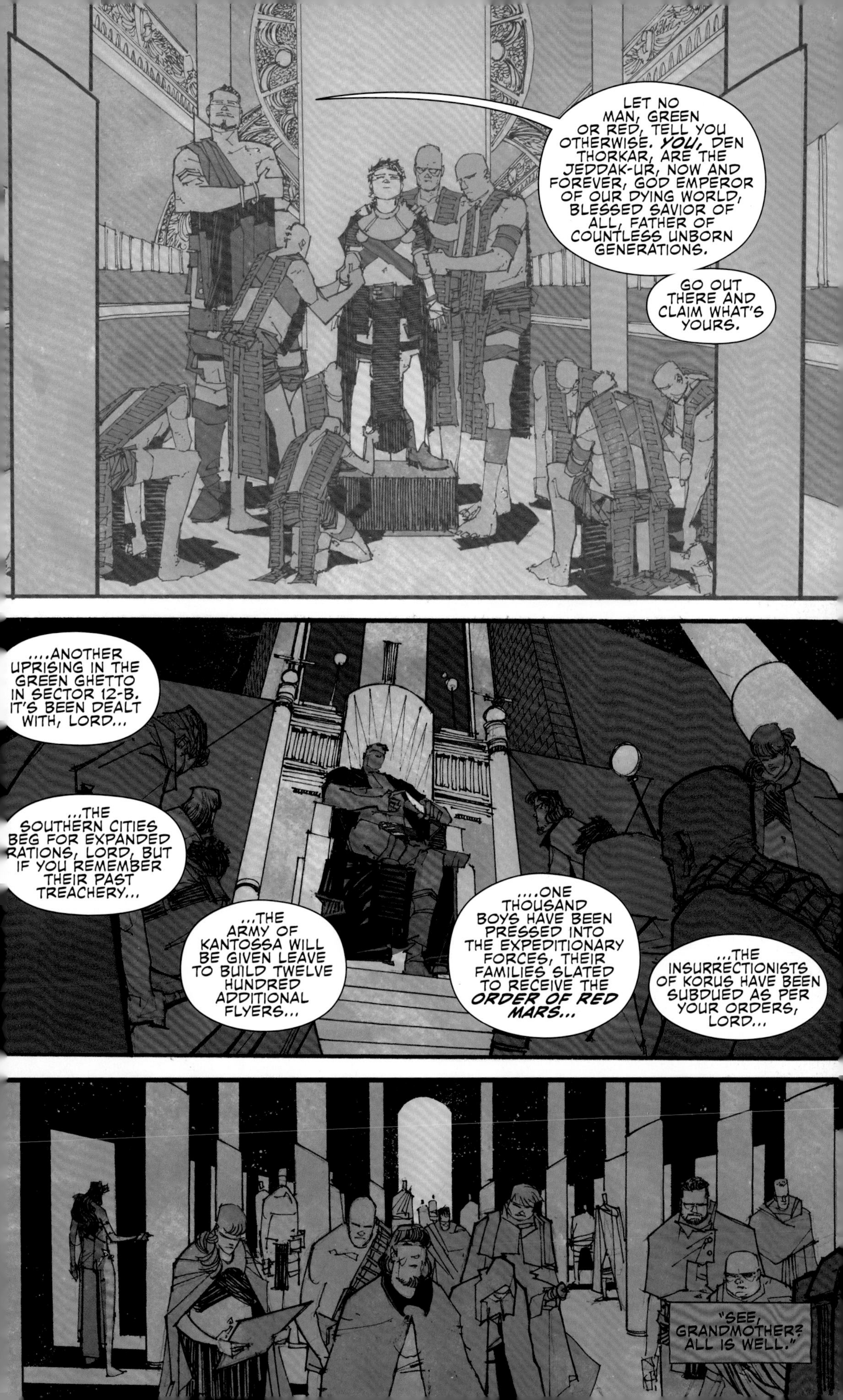
LET NO MAN, GREEN OR RED, TELL YOU OTHERWISE. YOU, DEN THORKAR, ARE THE JEDDAK-UR, NOW AND FOREVER, GOD EMPEROR OF OUR DYING WORLD, BLESSED SAVIOR OF ALL, FATHER OF COUNTLESS UNBORN GENERATIONS.
GO OUT THERE AND CLAIM WHAT'S YOURS.
....ANOTHER UPRISING IN THE GREEN GHETTO IN SECTOR 12-B. IT'S BEEN DEALT WITH, LORD...
...THE SOUTHERN CITIES BEG FOR EXPANDED RATIONS, LORD, BUT IF YOU REMEMBER THEIR PAST TREACHERY...
...THE ARMY OF KANTOSSA WILL BE GIVEN LEAVE TO BUILD TWELVE HUNDRED ADDITIONAL FLYERS...
....ONE THOUSAND BOYS HAVE BEEN PRESSED INTO THE EXPEDITIONARY FORCES, THEIR FAMILIES SLATED TO RECEIVE THE ORDER OF RED MARS...
...THE INSURRECTIONISTS OF KORUS HAVE BEEN SUBDUED AS PER YOUR ORDERS, LORD...
"SEE, GRANDMOTHER? ALL IS WELL."

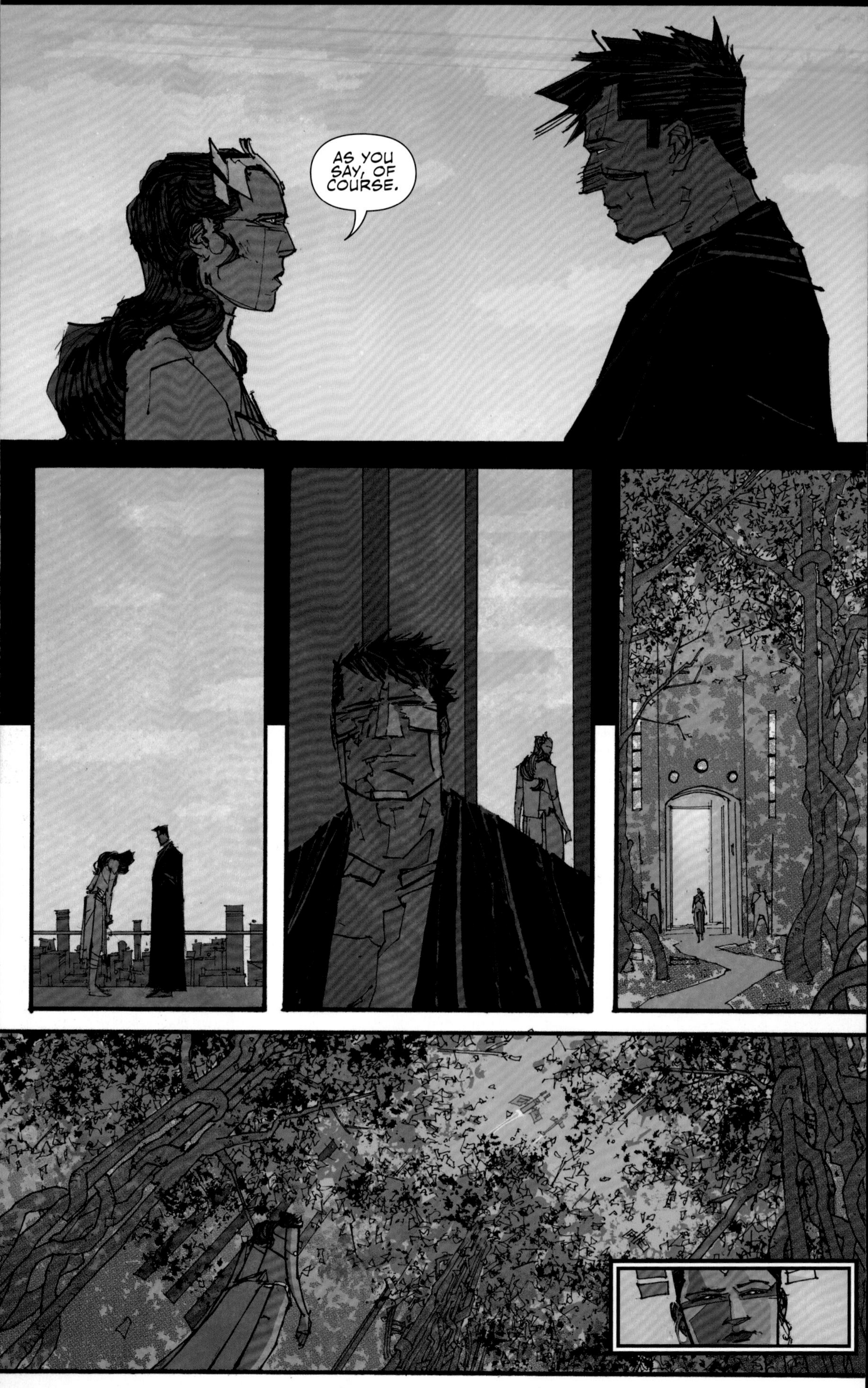
AS YOU SAY, OF COURSE.

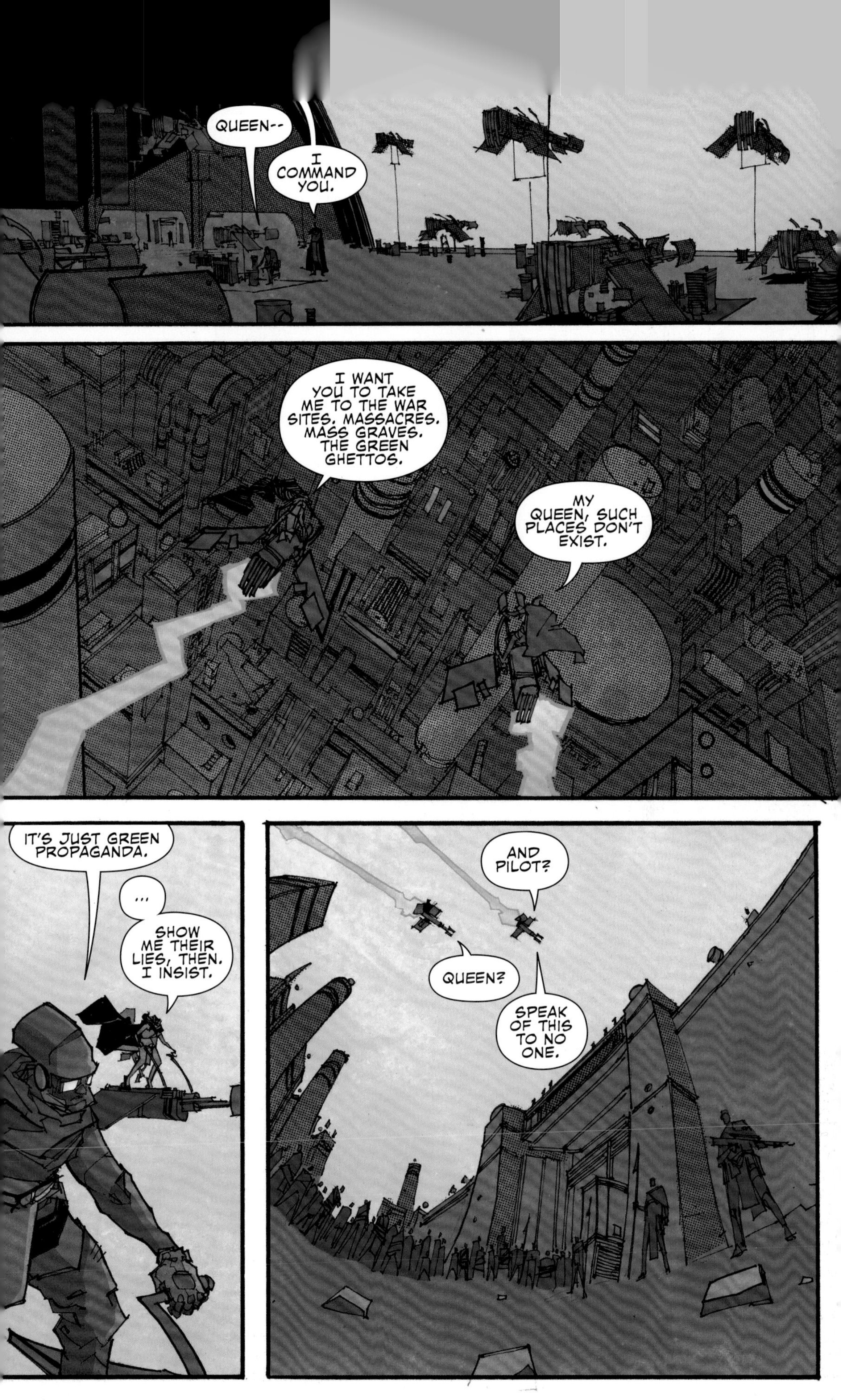
QUEEN--
I COMMAND YOU.
I WANT YOU TO TAKE ME TO THE WAR SITES. MASSACRES. MASS GRAVES. THE GREEN GHETTOS.
MY QUEEN, SUCH PLACES DON'T EXIST.
IT'S JUST GREEN PROPAGANDA.
...
SHOW ME THEIR LIES, THEN. I INSIST.
AND PILOT?
QUEEN?
SPEAK OF THIS TO NO ONE.

IT'S THE DAMNED GREENS! THE *SWORDS OF OLD BARSOOM!* WE'RE BESIEGED!

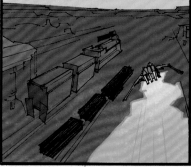

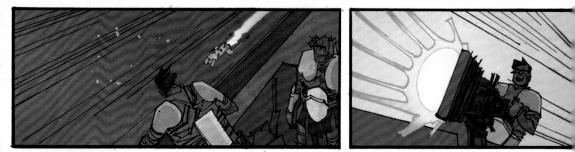

BRING UP THE OVER-SHIELDS!

THIS WON'T SLOW THEM DOWN FOR VERY LONG.

I KNOW...

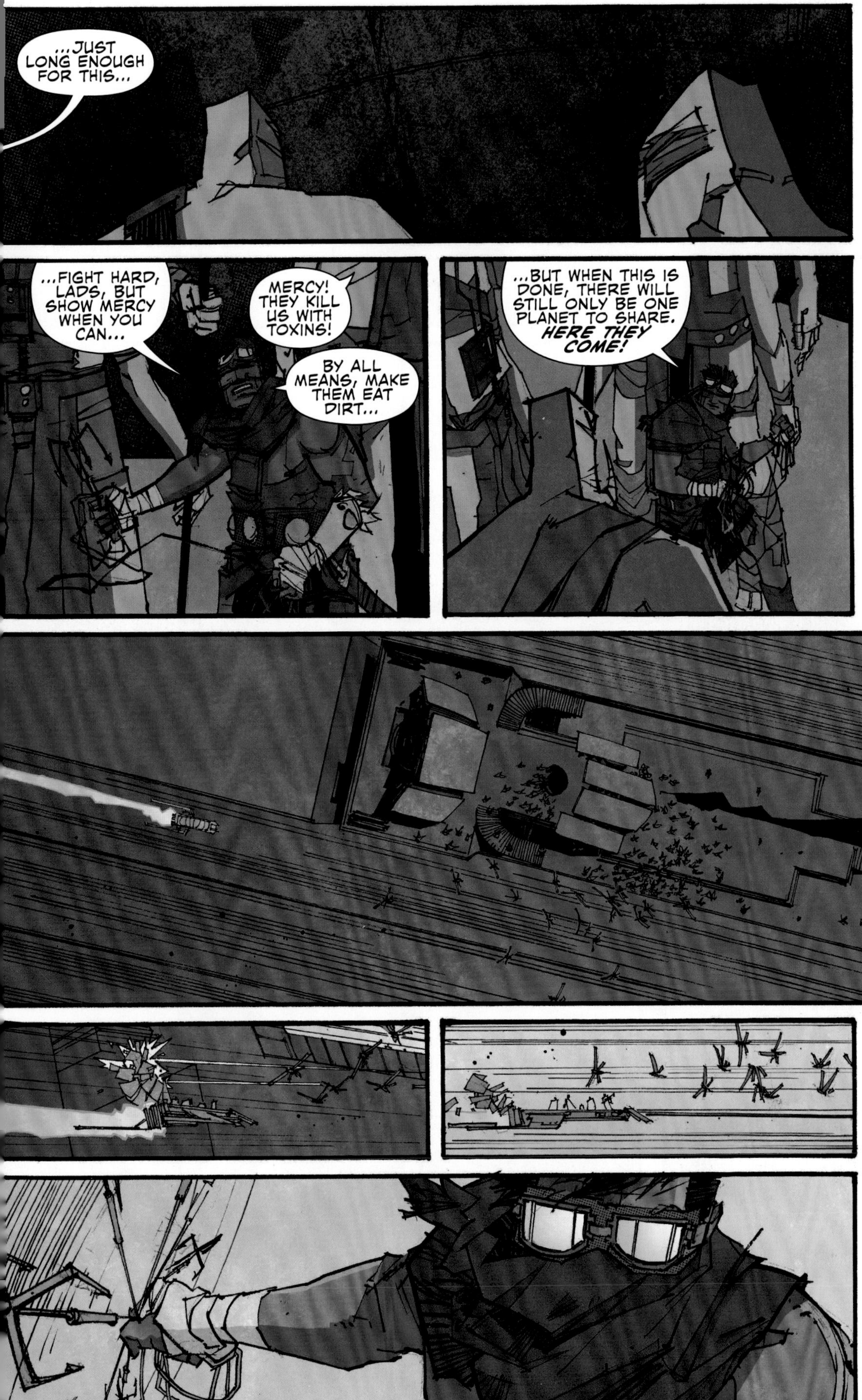
...JUST LONG ENOUGH FOR THIS...
...FIGHT HARD, LADS, BUT SHOW MERCY WHEN YOU CAN...
MERCY! THEY KILL US WITH TOXINS!
BY ALL MEANS, MAKE THEM EAT DIRT...
...BUT WHEN THIS IS DONE, THERE WILL STILL ONLY BE ONE PLANET TO SHARE. HERE THEY COME!

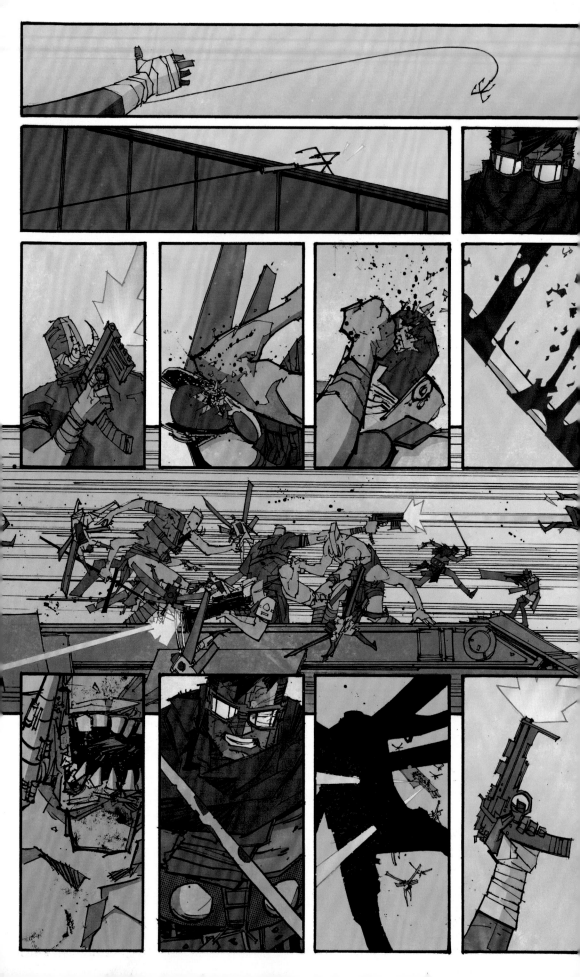

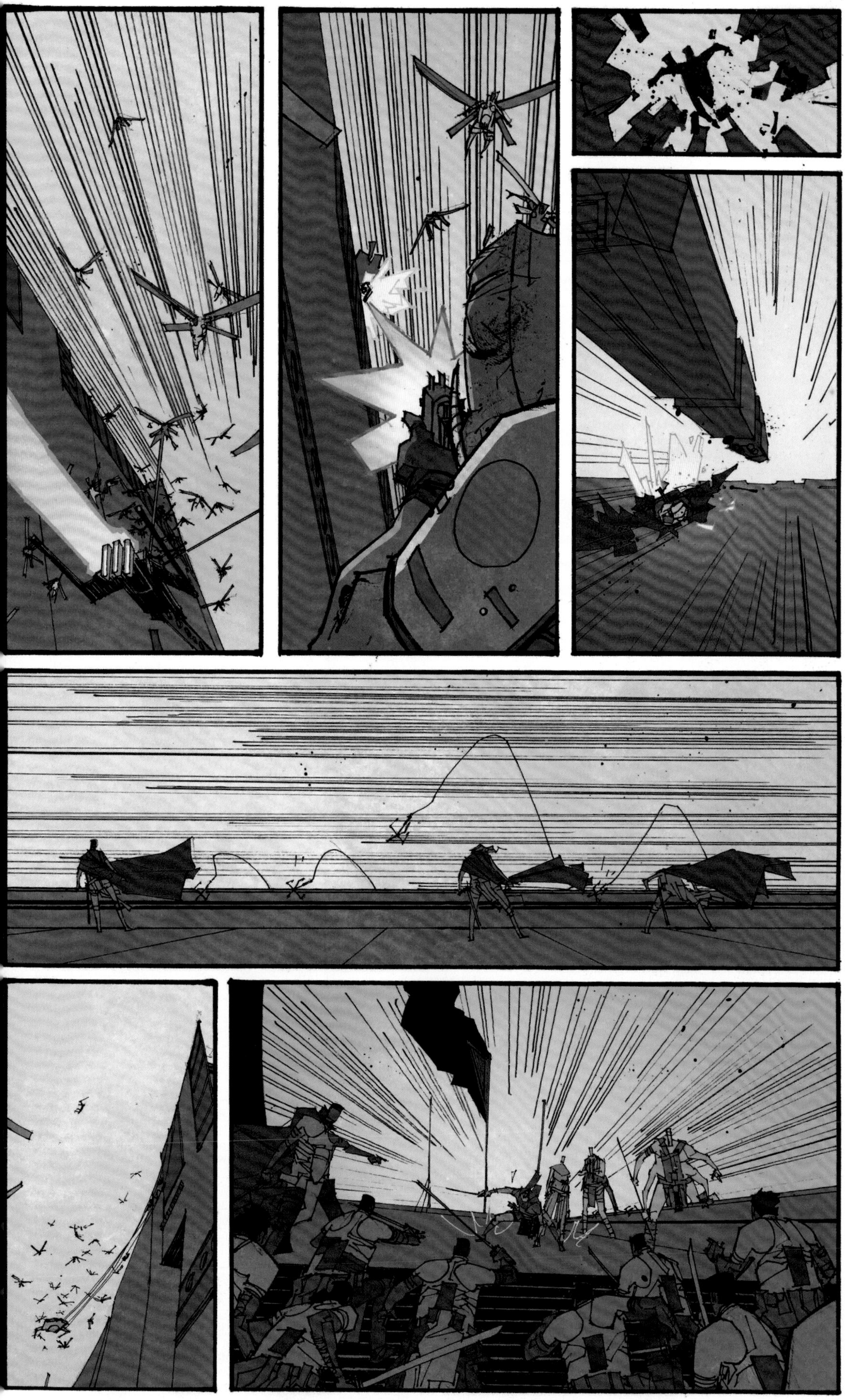

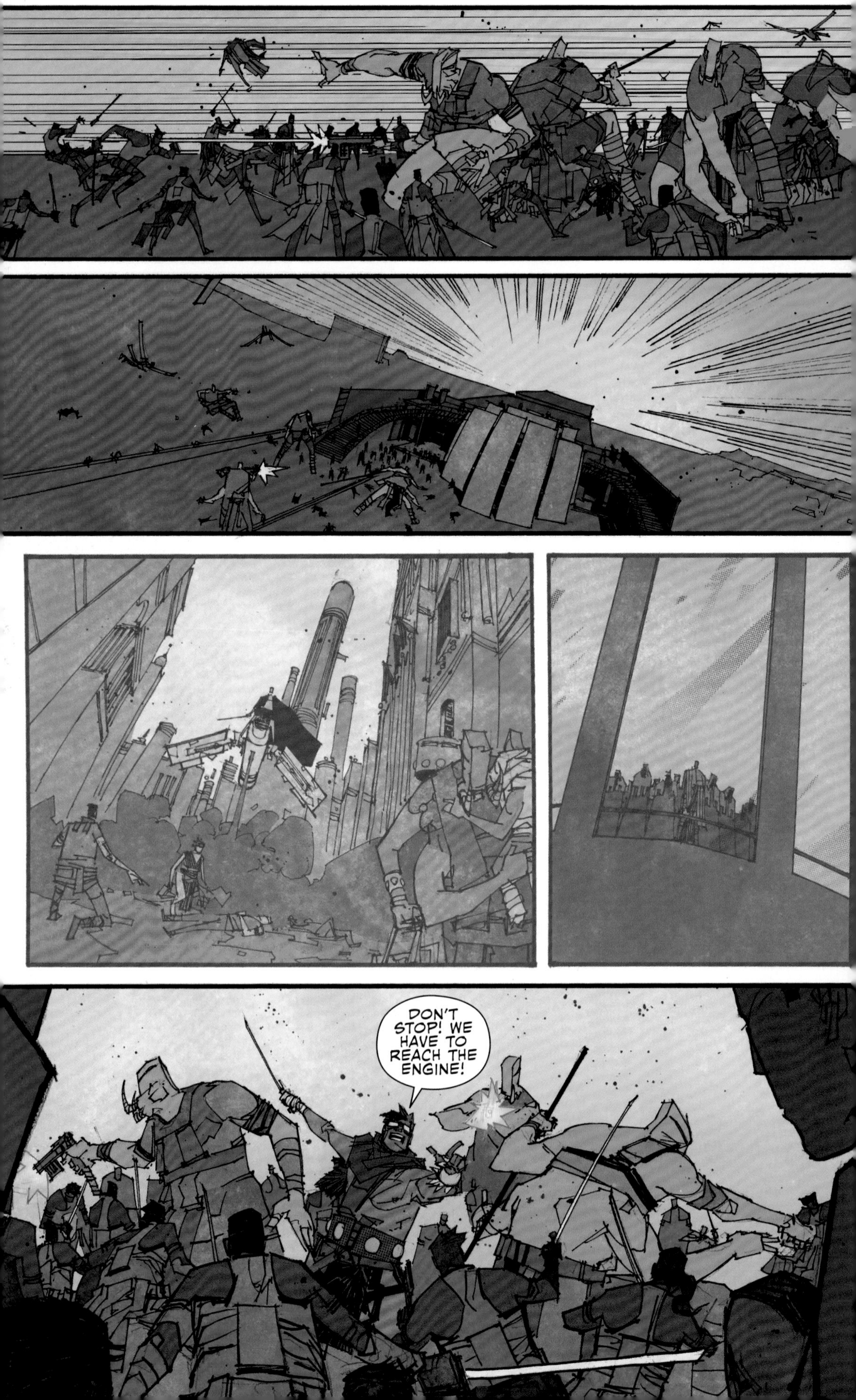
DON'T STOP! WE HAVE TO REACH THE ENGINE!

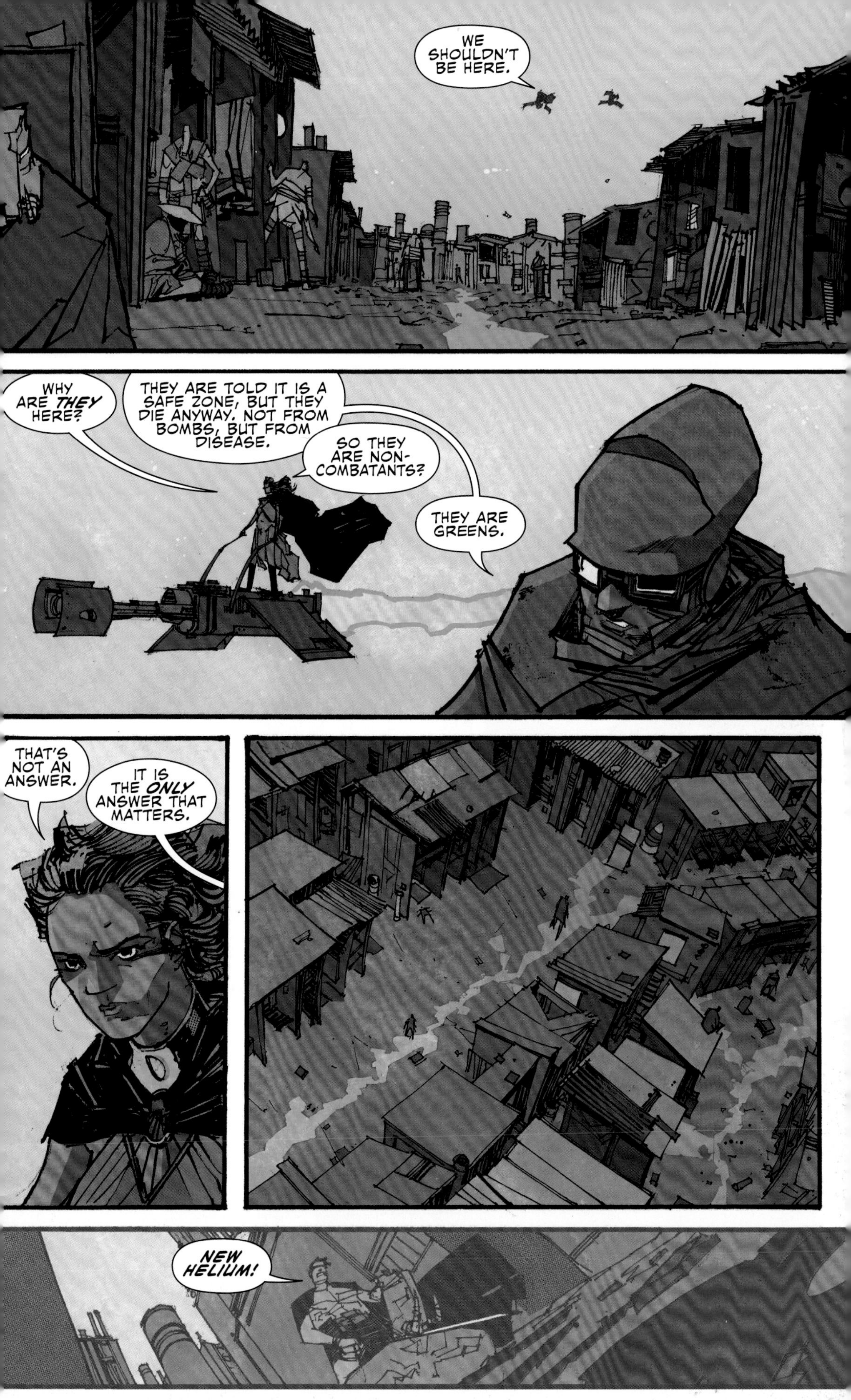
WE SHOULDN'T BE HERE.
WHY ARE THEY HERE?
THEY ARE TOLD IT IS A SAFE ZONE, BUT THEY DIE ANYWAY. NOT FROM BOMBS, BUT FROM DISEASE.
SO THEY ARE NON-COMBATANTS?
THEY ARE GREENS.
THAT'S NOT AN ANSWER.
IT IS THE ONLY ANSWER THAT MATTERS.
NEW HELIUM!

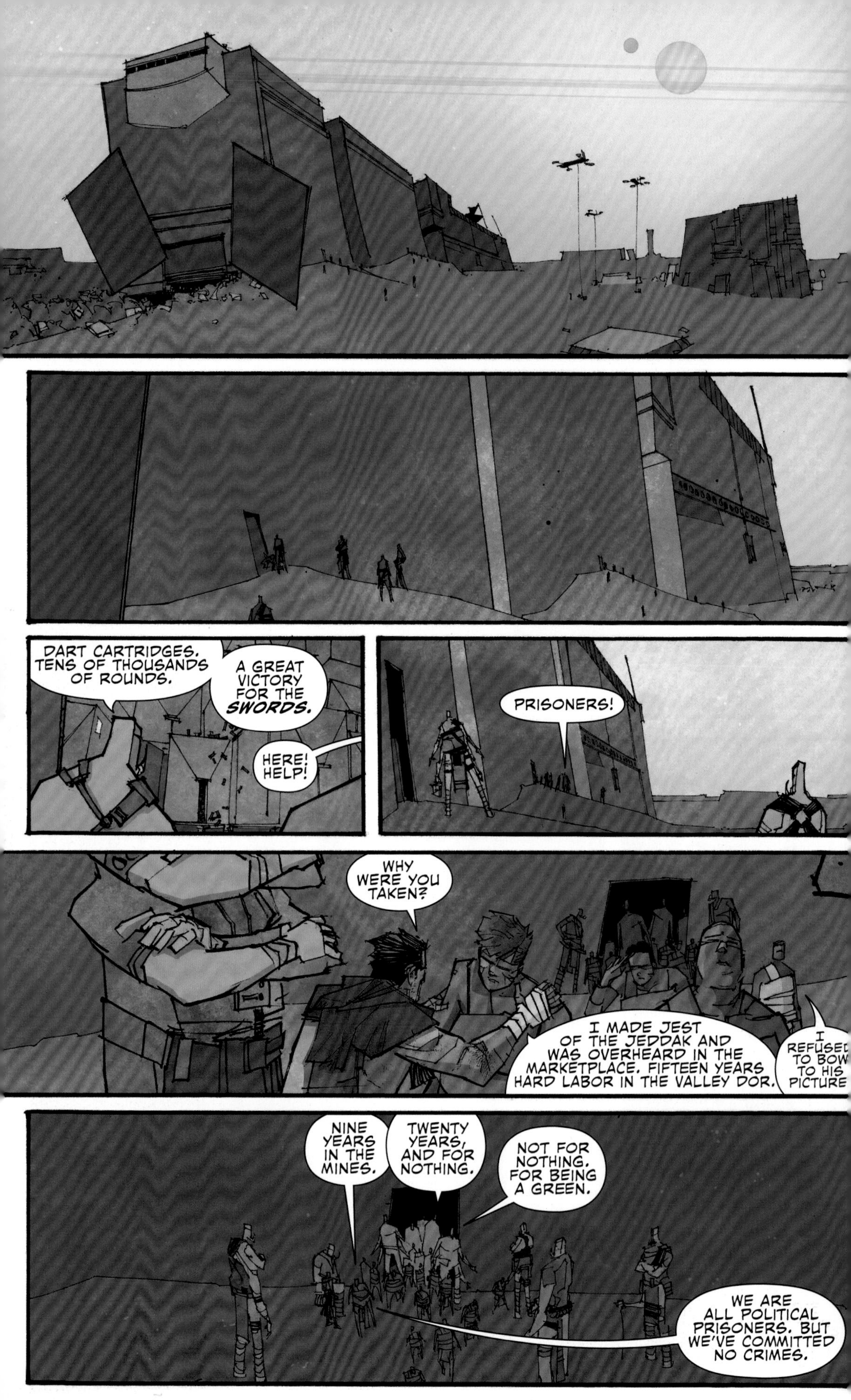
DART CARTRIDGES. TENS OF THOUSANDS OF ROUNDS.
A GREAT VICTORY FOR THE SWORDS.
HERE! HELP!
PRISONERS!
WHY WERE YOU TAKEN?
I MADE JEST OF THE JEDDAK AND WAS OVERHEARD IN THE MARKETPLACE. FIFTEEN YEARS HARD LABOR IN THE VALLEY DOR.
I REFUSED TO BOW TO HIS PICTURE
NINE YEARS IN THE MINES.
TWENTY YEARS, AND FOR NOTHING.
NOT FOR NOTHING. FOR BEING A GREEN.
WE ARE ALL POLITICAL PRISONERS. BUT WE'VE COMMITTED NO CRIMES.

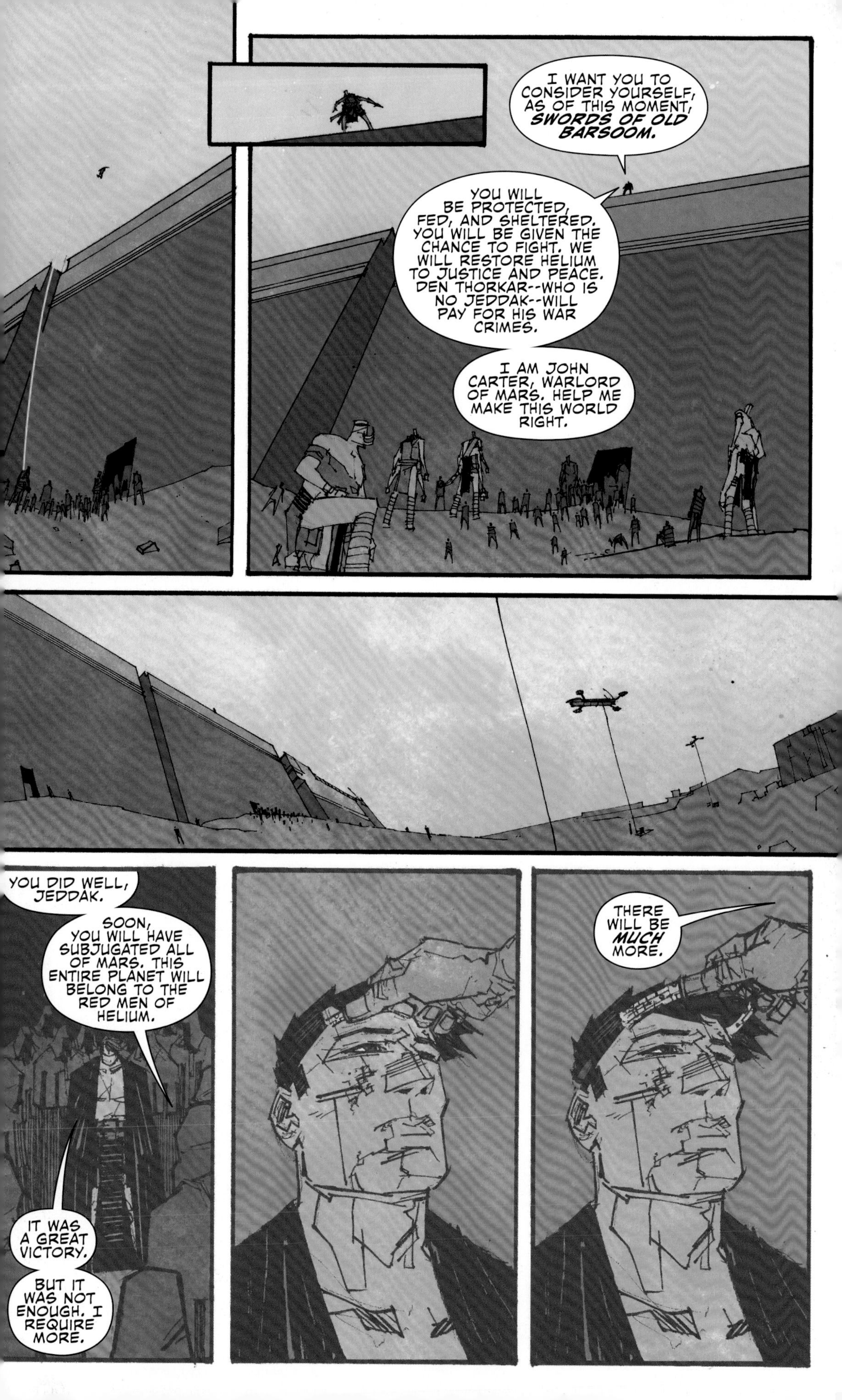

I WANT YOU TO CONSIDER YOURSELF, AS OF THIS MOMENT, ***SWORDS OF OLD BARSOOM.***
YOU WILL BE PROTECTED, FED, AND SHELTERED. YOU WILL BE GIVEN THE CHANCE TO FIGHT. WE WILL RESTORE HELIUM TO JUSTICE AND PEACE. DEN THORKAR--WHO IS NO JEDDAK--WILL PAY FOR HIS WAR CRIMES.
I AM JOHN CARTER, WARLORD OF MARS. HELP ME MAKE THIS WORLD RIGHT.
YOU DID WELL, JEDDAK.
SOON, YOU WILL HAVE SUBJUGATED ALL OF MARS. THIS ENTIRE PLANET WILL BELONG TO THE RED MEN OF HELIUM.
IT WAS A GREAT VICTORY.
BUT IT WAS NOT ENOUGH. I REQUIRE MORE.
THERE WILL BE *MUCH* MORE.

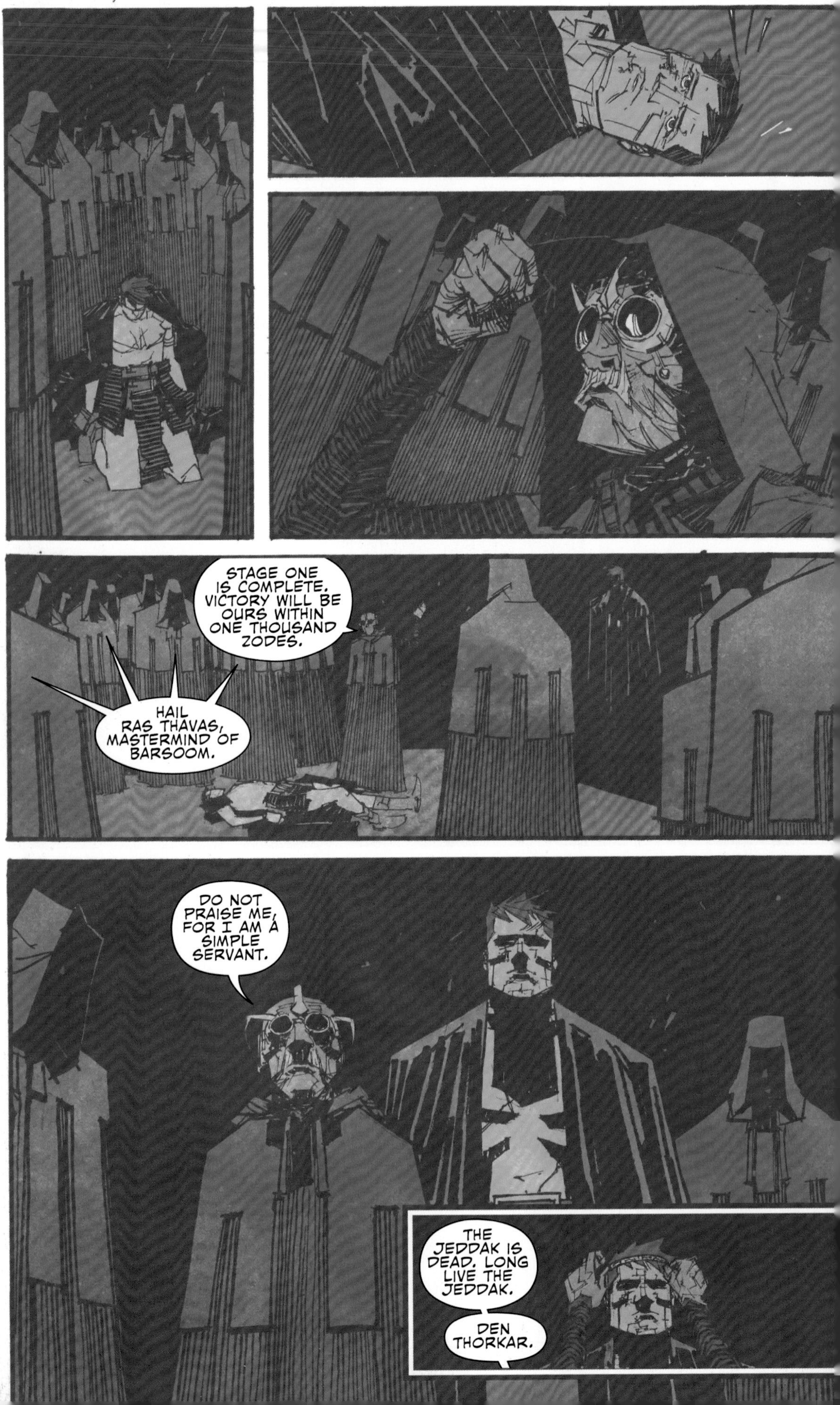
STAGE ONE IS COMPLETE. VICTORY WILL BE OURS WITHIN ONE THOUSAND ZODES.
HAIL RAS THAVAS, MASTERMIND OF BARSOOM.
DO NOT PRAISE ME, FOR I AM A SIMPLE SERVANT.
THE JEDDAK IS DEAD. LONG LIVE THE JEDDAK.
DEN THORKAR.

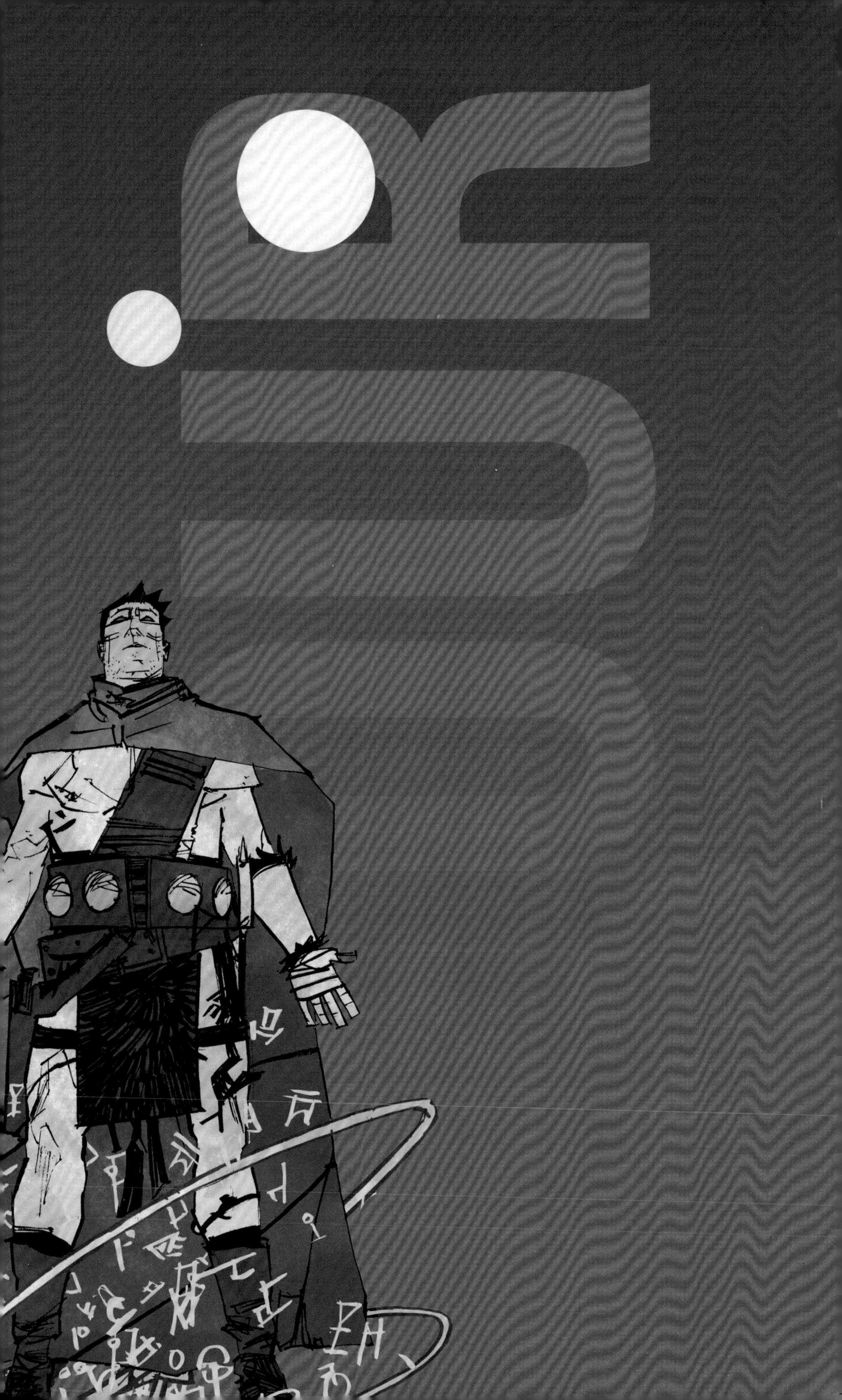

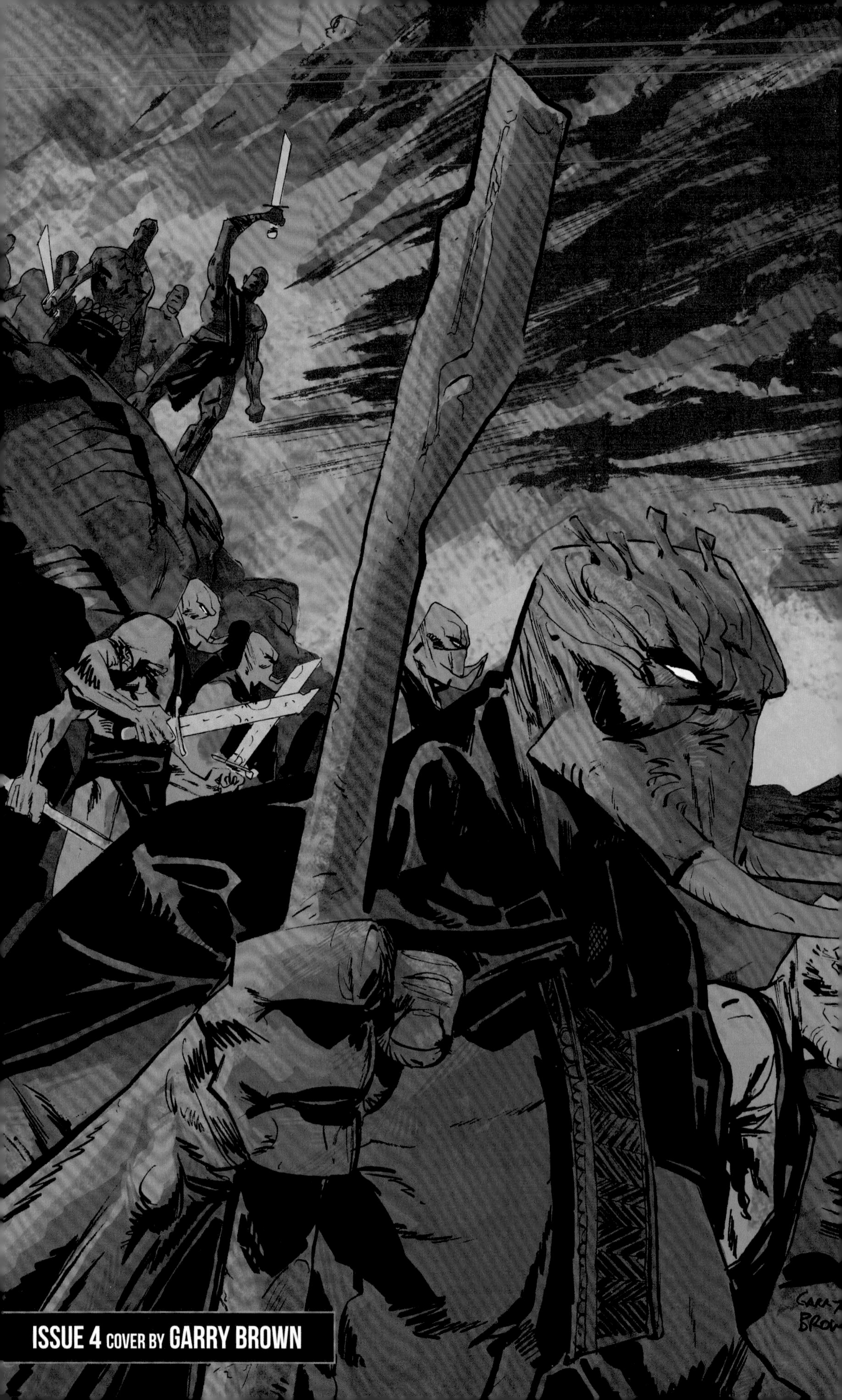

ISSUE 4 COVER BY GARRY BROWN

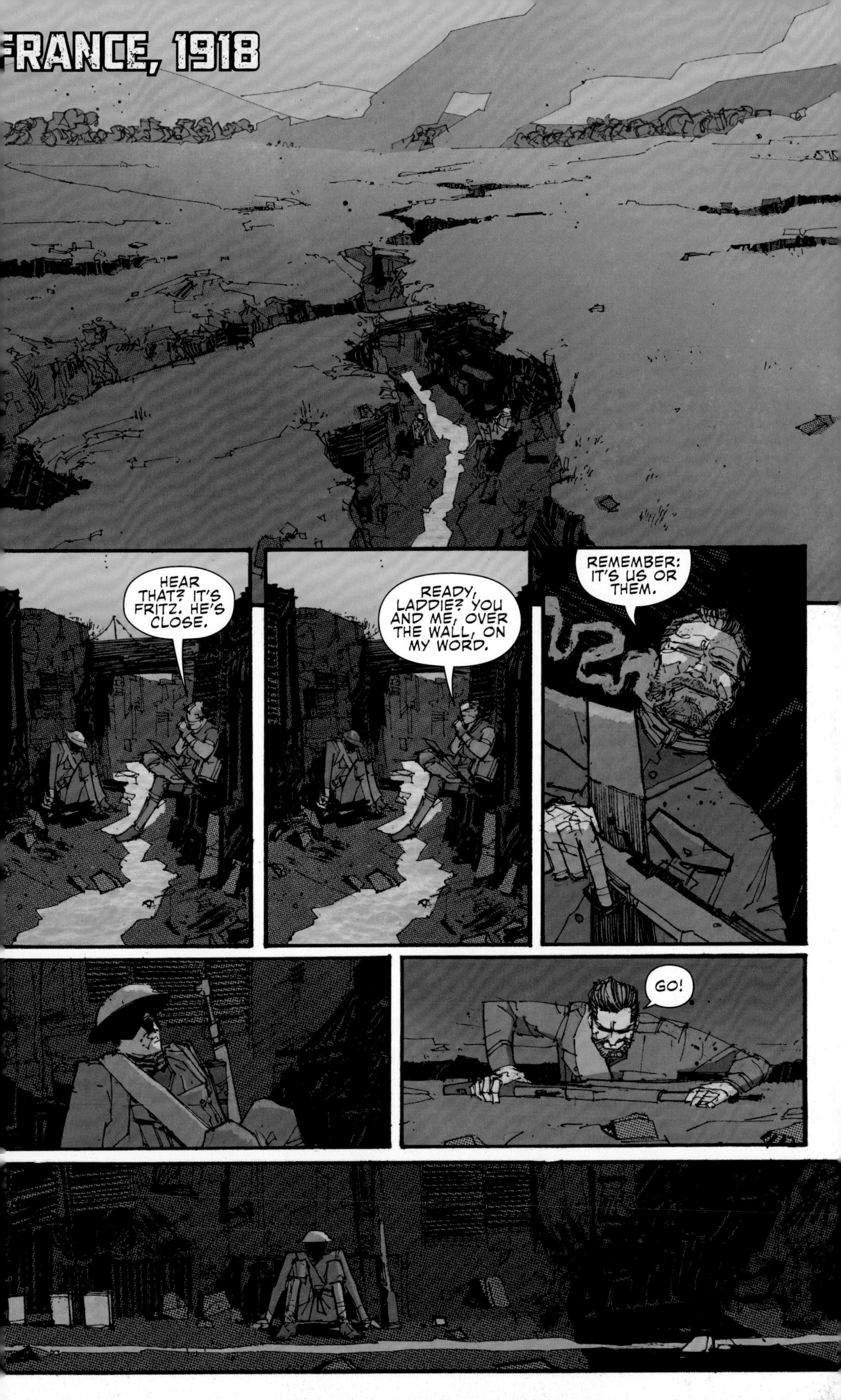

FRANCE, 1918
HEAR THAT? IT'S FRITZ. HE'S CLOSE.
READY, LADDIE? YOU AND ME, OVER THE WALL, ON MY WORD.
REMEMBER: IT'S US OR THEM.
GO!

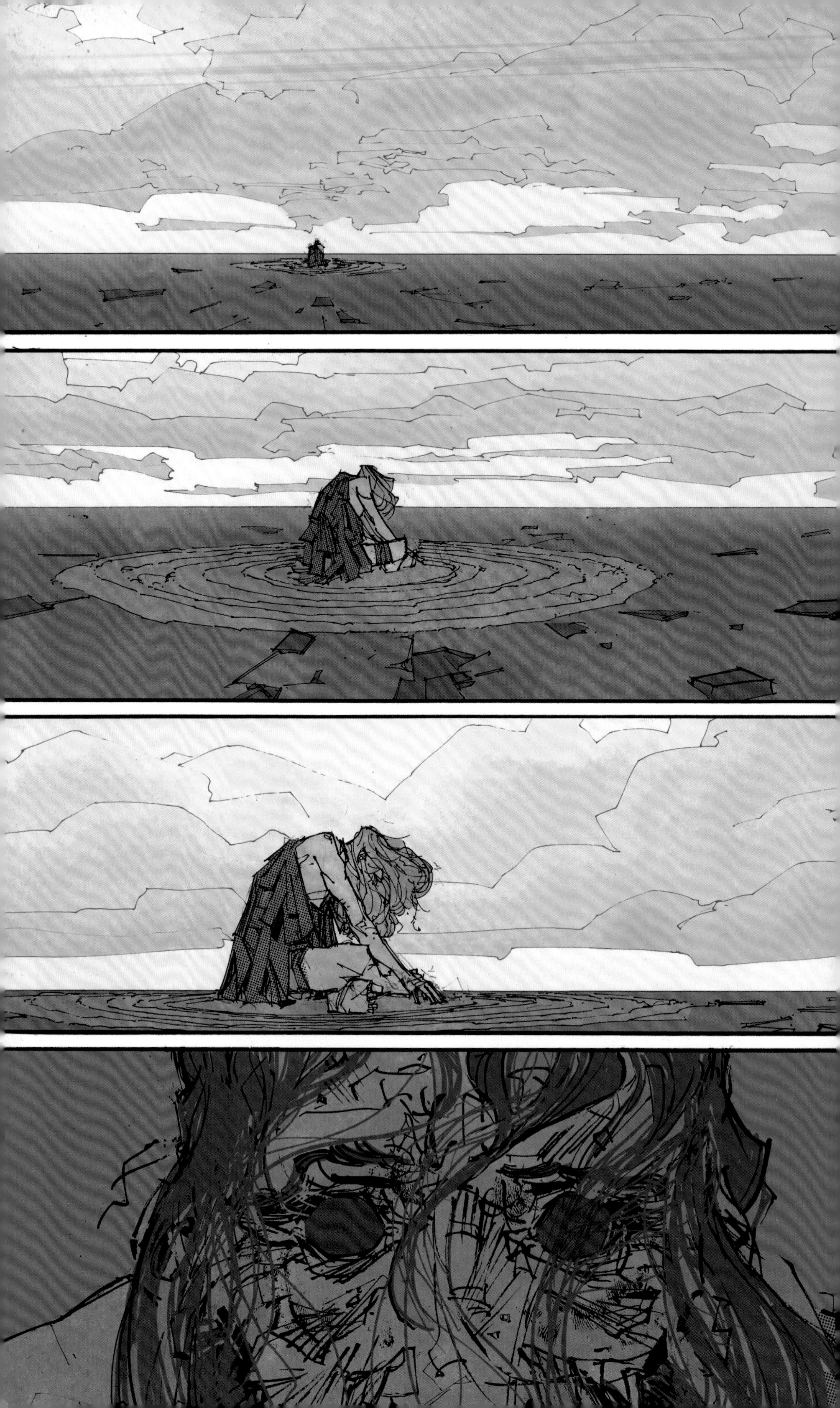

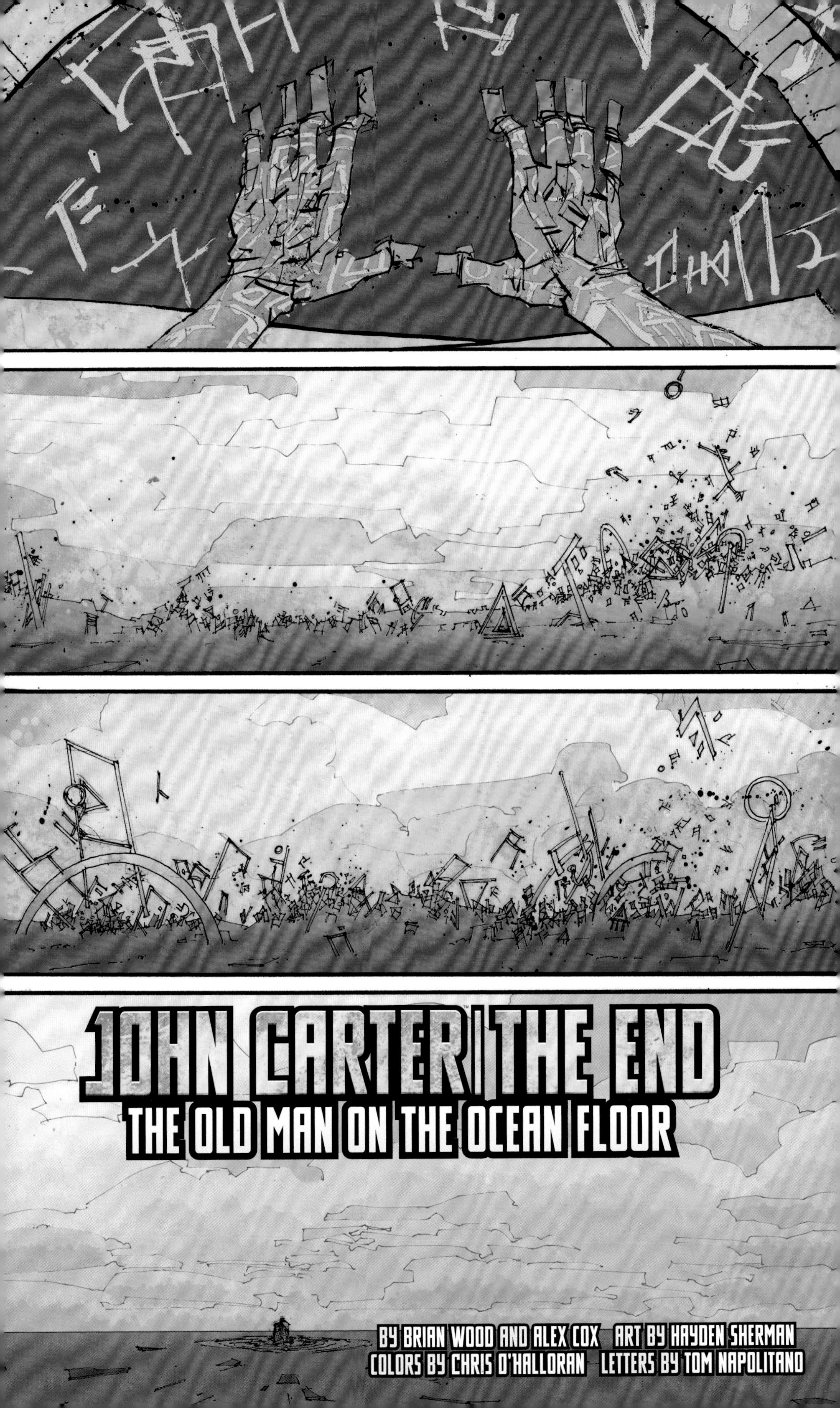

JOHN CARTER™ THE END
THE OLD MAN ON THE OCEAN FLOOR
BY BRIAN WOOD AND ALEX COX ART BY HAYDEN SHERMAN
COLORS BY CHRIS O'HALLORAN LETTERS BY TOM NAPOLITANO

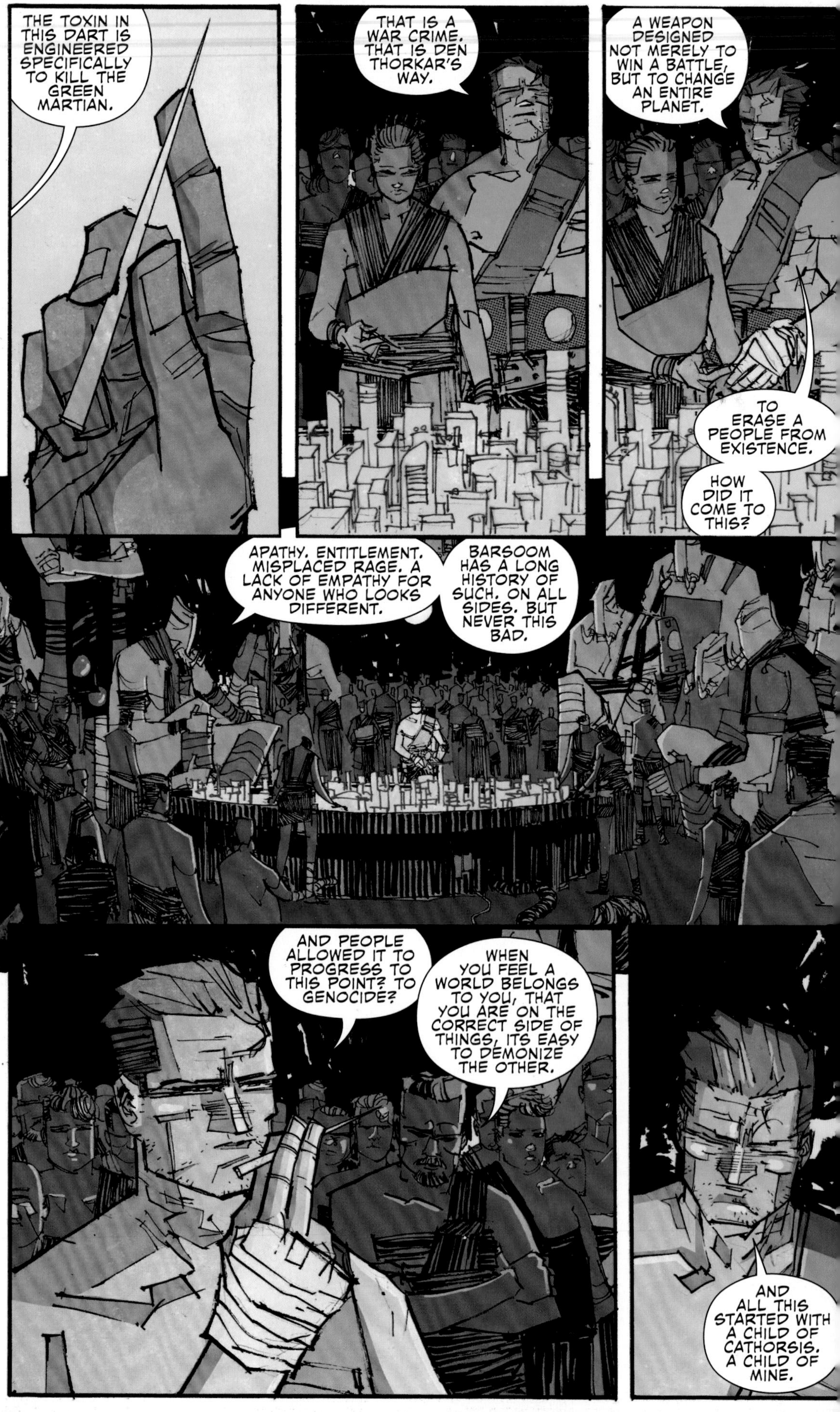

THE TOXIN IN THIS DART IS ENGINEERED SPECIFICALLY TO KILL THE GREEN MARTIAN.
THAT IS A WAR CRIME. THAT IS DEN THORKAR'S WAY.
A WEAPON DESIGNED NOT MERELY TO WIN A BATTLE, BUT TO CHANGE AN ENTIRE PLANET.
TO ERASE A PEOPLE FROM EXISTENCE.
HOW DID IT COME TO THIS?
APATHY. ENTITLEMENT. MISPLACED RAGE. A LACK OF EMPATHY FOR ANYONE WHO LOOKS DIFFERENT.
BARSOOM HAS A LONG HISTORY OF SUCH. ON ALL SIDES. BUT NEVER THIS BAD.
AND PEOPLE ALLOWED IT TO PROGRESS TO THIS POINT? TO GENOCIDE?
WHEN YOU FEEL A WORLD BELONGS TO YOU, THAT YOU ARE ON THE CORRECT SIDE OF THINGS, ITS EASY TO DEMONIZE THE OTHER.
AND ALL THIS STARTED WITH A CHILD OF CATHORSIS. A CHILD OF MINE.

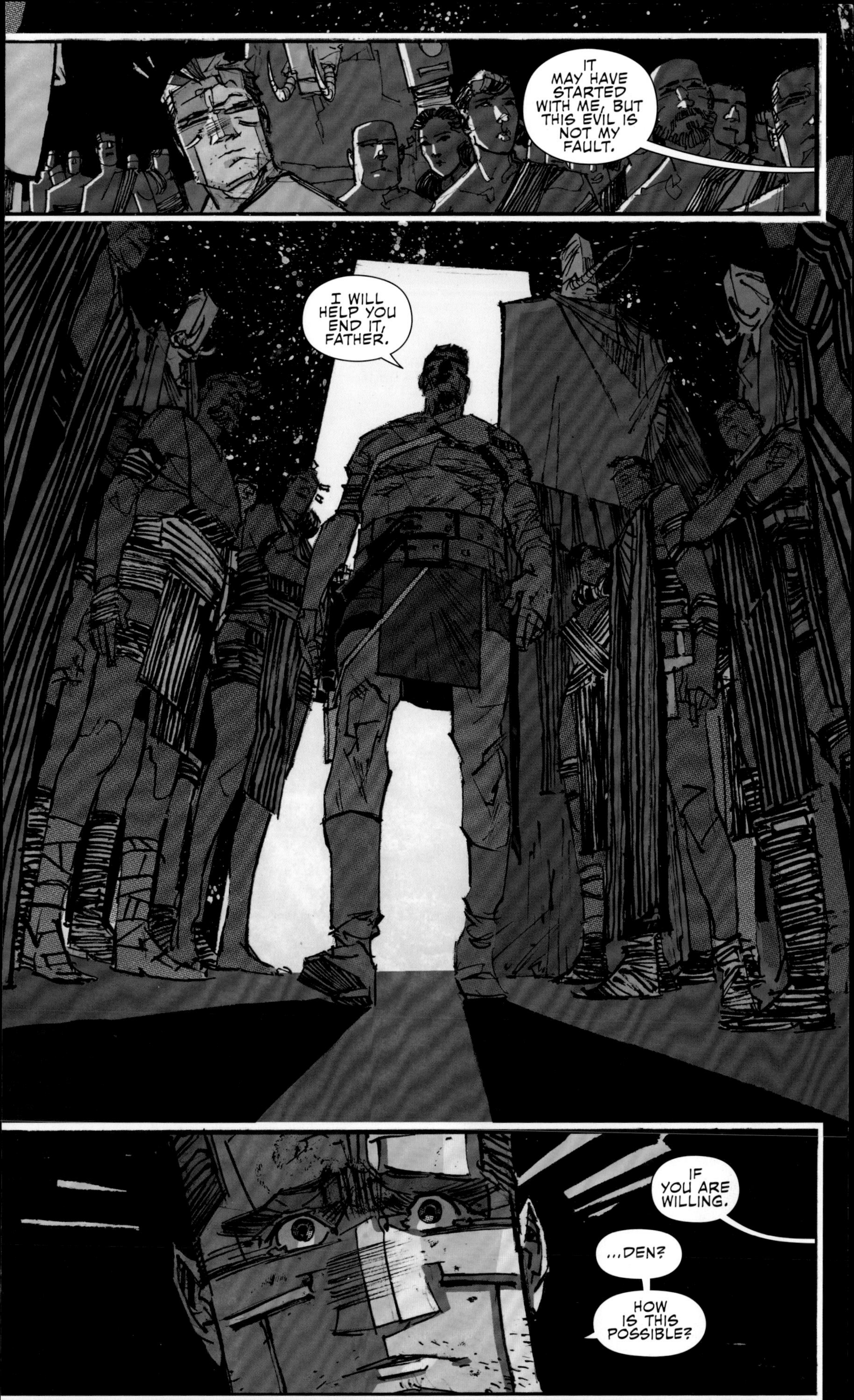
IT MAY HAVE STARTED WITH ME, BUT THIS EVIL IS NOT MY FAULT.
I WILL HELP YOU END IT, FATHER.
IF YOU ARE WILLING.
...DEN?
HOW IS THIS POSSIBLE?

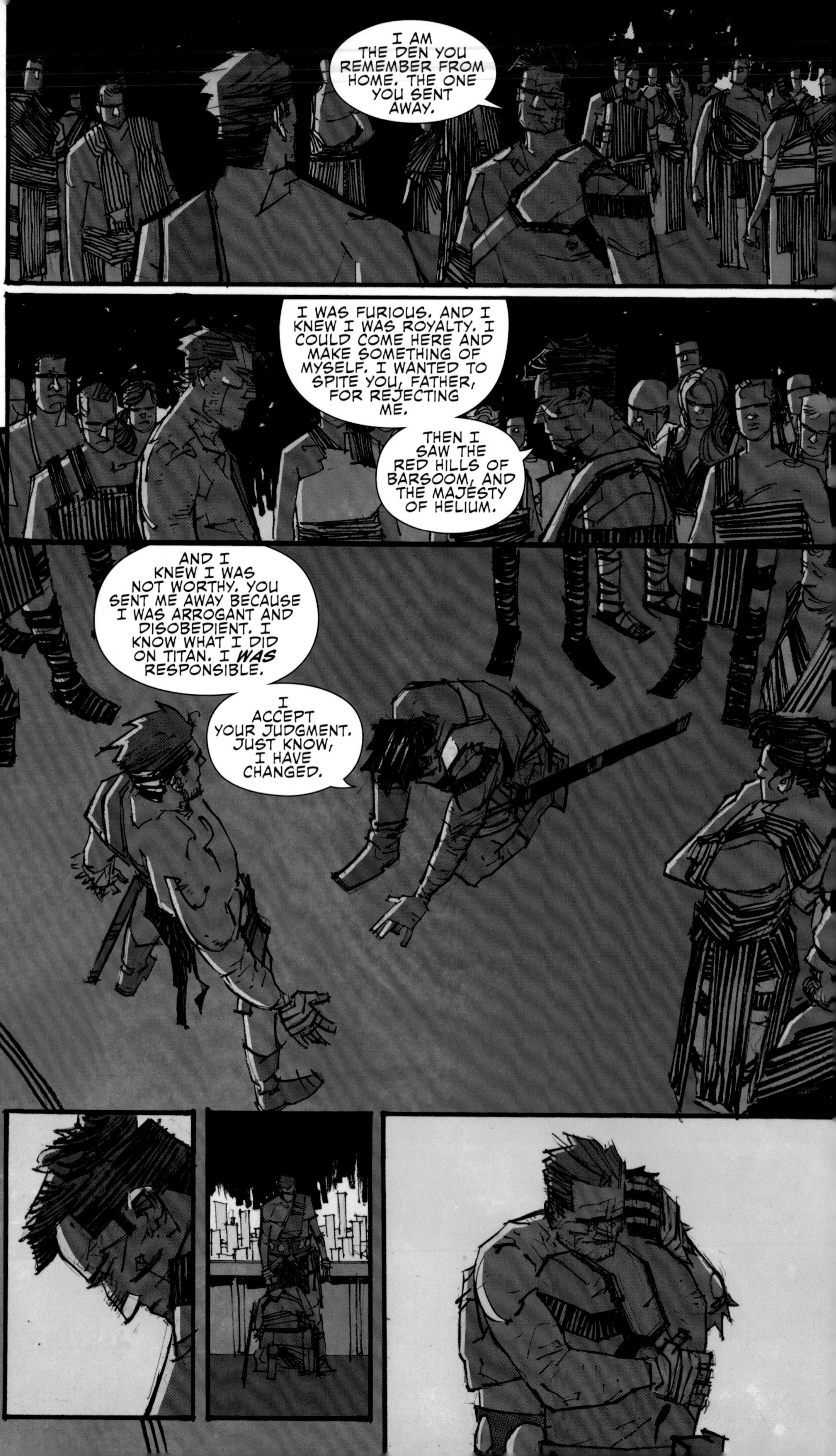
I AM THE DEN YOU REMEMBER FROM HOME. THE ONE YOU SENT AWAY.
I WAS FURIOUS. AND I KNEW I WAS ROYALTY. I COULD COME HERE AND MAKE SOMETHING OF MYSELF. I WANTED TO SPITE YOU, FATHER, FOR REJECTING ME.
THEN I SAW THE RED HILLS OF BARSOOM, AND THE MAJESTY OF HELIUM.
AND I KNEW I WAS NOT WORTHY. YOU SENT ME AWAY BECAUSE I WAS ARROGANT AND DISOBEDIENT. I KNOW WHAT I DID ON TITAN. I *WAS* RESPONSIBLE.
I ACCEPT YOUR JUDGMENT. JUST KNOW, I HAVE CHANGED.

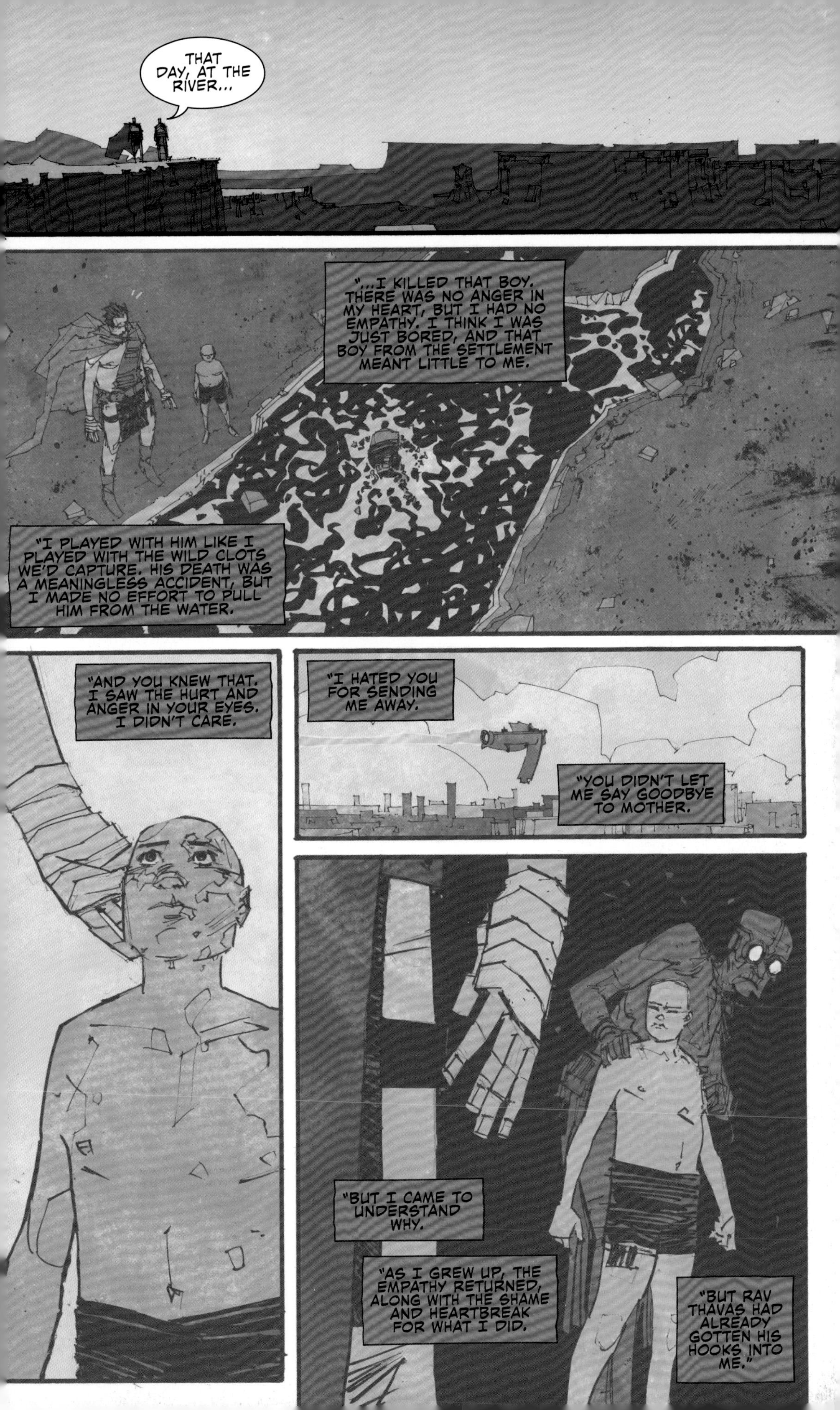
THAT DAY, AT THE RIVER...
"...I KILLED THAT BOY. THERE WAS NO ANGER IN MY HEART, BUT I HAD NO EMPATHY. I THINK I WAS JUST BORED, AND THAT BOY FROM THE SETTLEMENT MEANT LITTLE TO ME.
"I PLAYED WITH HIM LIKE I PLAYED WITH THE WILD CLOTS WE'D CAPTURE. HIS DEATH WAS A MEANINGLESS ACCIDENT, BUT I MADE NO EFFORT TO PULL HIM FROM THE WATER.
"AND YOU KNEW THAT. I SAW THE HURT AND ANGER IN YOUR EYES. I DIDN'T CARE.
"I HATED YOU FOR SENDING ME AWAY.
"YOU DIDN'T LET ME SAY GOODBYE TO MOTHER.
"BUT I CAME TO UNDERSTAND WHY.
"AS I GREW UP, THE EMPATHY RETURNED, ALONG WITH THE SHAME AND HEARTBREAK FOR WHAT I DID.
"BUT RAV THAVAS HAD ALREADY GOTTEN HIS HOOKS INTO ME."

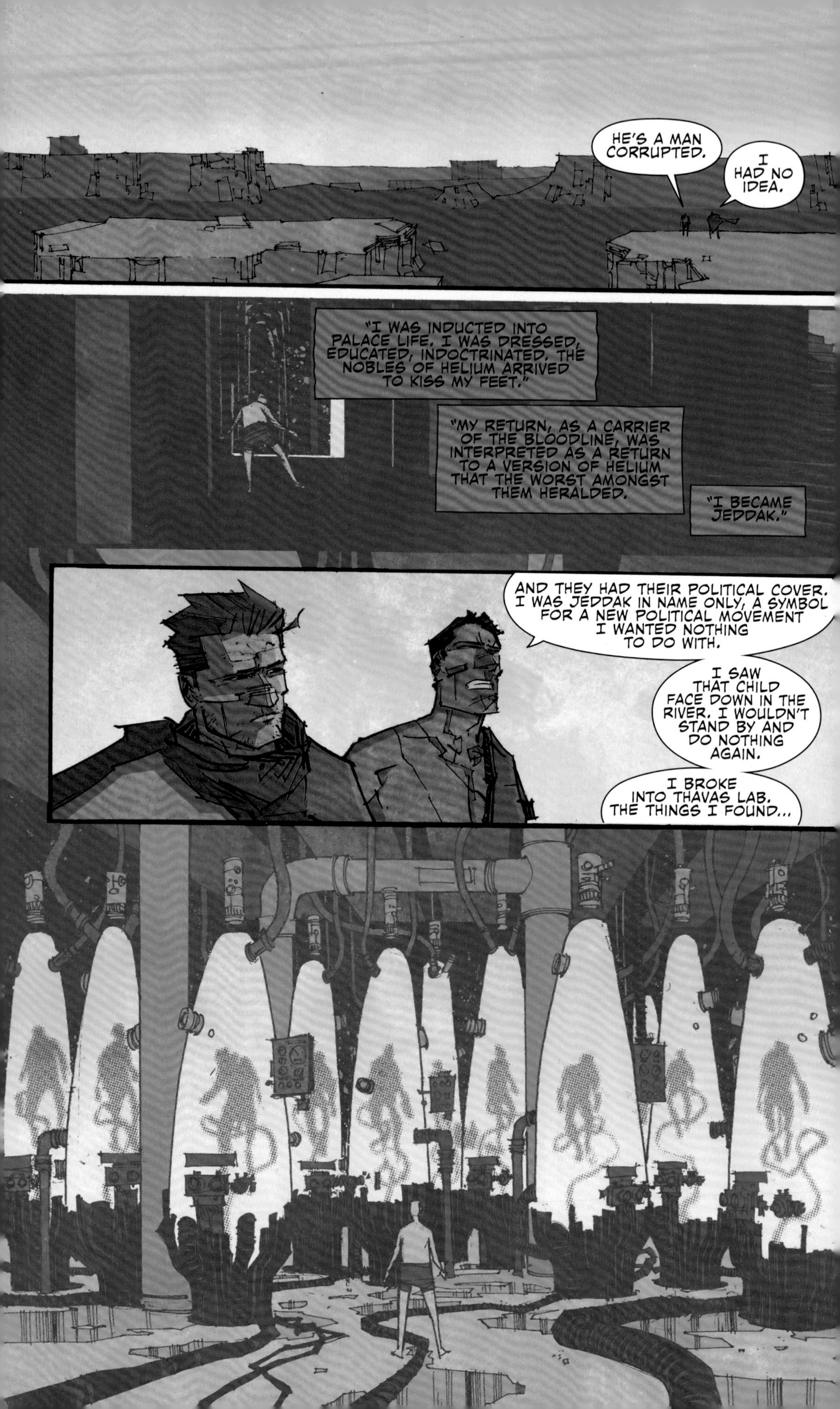
HE'S A MAN CORRUPTED.
I HAD NO IDEA.
"I WAS INDUCTED INTO PALACE LIFE. I WAS DRESSED, EDUCATED, INDOCTRINATED. THE NOBLES OF HELIUM ARRIVED TO KISS MY FEET."
"MY RETURN, AS A CARRIER OF THE BLOODLINE, WAS INTERPRETED AS A RETURN TO A VERSION OF HELIUM THAT THE WORST AMONGST THEM HERALDED.
"I BECAME JEDDAK."
AND THEY HAD THEIR POLITICAL COVER. I WAS JEDDAK IN NAME ONLY, A SYMBOL FOR A NEW POLITICAL MOVEMENT I WANTED NOTHING TO DO WITH.
I SAW THAT CHILD FACE DOWN IN THE RIVER. I WOULDN'T STAND BY AND DO NOTHING AGAIN.
I BROKE INTO THAVAS LAB. THE THINGS I FOUND...

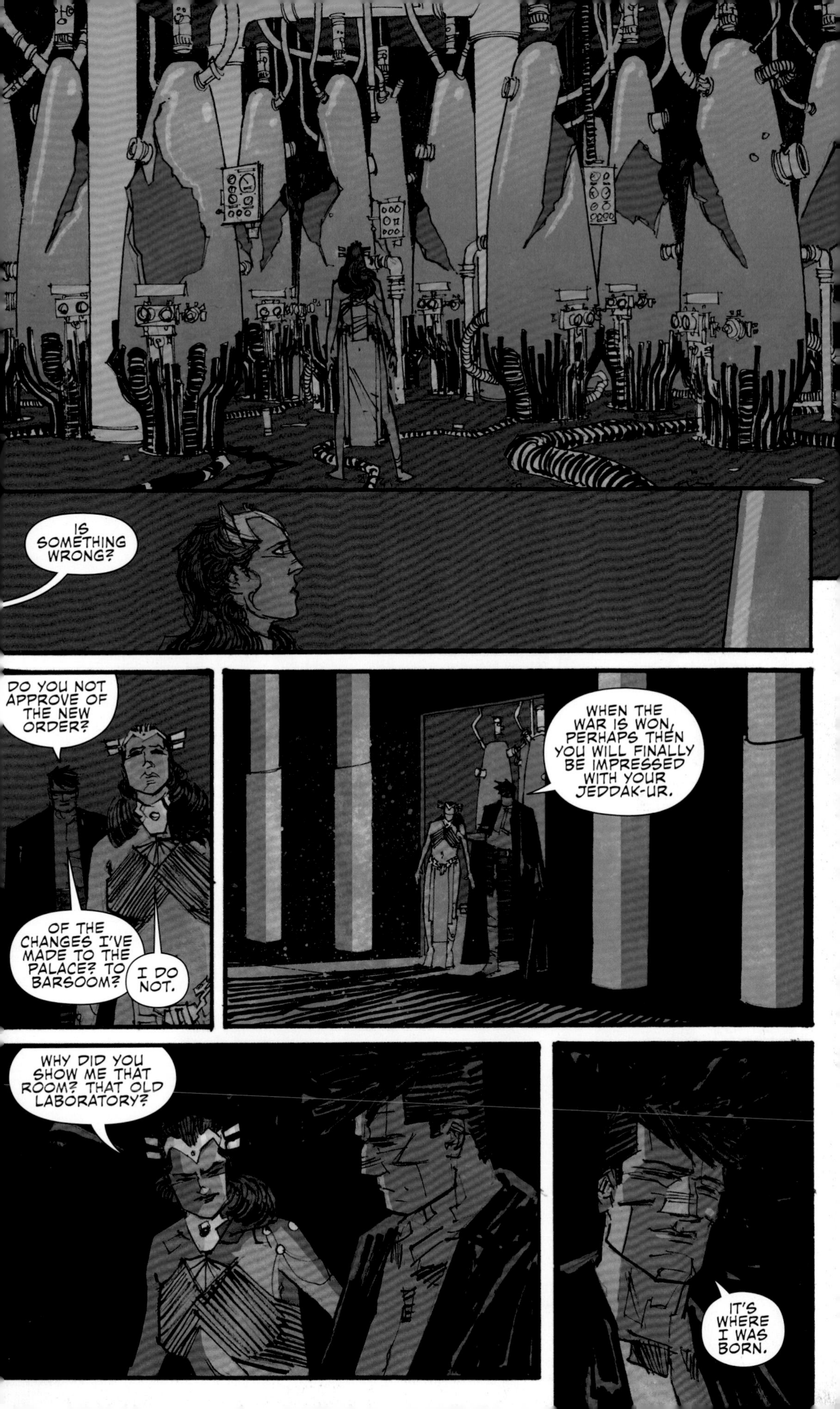

IS SOMETHING WRONG?
DO YOU NOT APPROVE OF THE NEW ORDER?
OF THE CHANGES I'VE MADE TO THE PALACE? TO BARSOOM?
I DO NOT.
WHEN THE WAR IS WON, PERHAPS THEN YOU WILL FINALLY BE IMPRESSED WITH YOUR JEDDAK-UR.
WHY DID YOU SHOW ME THAT ROOM? THAT OLD LABORATORY?
IT'S WHERE I WAS BORN.

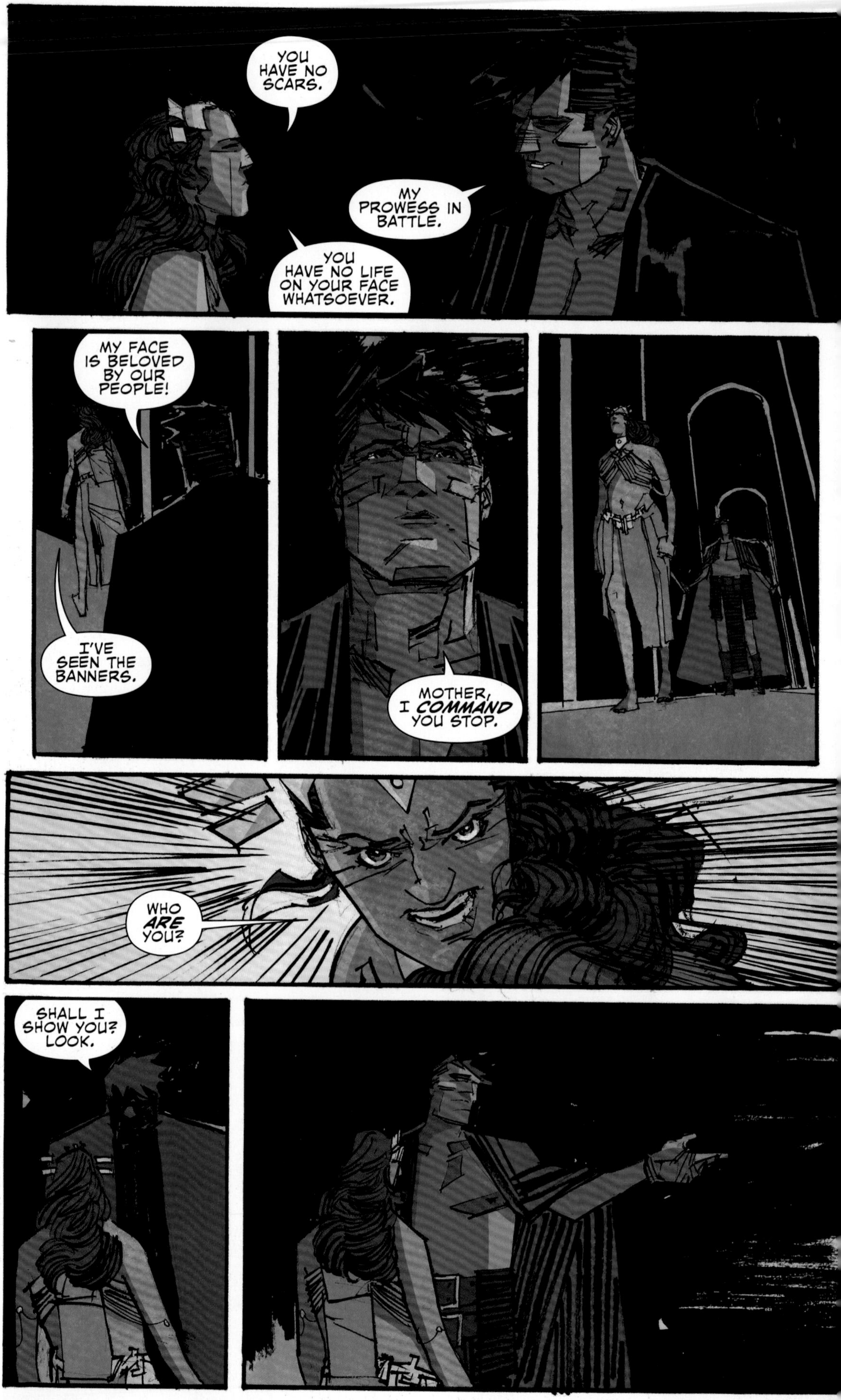
YOU HAVE NO SCARS.
MY PROWESS IN BATTLE.
YOU HAVE NO LIFE ON YOUR FACE WHATSOEVER.
MY FACE IS BELOVED BY OUR PEOPLE!
I'VE SEEN THE BANNERS.
MOTHER, I *COMMAND* YOU STOP.
WHO *ARE* YOU?
SHALL I SHOW YOU? LOOK.

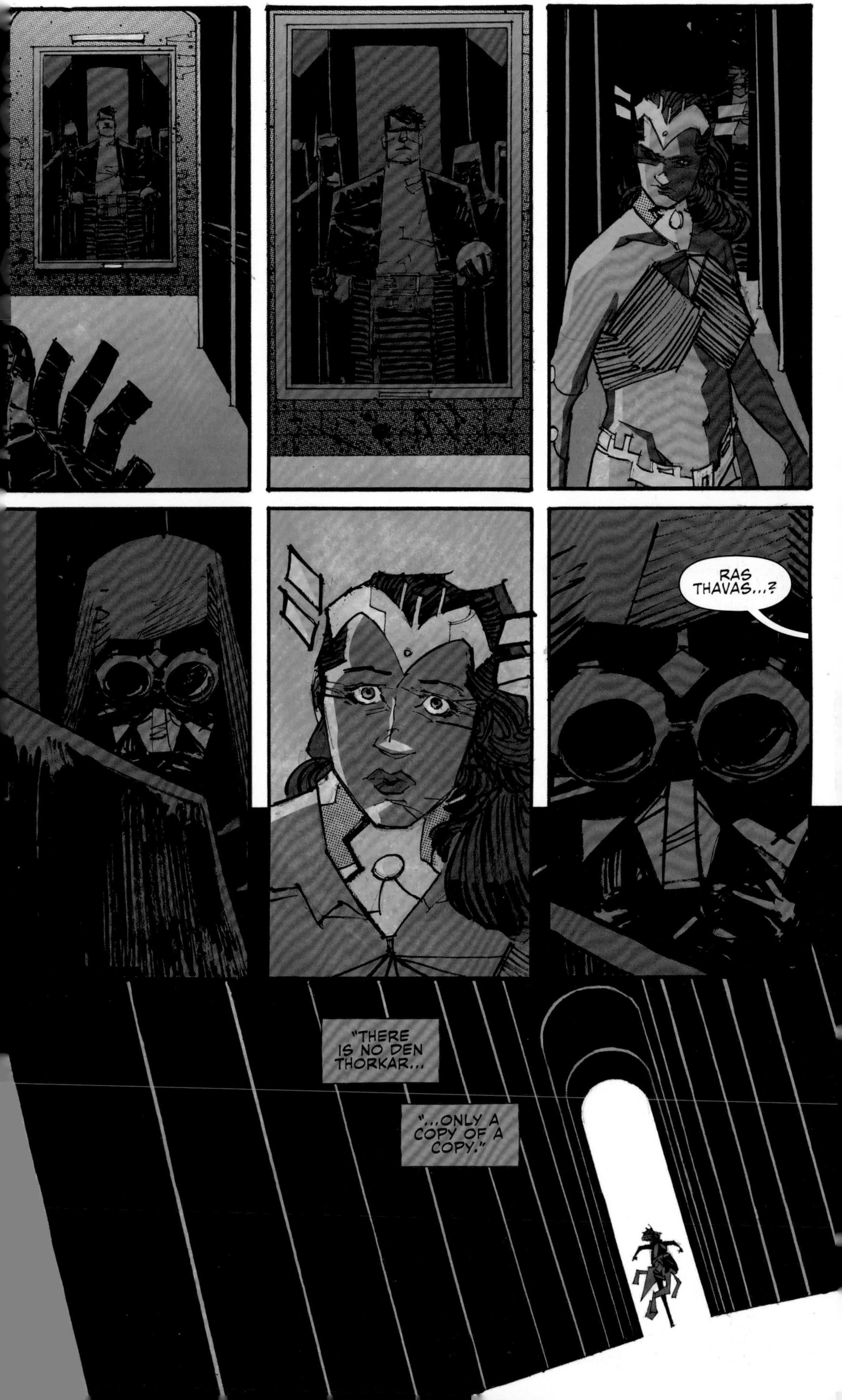
RAS THAVAS...?
"THERE IS NO DEN THORKAR...
"...ONLY A COPY OF A COPY."

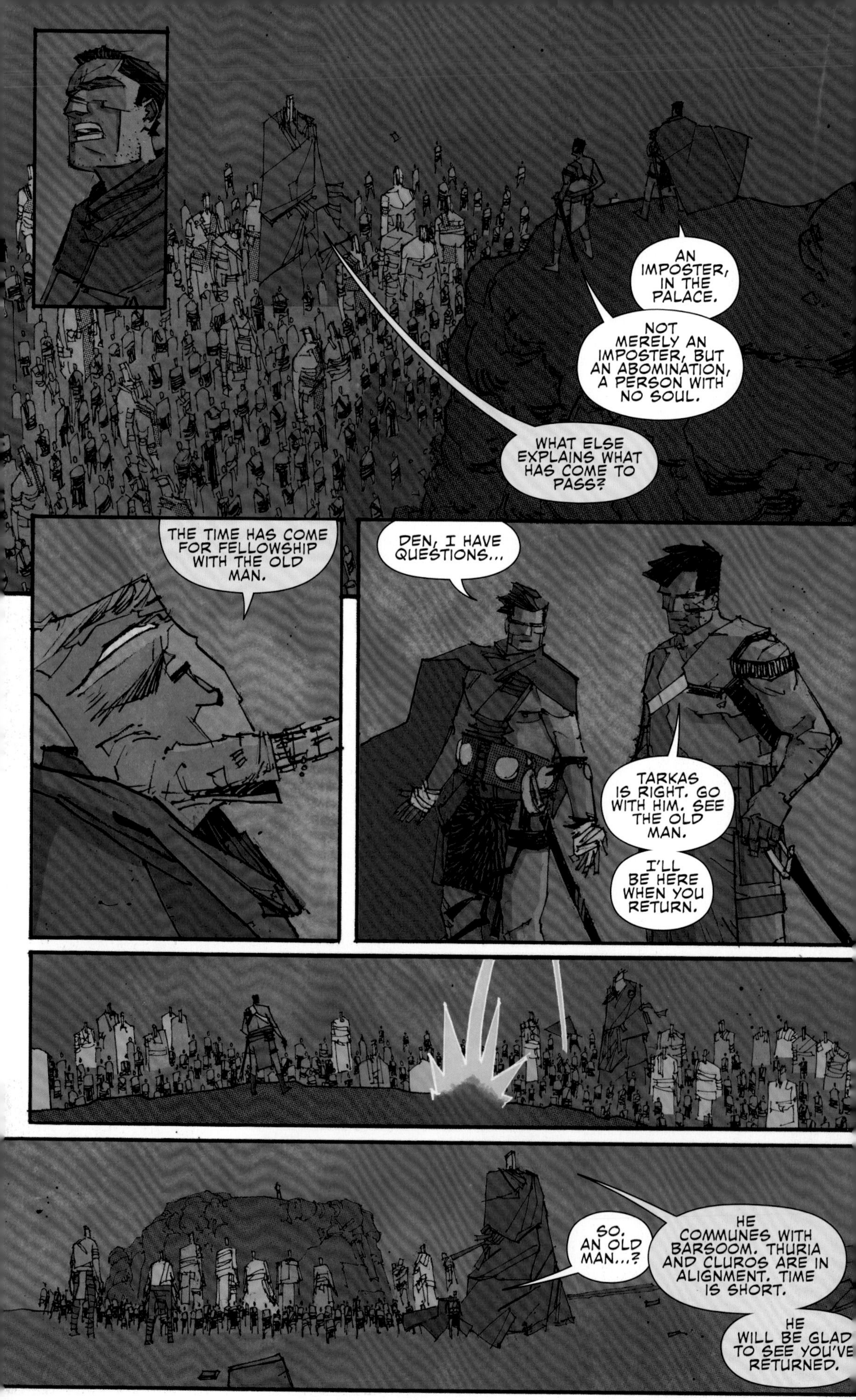
AN IMPOSTER, IN THE PALACE.
NOT MERELY AN IMPOSTER, BUT AN ABOMINATION, A PERSON WITH NO SOUL.
WHAT ELSE EXPLAINS WHAT HAS COME TO PASS?
THE TIME HAS COME FOR FELLOWSHIP WITH THE OLD MAN.
DEN, I HAVE QUESTIONS...
TARKAS IS RIGHT. GO WITH HIM. SEE THE OLD MAN.
I'LL BE HERE WHEN YOU RETURN.
SO. AN OLD MAN...?
HE COMMUNES WITH BARSOOM. THURIA AND CLUROS ARE IN ALIGNMENT. TIME IS SHORT.
HE WILL BE GLAD TO SEE YOU'VE RETURNED.

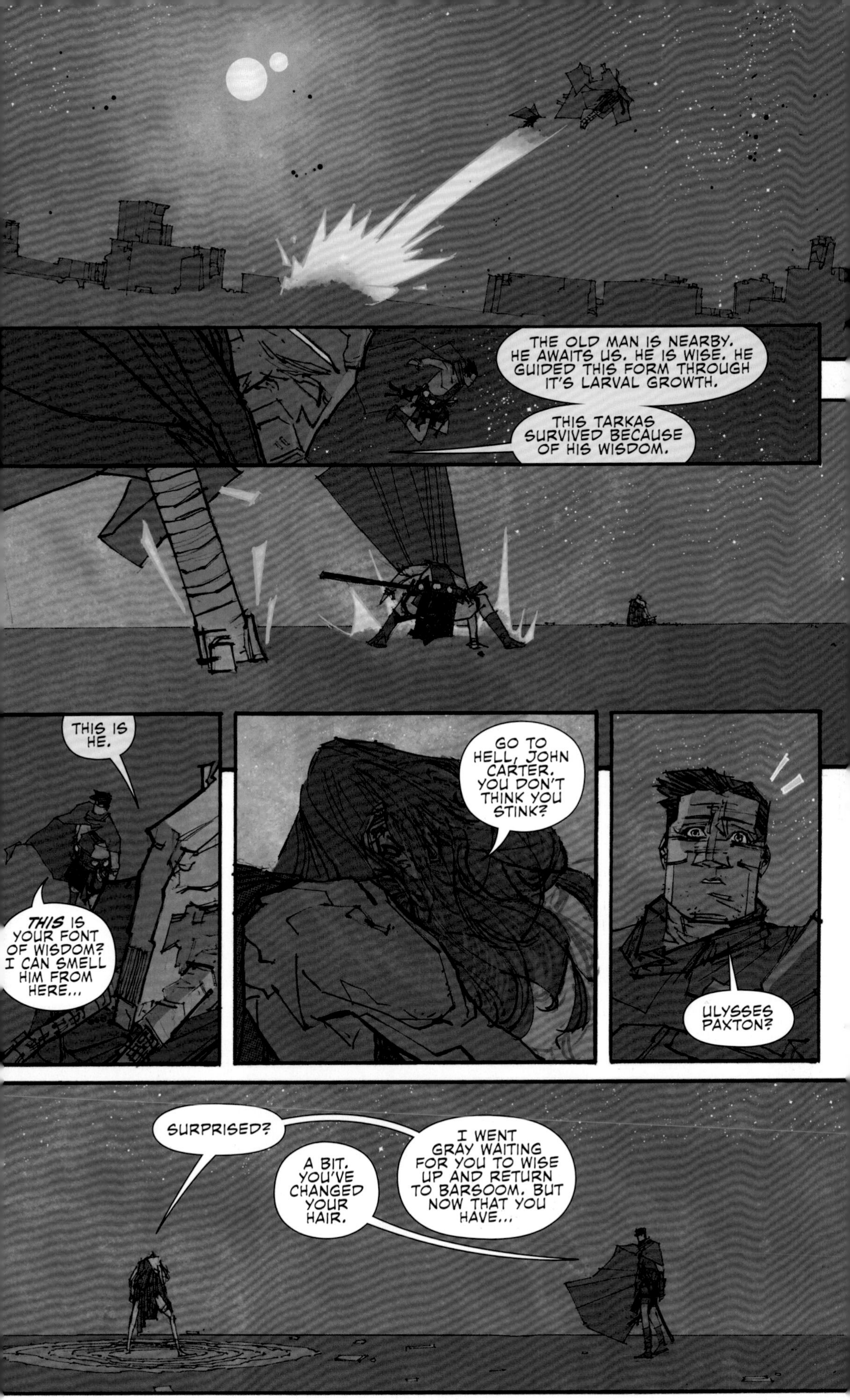
THE OLD MAN IS NEARBY. HE AWAITS US. HE IS WISE. HE GUIDED THIS FORM THROUGH IT'S LARVAL GROWTH.
THIS TARKAS SURVIVED BECAUSE OF HIS WISDOM.
THIS IS HE.
THIS IS YOUR FONT OF WISDOM? I CAN SMELL HIM FROM HERE...
GO TO HELL, JOHN CARTER. YOU DON'T THINK YOU STINK?
ULYSSES PAXTON?
SURPRISED?
A BIT. YOU'VE CHANGED YOUR HAIR.
I WENT GRAY WAITING FOR YOU TO WISE UP AND RETURN TO BARSOOM. BUT NOW THAT YOU HAVE...

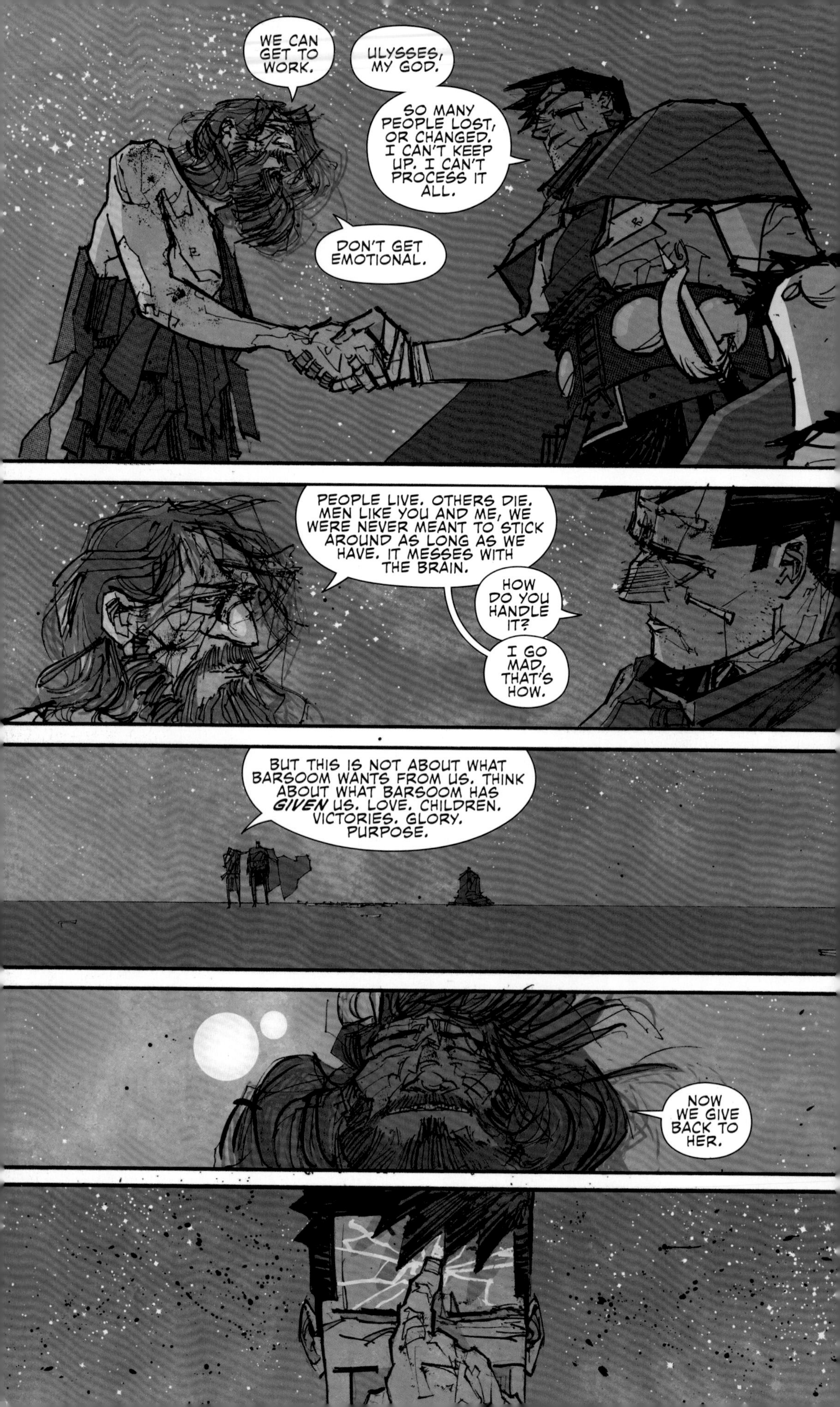
WE CAN GET TO WORK.
ULYSSES, MY GOD.
SO MANY PEOPLE LOST, OR CHANGED. I CAN'T KEEP UP. I CAN'T PROCESS IT ALL.
DON'T GET EMOTIONAL.
PEOPLE LIVE. OTHERS DIE. MEN LIKE YOU AND ME, WE WERE NEVER MEANT TO STICK AROUND AS LONG AS WE HAVE. IT MESSES WITH THE BRAIN.
HOW DO YOU HANDLE IT?
I GO MAD, THAT'S HOW.
BUT THIS IS NOT ABOUT WHAT BARSOOM WANTS FROM US. THINK ABOUT WHAT BARSOOM HAS *GIVEN* US. LOVE. CHILDREN. VICTORIES. GLORY. PURPOSE.
NOW WE GIVE BACK TO HER.

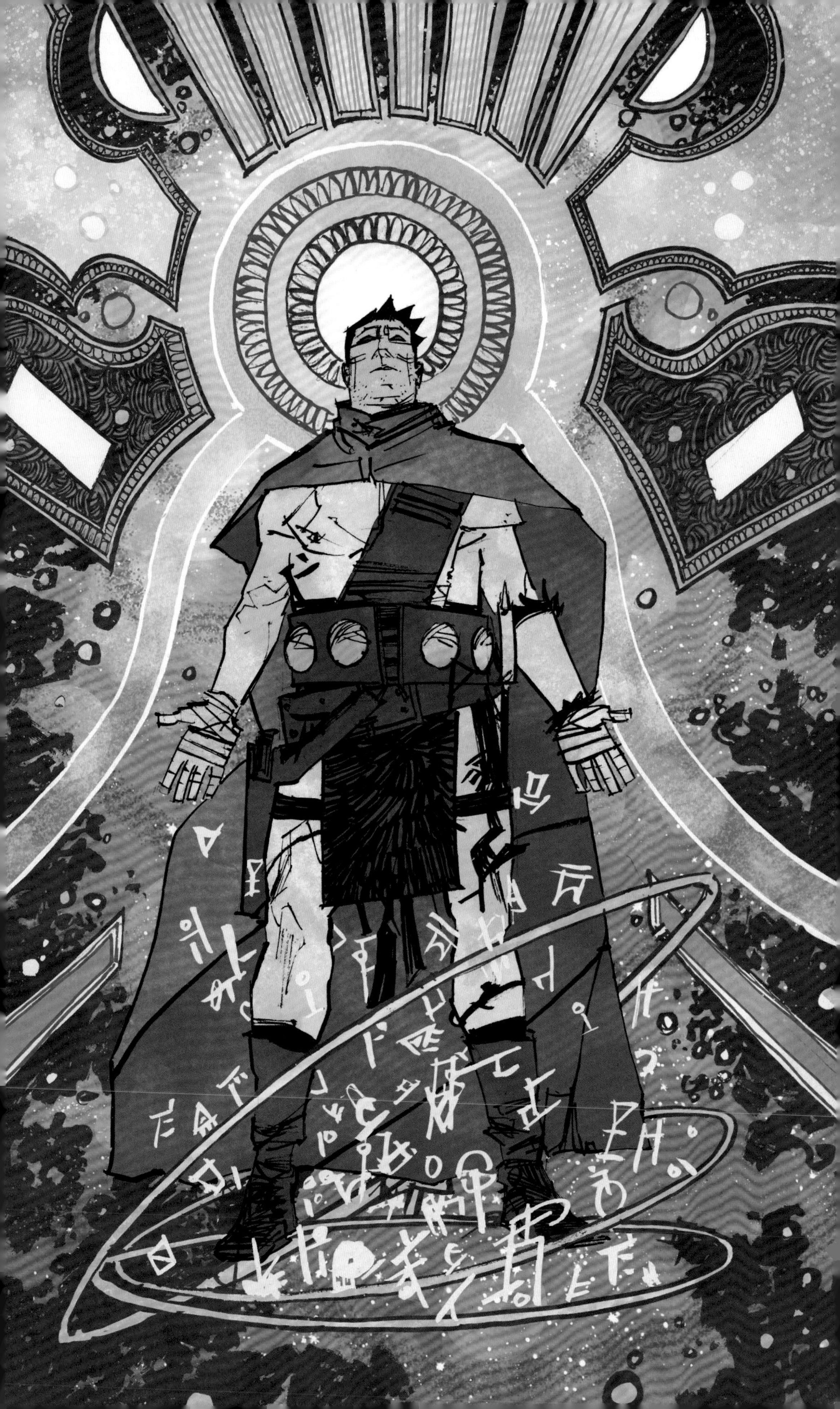

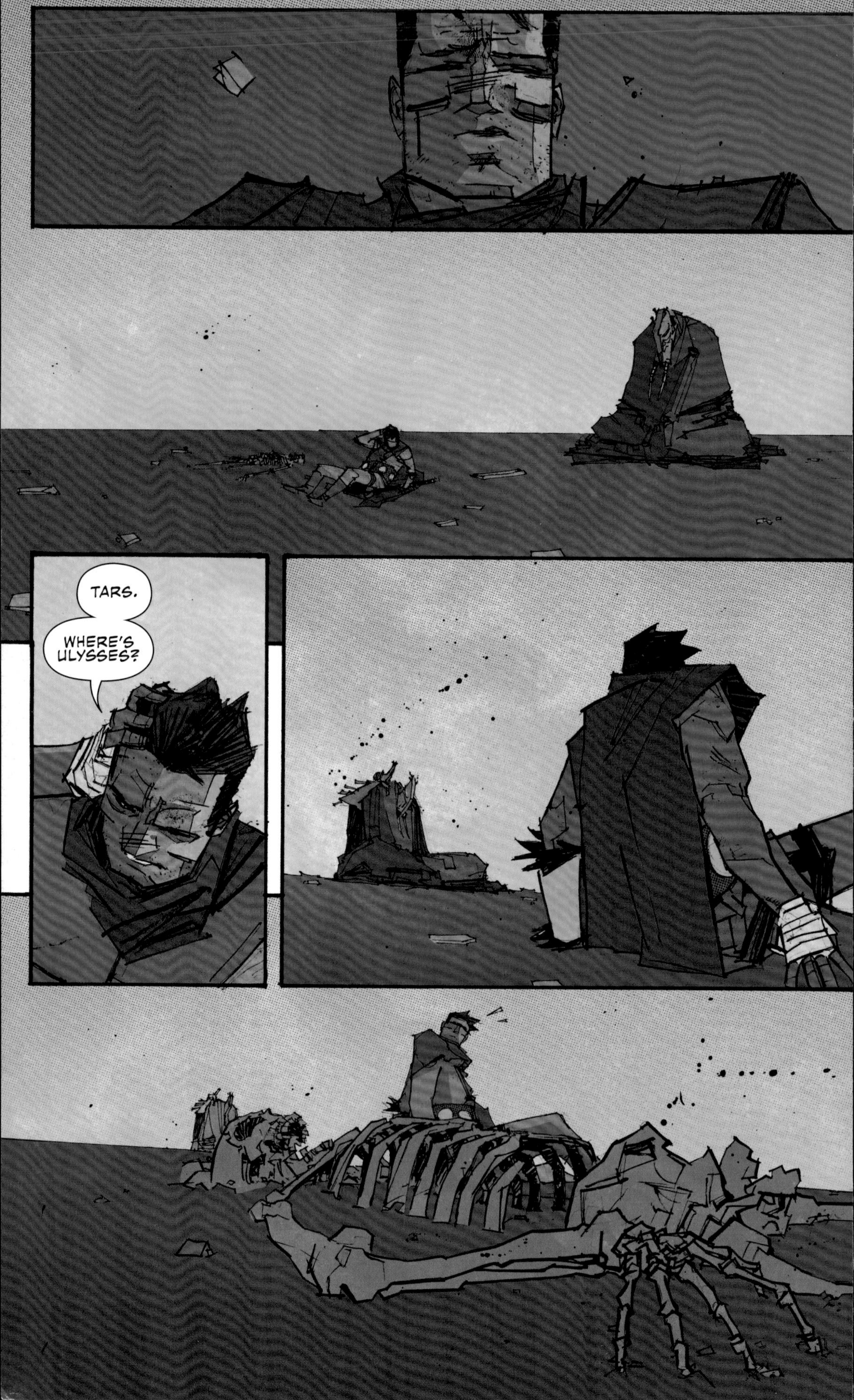
TARS.
WHERE'S ULYSSES?

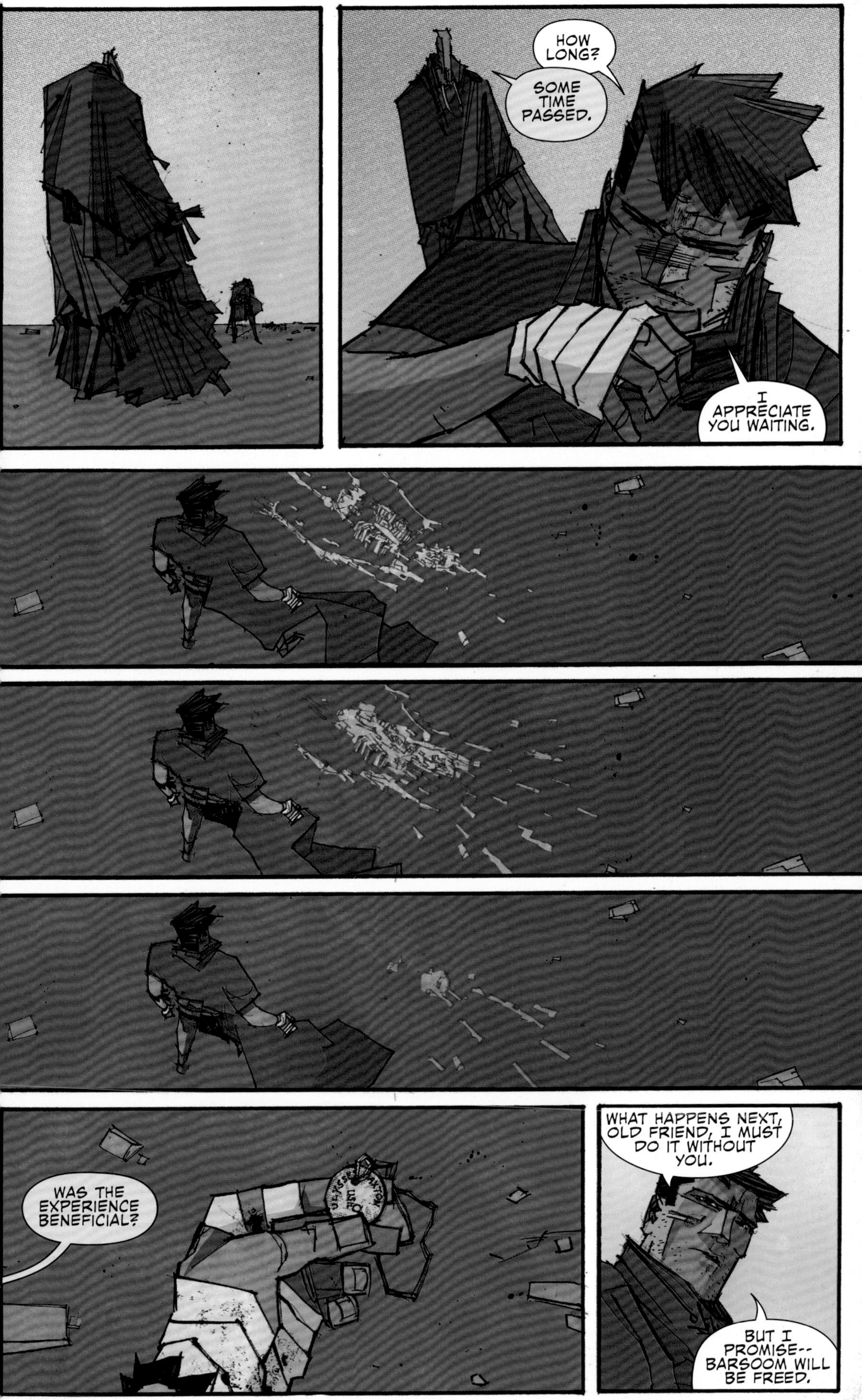
HOW LONG?
SOME TIME PASSED.
I APPRECIATE YOU WAITING.
WAS THE EXPERIENCE BENEFICIAL?
WHAT HAPPENS NEXT, OLD FRIEND, I MUST DO IT WITHOUT YOU.
BUT I PROMISE-- BARSOOM WILL BE FREED.

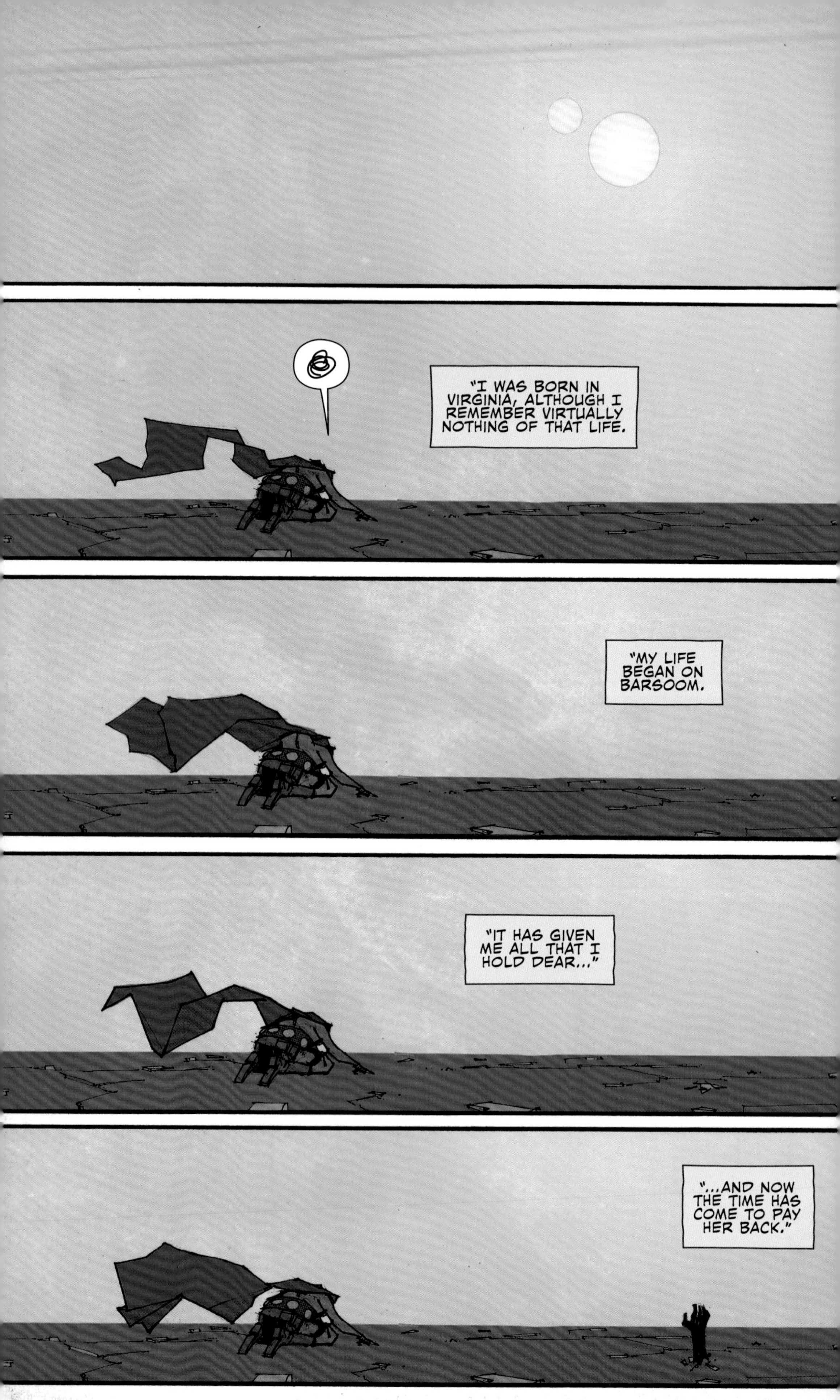
"I WAS BORN IN VIRGINIA, ALTHOUGH I REMEMBER VIRTUALLY NOTHING OF THAT LIFE.
"MY LIFE BEGAN ON BARSOOM.
"IT HAS GIVEN ME ALL THAT I HOLD DEAR..."
"...AND NOW THE TIME HAS COME TO PAY HER BACK."

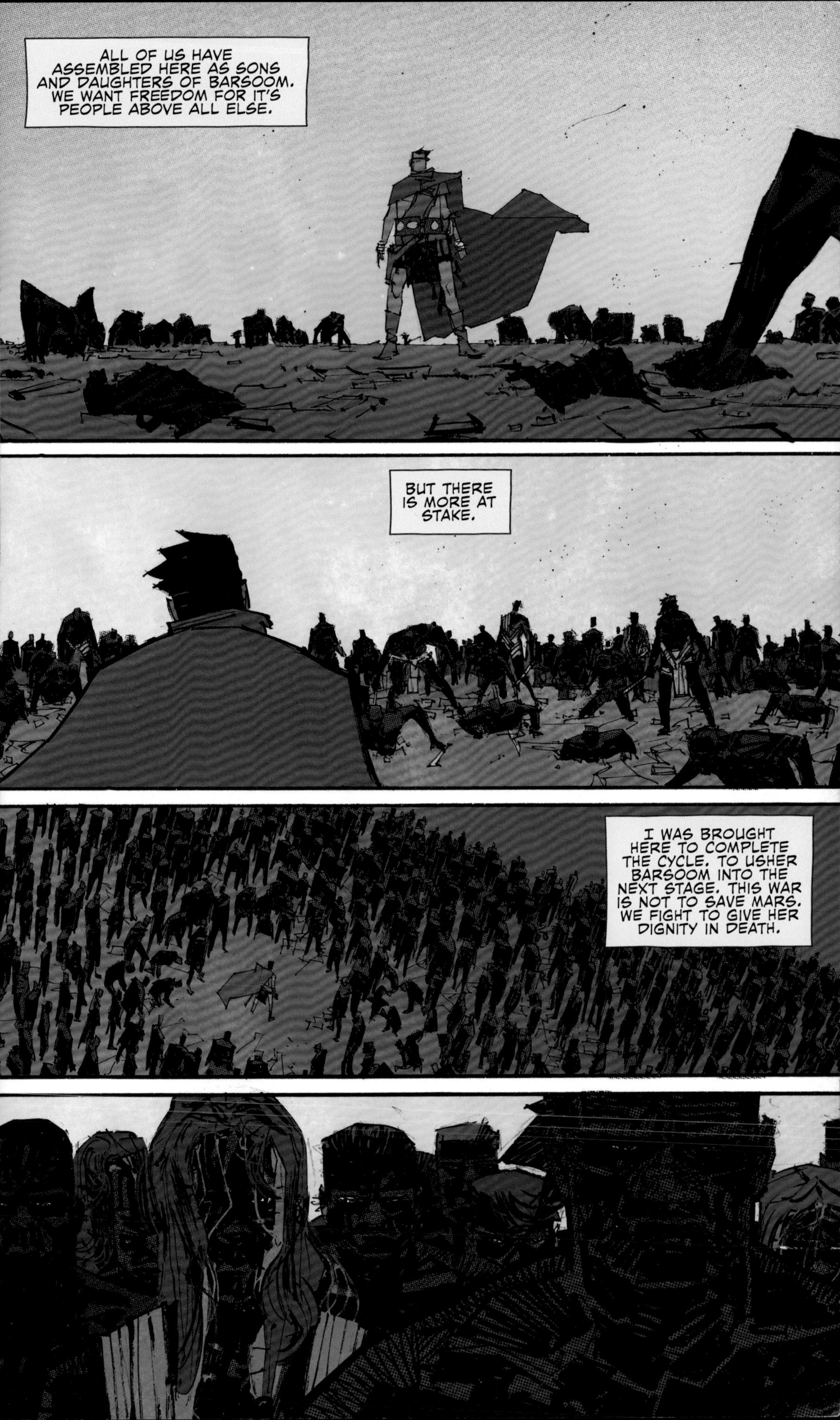
ALL OF US HAVE ASSEMBLED HERE AS SONS AND DAUGHTERS OF BARSOOM. WE WANT FREEDOM FOR IT'S PEOPLE ABOVE ALL ELSE.
BUT THERE IS MORE AT STAKE.
I WAS BROUGHT HERE TO COMPLETE THE CYCLE. TO USHER BARSOOM INTO THE NEXT STAGE. THIS WAR IS NOT TO SAVE MARS. WE FIGHT TO GIVE HER DIGNITY IN DEATH.

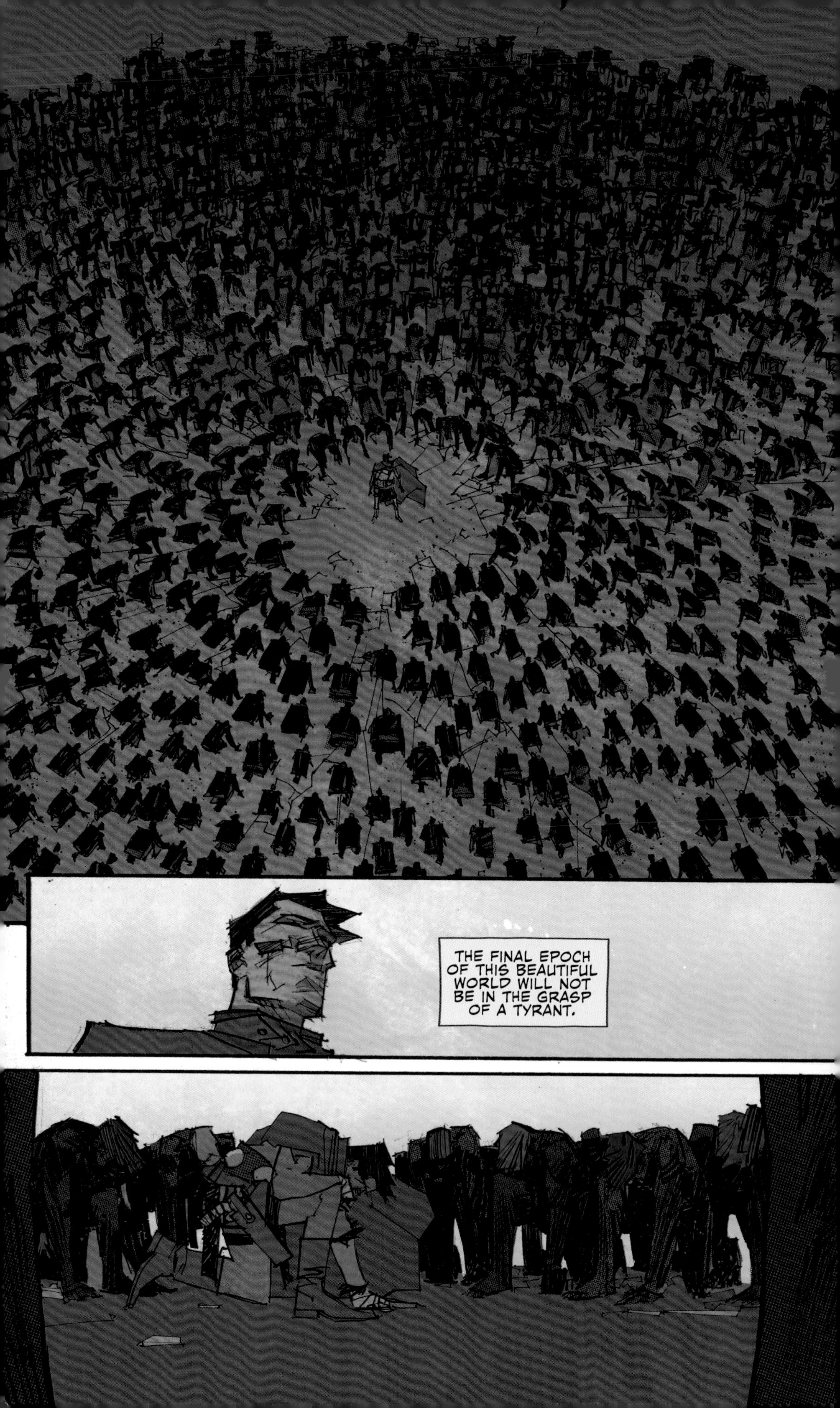
THE FINAL EPOCH OF THIS BEAUTIFUL WORLD WILL NOT BE IN THE GRASP OF A TYRANT.

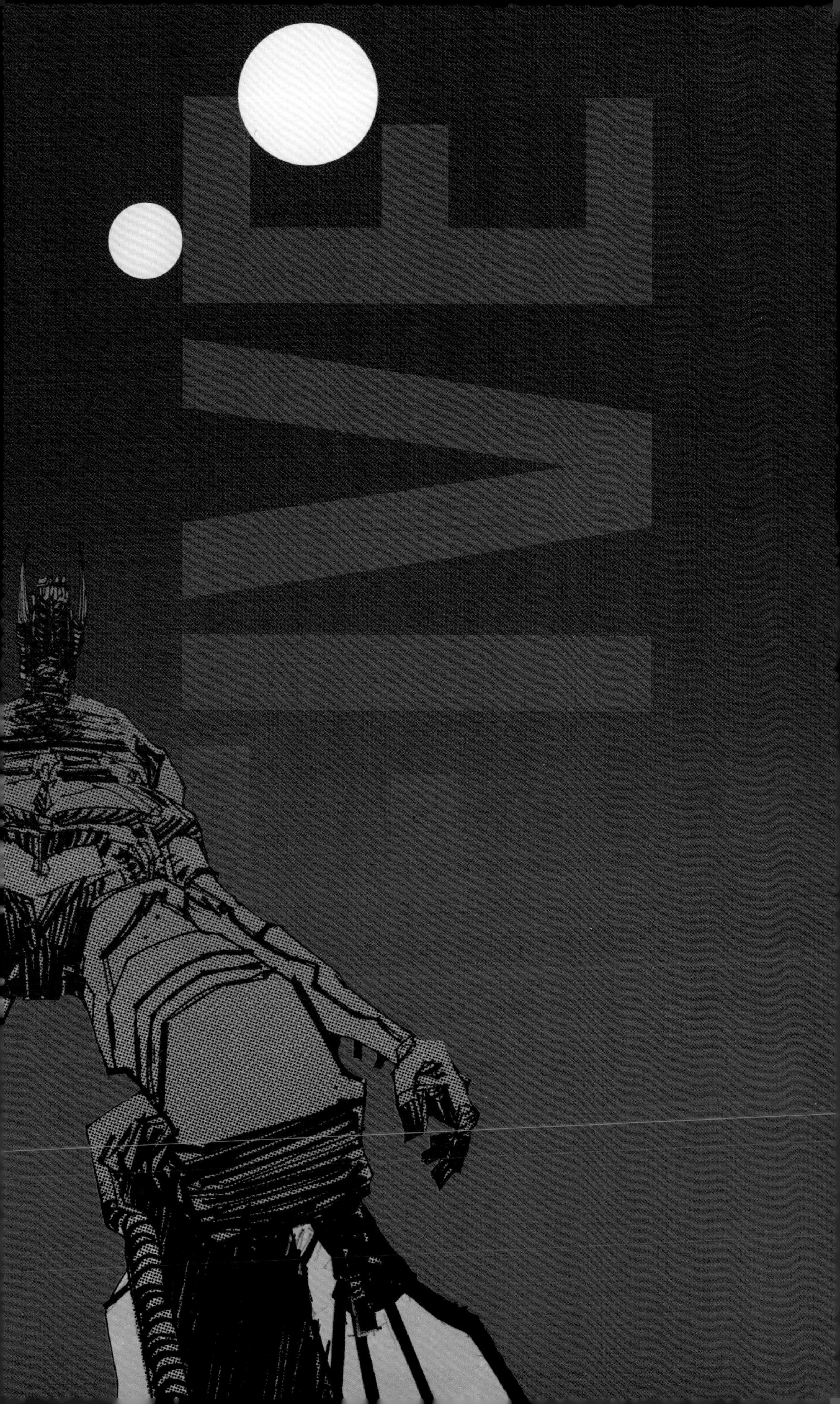

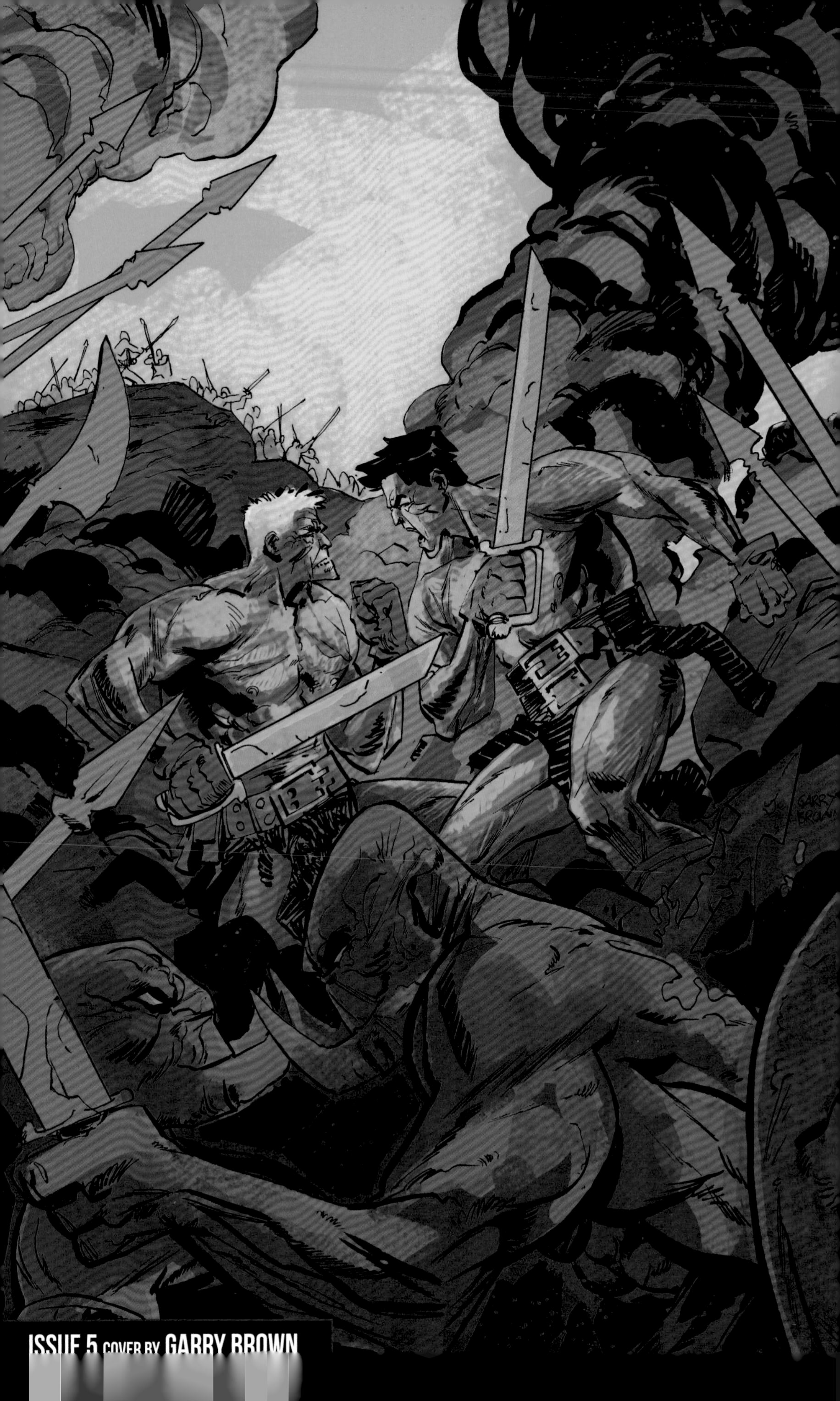
GARRY BROWN

ISSUE 5 COVER BY GARRY BROWN

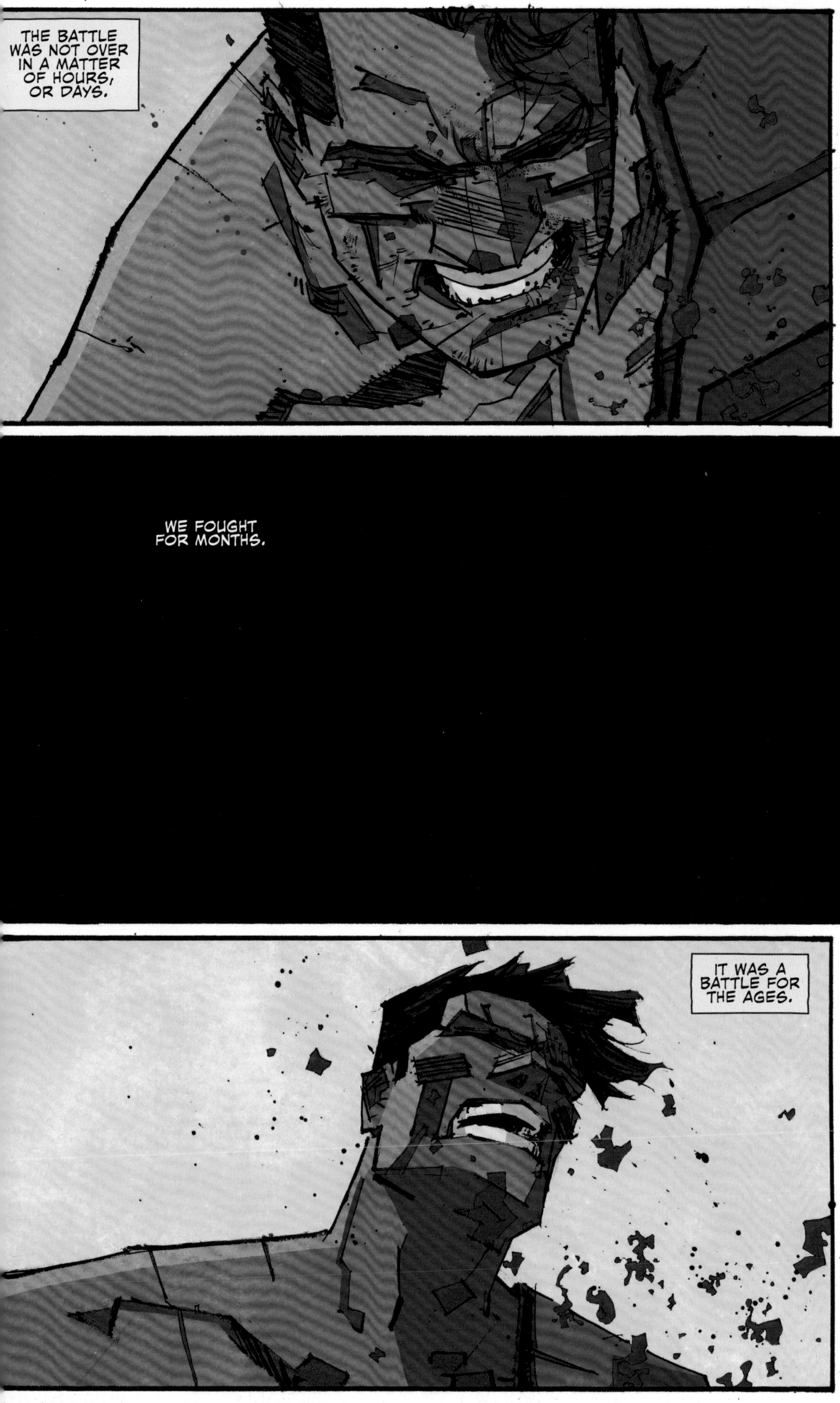
THE BATTLE WAS NOT OVER IN A MATTER OF HOURS, OR DAYS.
WE FOUGHT FOR MONTHS.
IT WAS A BATTLE FOR THE AGES.

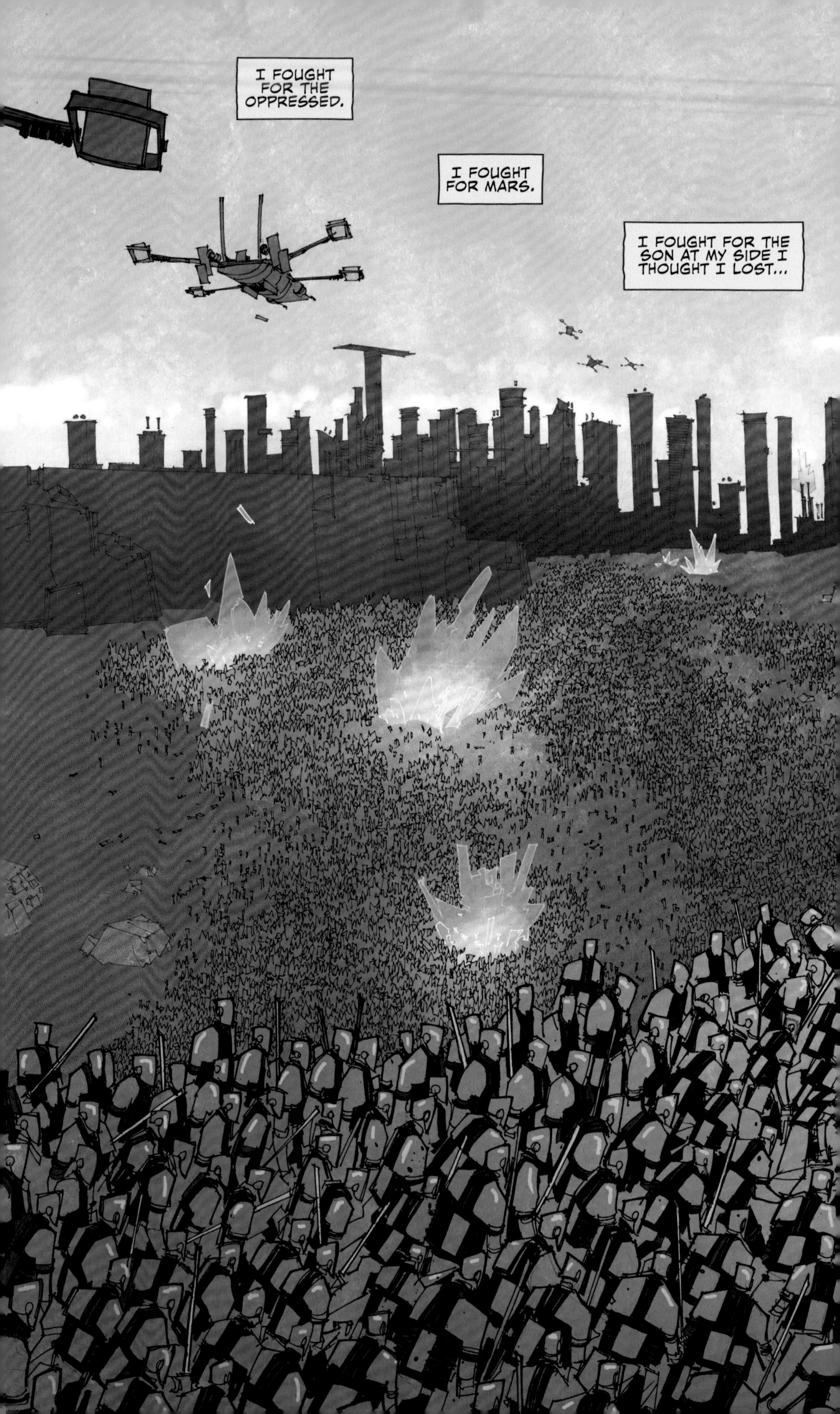
I FOUGHT FOR THE OPPRESSED.
I FOUGHT FOR MARS.
I FOUGHT FOR THE SON AT MY SIDE I THOUGHT I LOST...

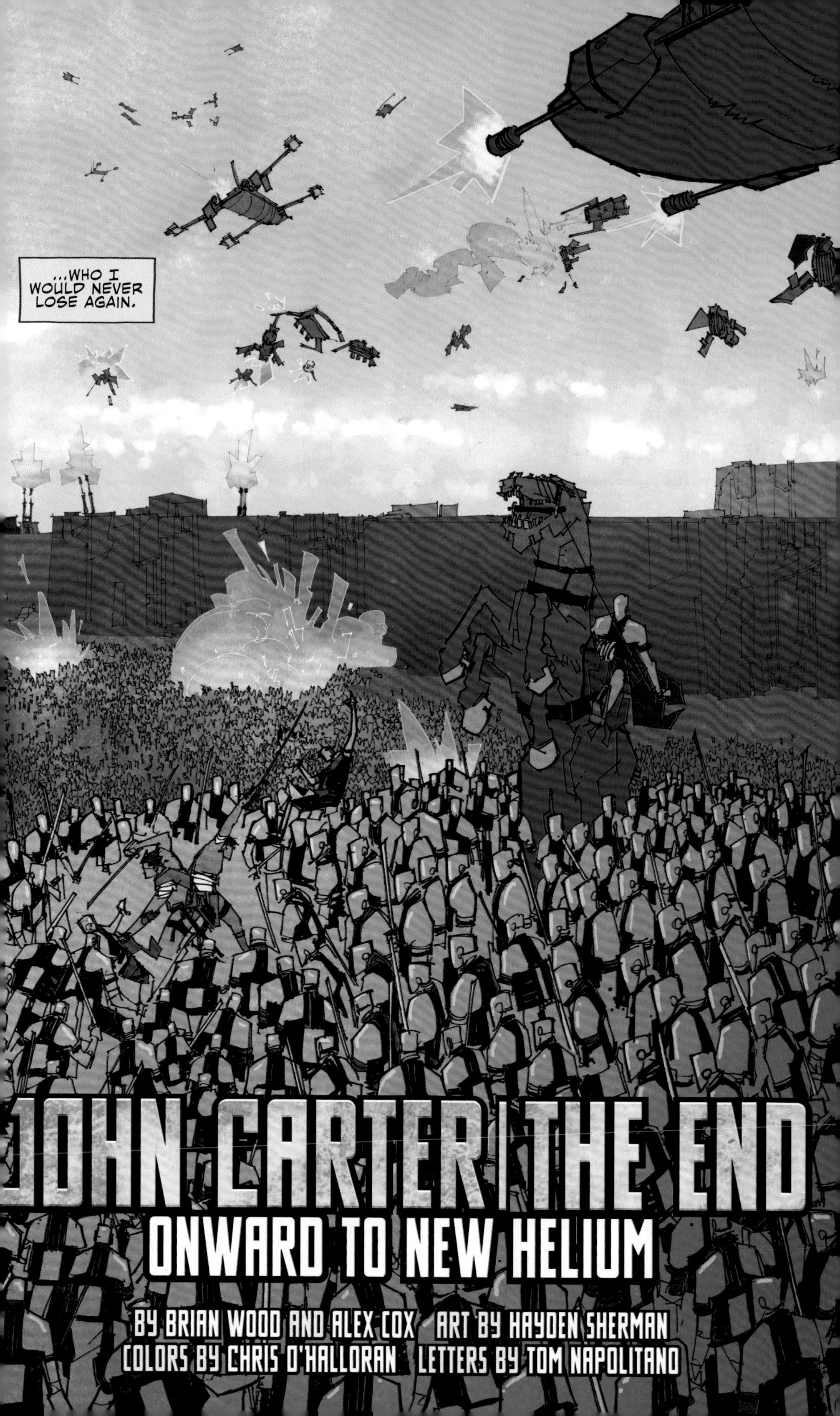
...WHO I WOULD NEVER LOSE AGAIN.
JOHN CARTER | THE END
ONWARD TO NEW HELIUM
BY BRIAN WOOD AND ALEX COX ART BY HAYDEN SHERMAN
COLORS BY CHRIS O'HALLORAN LETTERS BY TOM NAPOLITANO

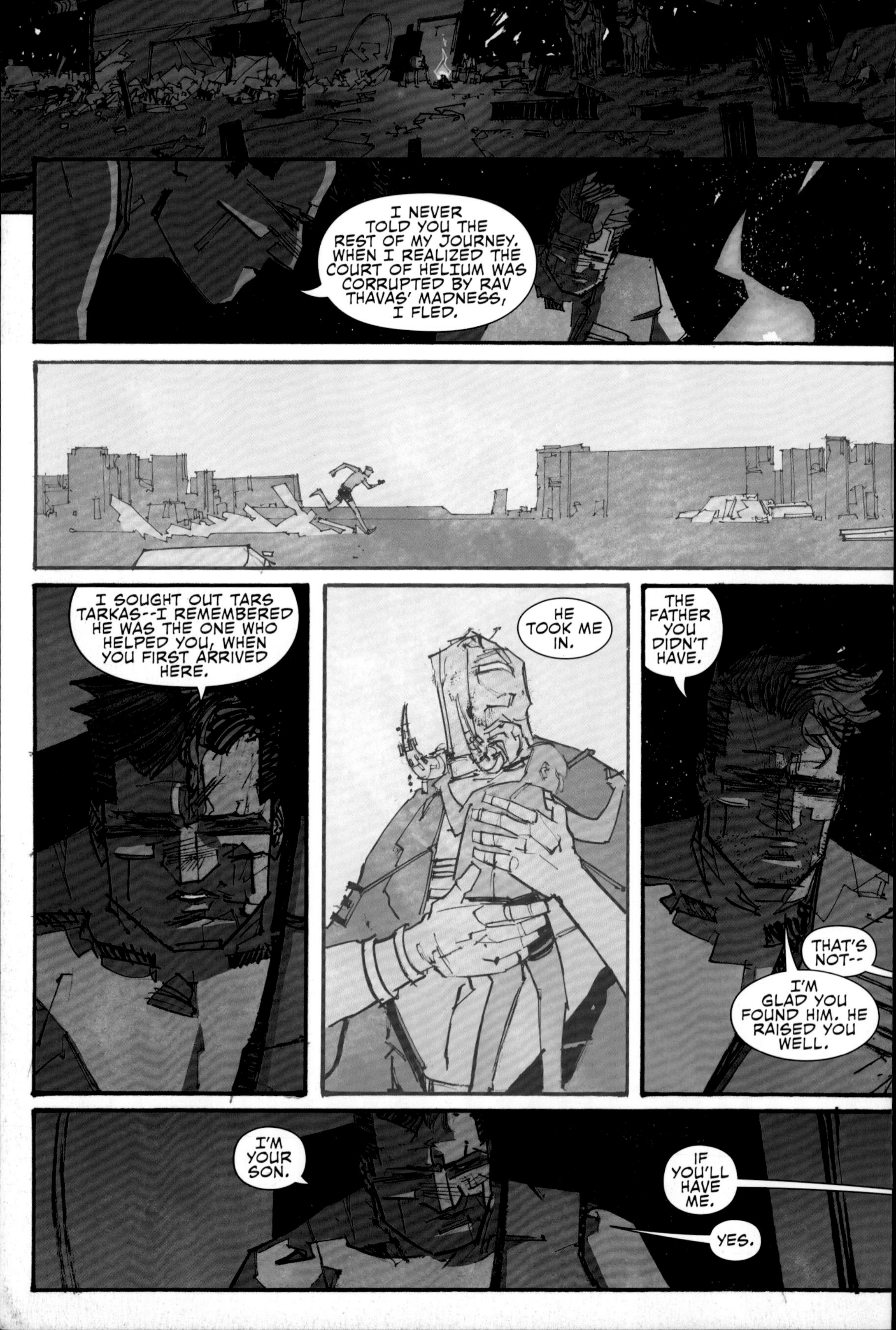
I NEVER TOLD YOU THE REST OF MY JOURNEY. WHEN I REALIZED THE COURT OF HELIUM WAS CORRUPTED BY RAV THAVAS' MADNESS, I FLED.
I SOUGHT OUT TARS TARKAS--I REMEMBERED HE WAS THE ONE WHO HELPED YOU, WHEN YOU FIRST ARRIVED HERE.
HE TOOK ME IN.
THE FATHER YOU DIDN'T HAVE.
THAT'S NOT--
I'M GLAD YOU FOUND HIM. HE RAISED YOU WELL.
I'M YOUR SON.
IF YOU'LL HAVE ME.
YES.

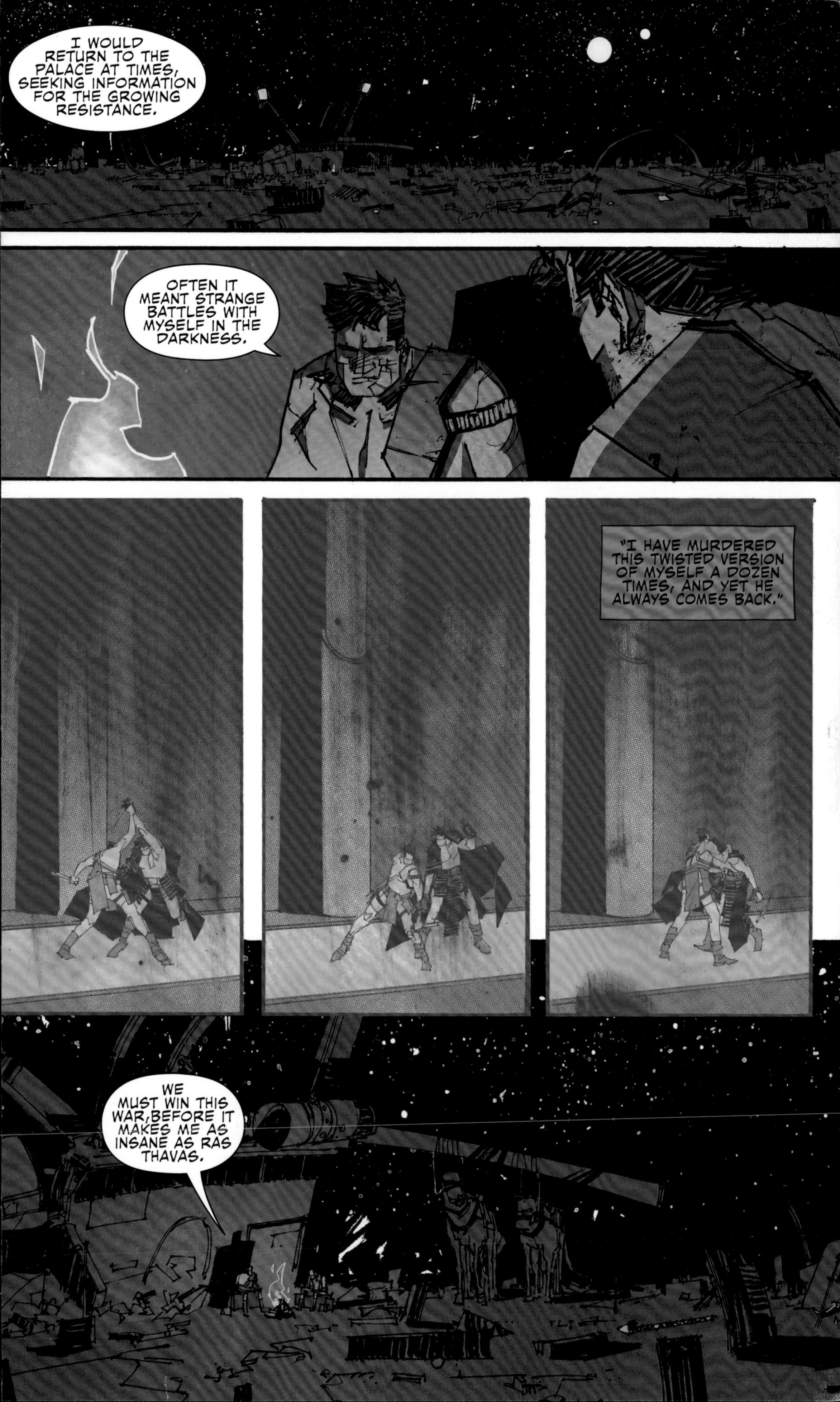
I WOULD RETURN TO THE PALACE AT TIMES, SEEKING INFORMATION FOR THE GROWING RESISTANCE.
OFTEN IT MEANT STRANGE BATTLES WITH MYSELF IN THE DARKNESS.
"I HAVE MURDERED THIS TWISTED VERSION OF MYSELF A DOZEN TIMES, AND YET HE ALWAYS COMES BACK."
WE MUST WIN THIS WAR,BEFORE IT MAKES ME AS INSANE AS RAS THAVAS.

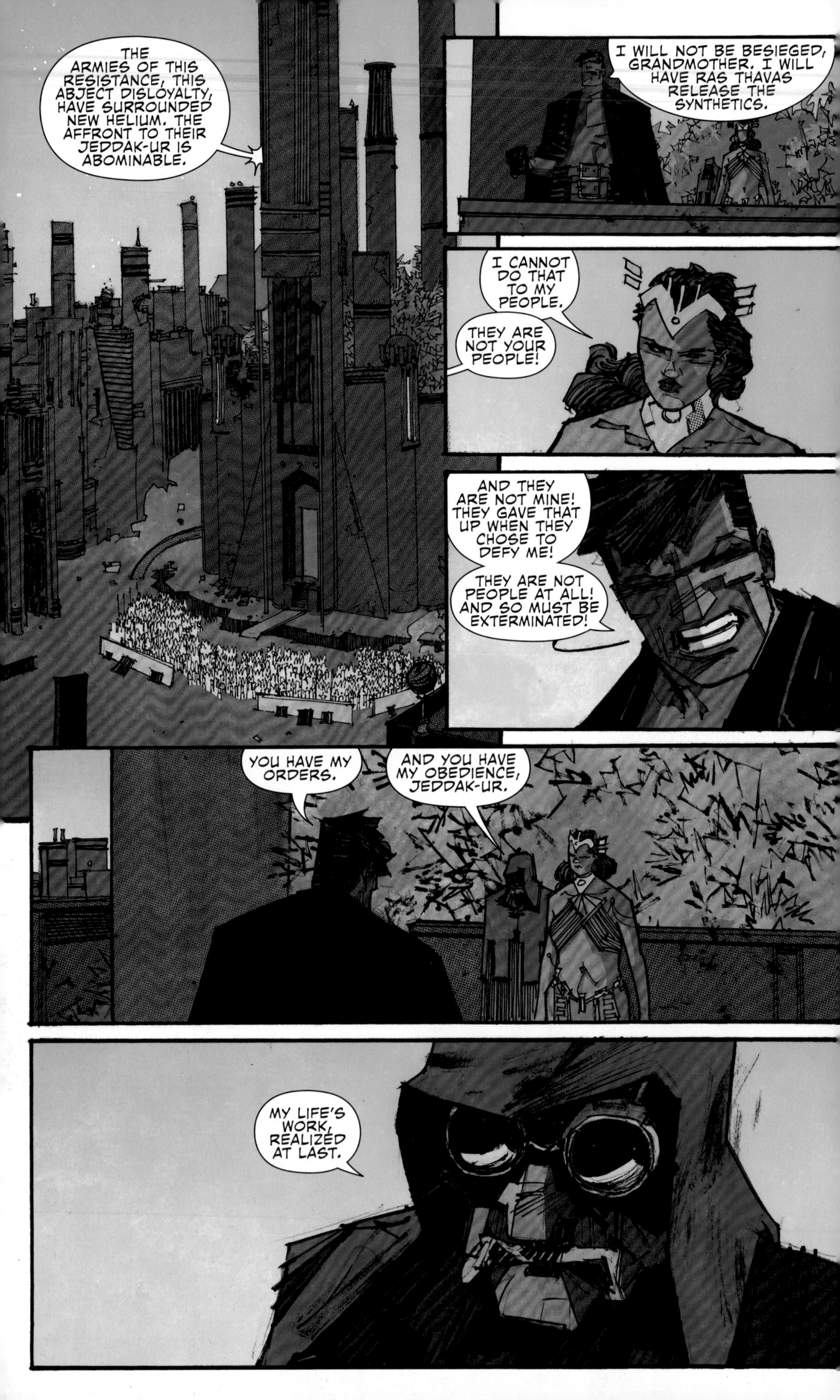
THE ARMIES OF THIS RESISTANCE, THIS ABJECT DISLOYALTY, HAVE SURROUNDED NEW HELIUM. THE AFFRONT TO THEIR JEDDAK-UR IS ABOMINABLE.
I WILL NOT BE BESIEGED, GRANDMOTHER. I WILL HAVE RAS THAVAS RELEASE THE SYNTHETICS.
I CANNOT DO THAT TO MY PEOPLE.
THEY ARE NOT YOUR PEOPLE!
AND THEY ARE NOT MINE! THEY GAVE THAT UP WHEN THEY CHOSE TO DEFY ME!
THEY ARE NOT PEOPLE AT ALL! AND SO MUST BE EXTERMINATED!
YOU HAVE MY ORDERS.
AND YOU HAVE MY OBEDIENCE, JEDDAK-UR.
MY LIFE'S WORK, REALIZED AT LAST.

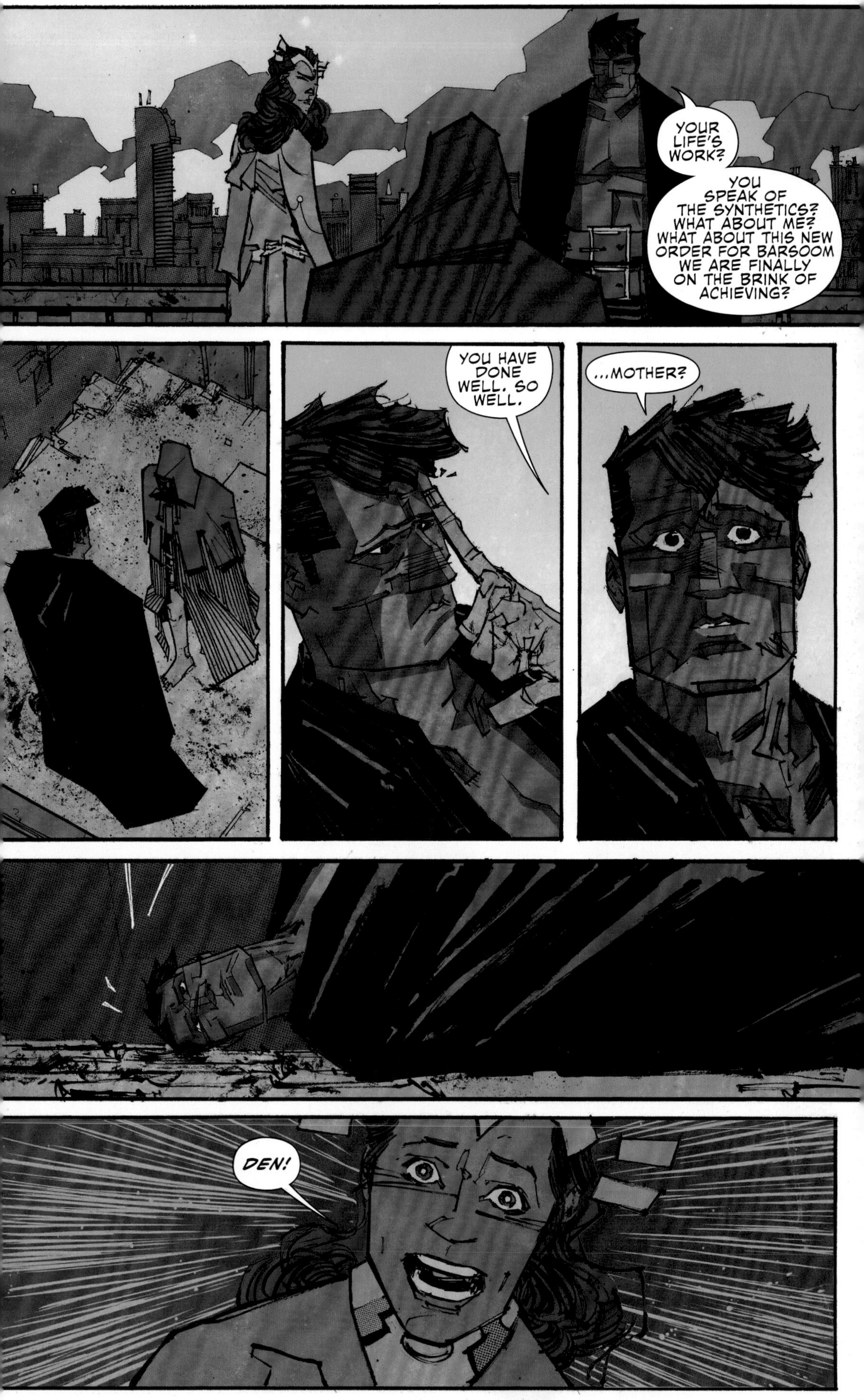
YOUR LIFE'S WORK?
YOU SPEAK OF THE SYNTHETICS? WHAT ABOUT ME? WHAT ABOUT THIS NEW ORDER FOR BARSOOM WE ARE FINALLY ON THE BRINK OF ACHIEVING?
YOU HAVE DONE WELL. SO WELL.
...MOTHER?
DEN!

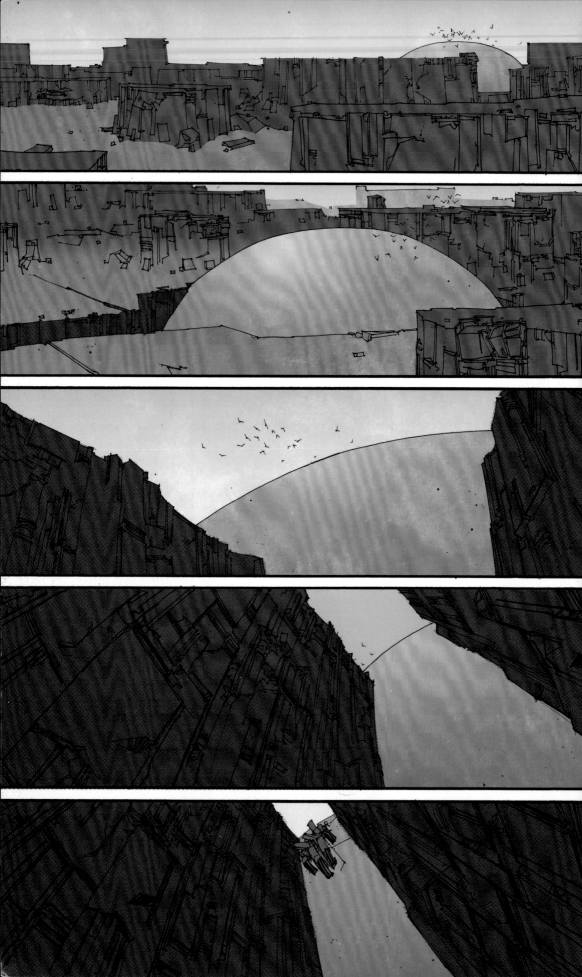

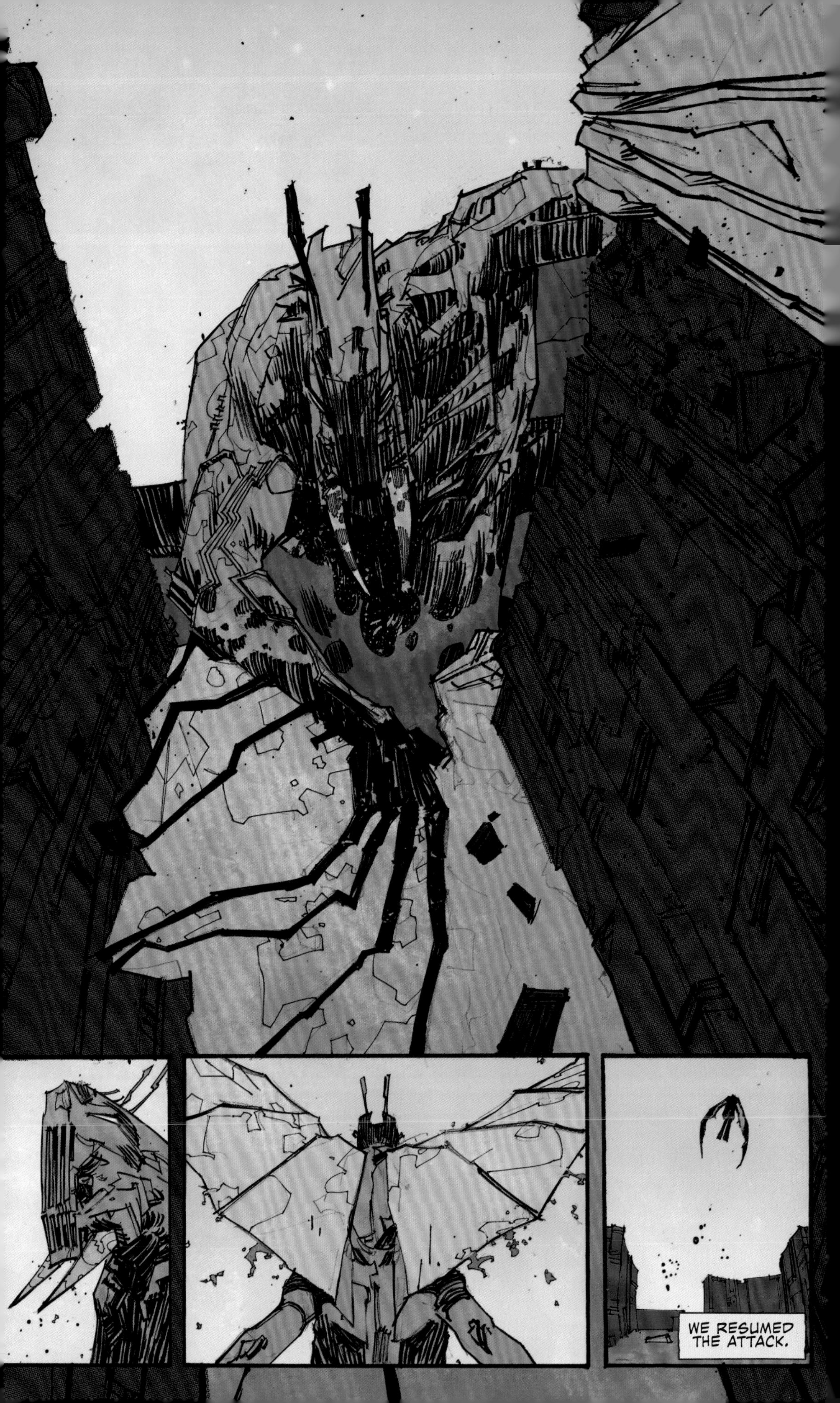
WE RESUMED THE ATTACK.

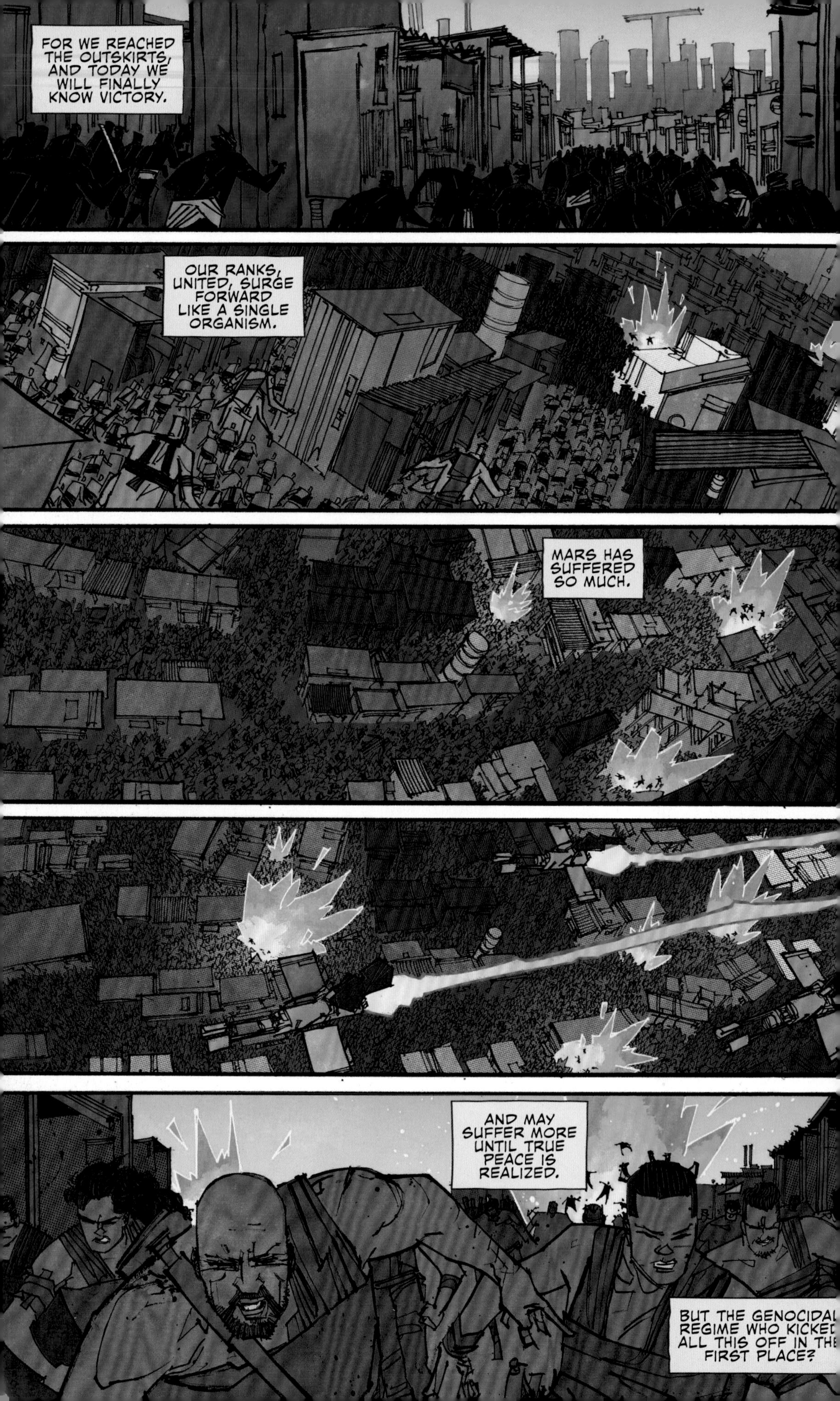
FOR WE REACHED THE OUTSKIRTS, AND TODAY WE WILL FINALLY KNOW VICTORY.
OUR RANKS, UNITED, SURGE FORWARD LIKE A SINGLE ORGANISM.
MARS HAS SUFFERED SO MUCH.
AND MAY SUFFER MORE UNTIL TRUE PEACE IS REALIZED.
BUT THE GENOCIDAL REGIME WHO KICKED ALL THIS OFF IN THE FIRST PLACE?

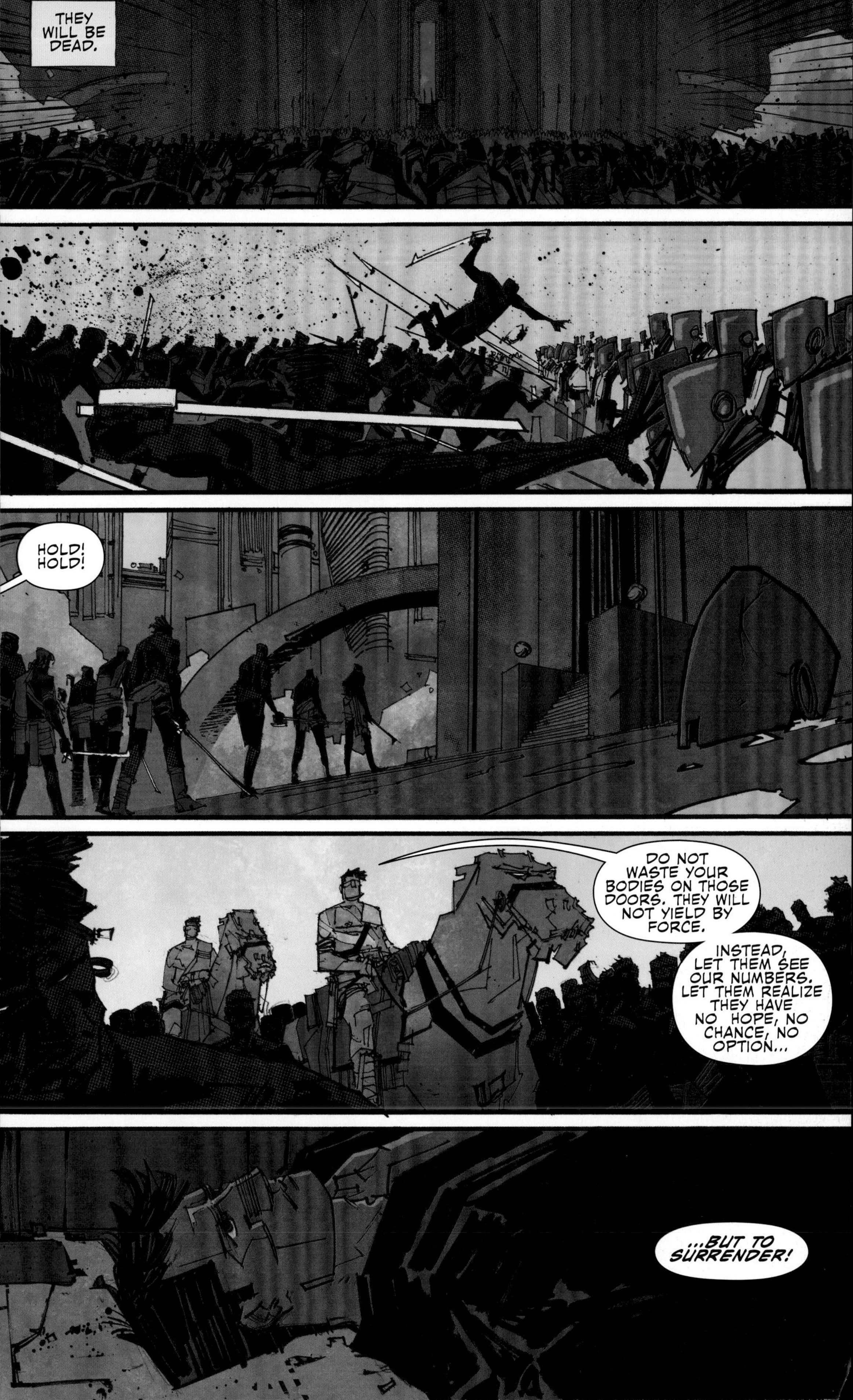
THEY WILL BE DEAD.
HOLD! HOLD!
DO NOT WASTE YOUR BODIES ON THOSE DOORS. THEY WILL NOT YIELD BY FORCE.
INSTEAD, LET THEM SEE OUR NUMBERS. LET THEM REALIZE THEY HAVE NO HOPE, NO CHANCE, NO OPTION...
...BUT TO SURRENDER!

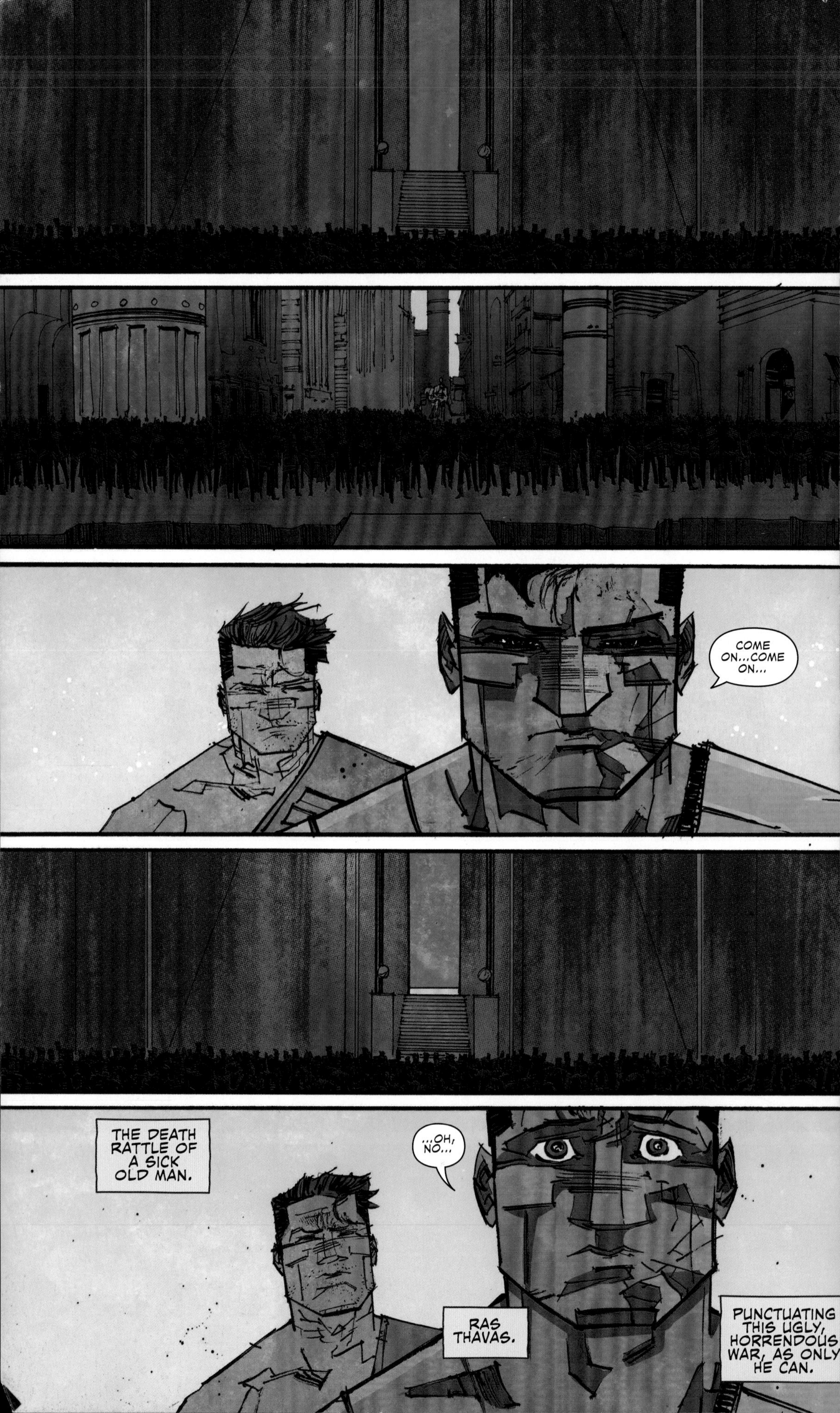
COME ON...COME ON...
THE DEATH RATTLE OF A SICK OLD MAN.
...OH, NO...
RAS THAVAS.
PUNCTUATING THIS UGLY, HORRENDOUS WAR, AS ONLY HE CAN.

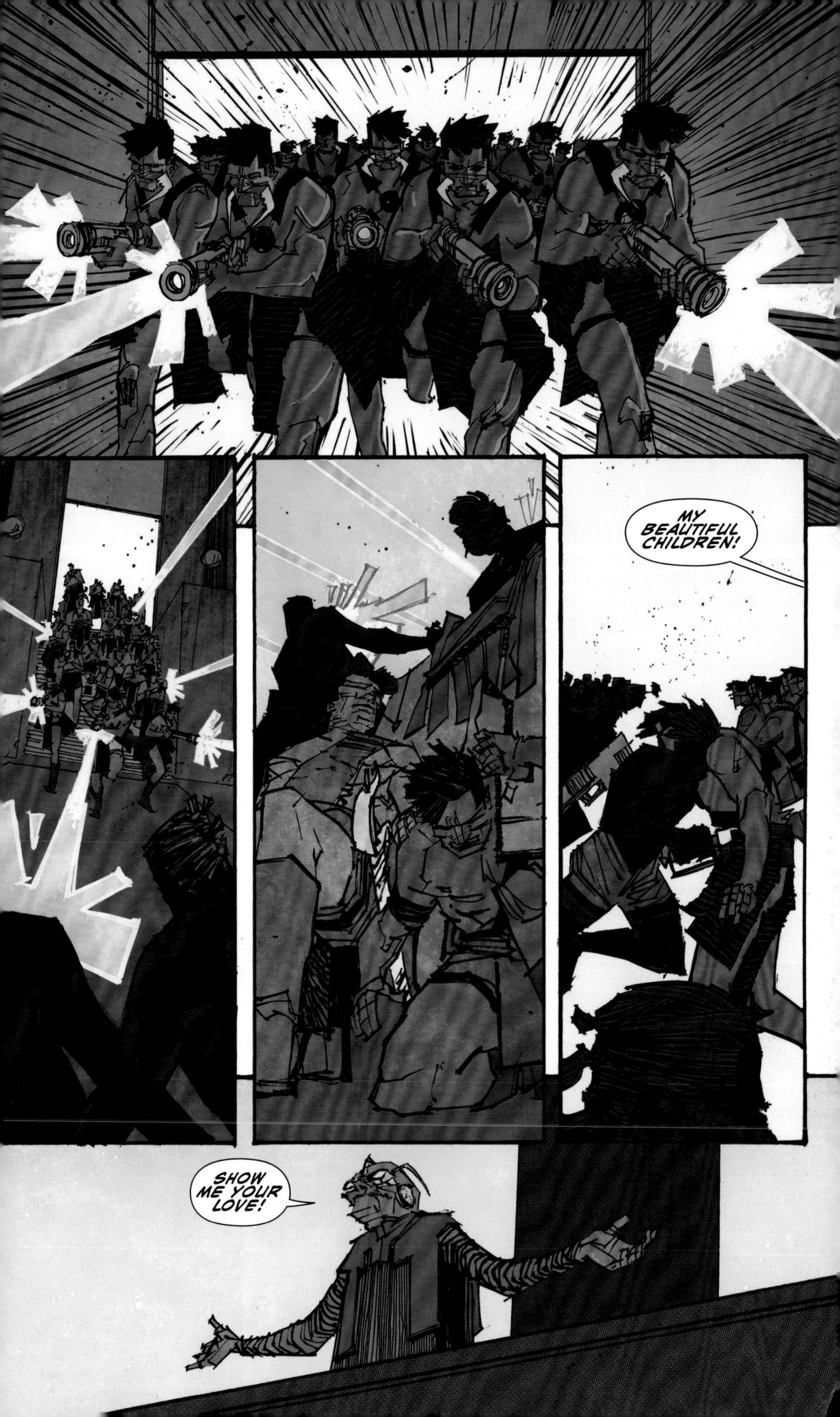
MY BEAUTIFUL CHILDREN!
SHOW ME YOUR LOVE!

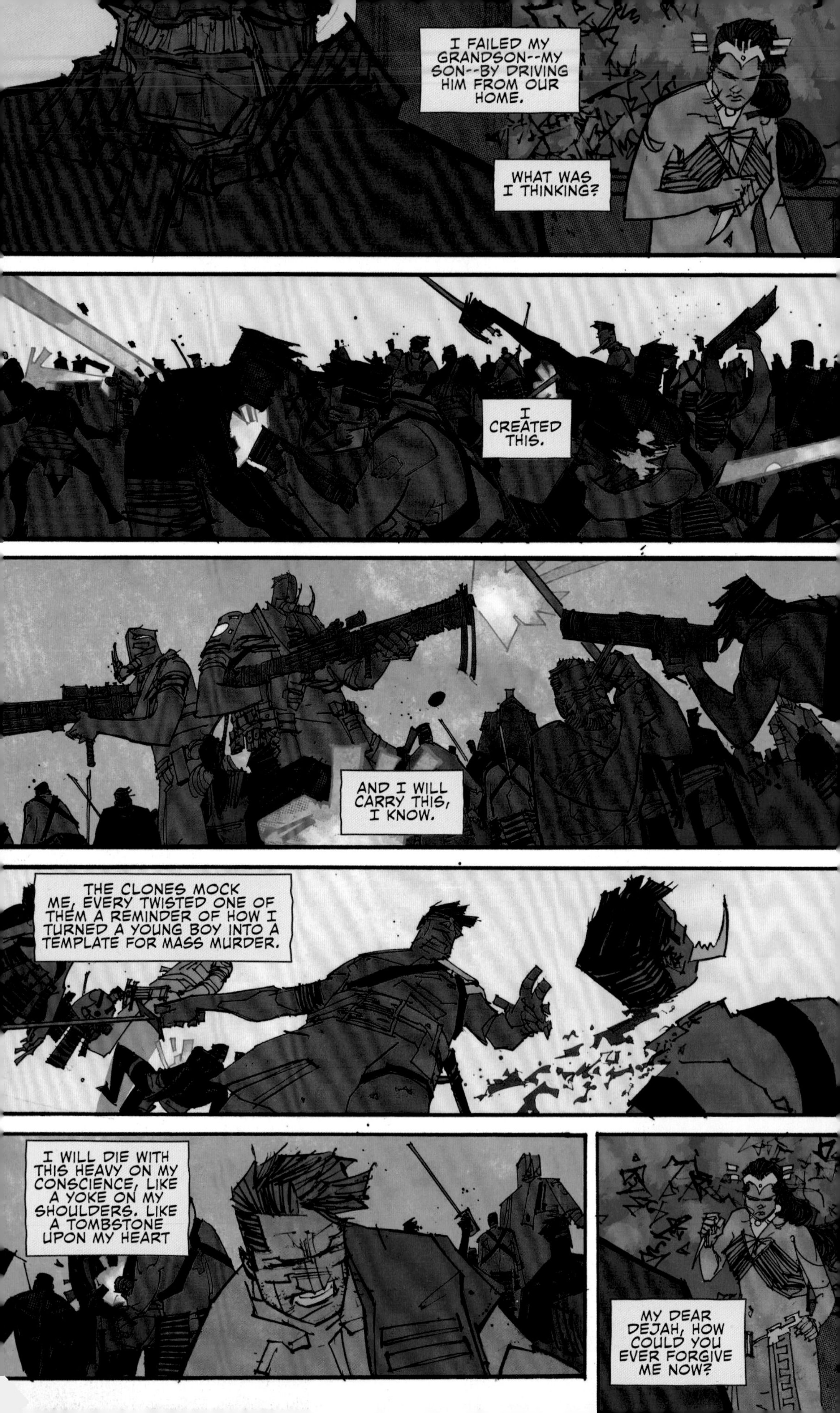
I FAILED MY GRANDSON--MY SON--BY DRIVING HIM FROM OUR HOME.
WHAT WAS I THINKING?
I CREATED THIS.
AND I WILL CARRY THIS, I KNOW.
THE CLONES MOCK ME, EVERY TWISTED ONE OF THEM A REMINDER OF HOW I TURNED A YOUNG BOY INTO A TEMPLATE FOR MASS MURDER.
I WILL DIE WITH THIS HEAVY ON MY CONSCIENCE, LIKE A YOKE ON MY SHOULDERS, LIKE A TOMBSTONE UPON MY HEART
MY DEAR DEJAH, HOW COULD YOU EVER FORGIVE ME NOW?

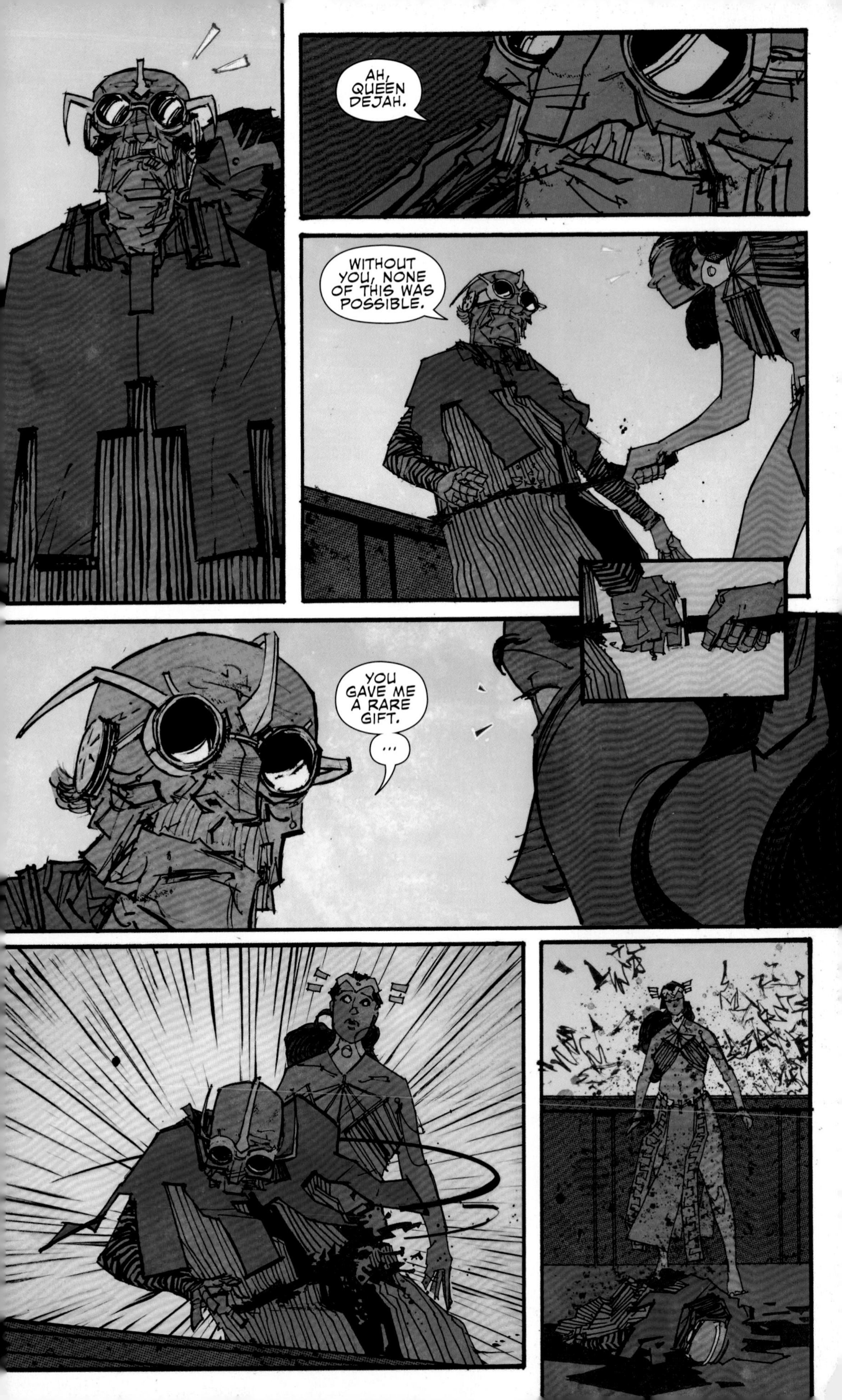

AH, QUEEN DEJAH.
WITHOUT YOU, NONE OF THIS WAS POSSIBLE.
YOU GAVE ME A RARE GIFT.
...

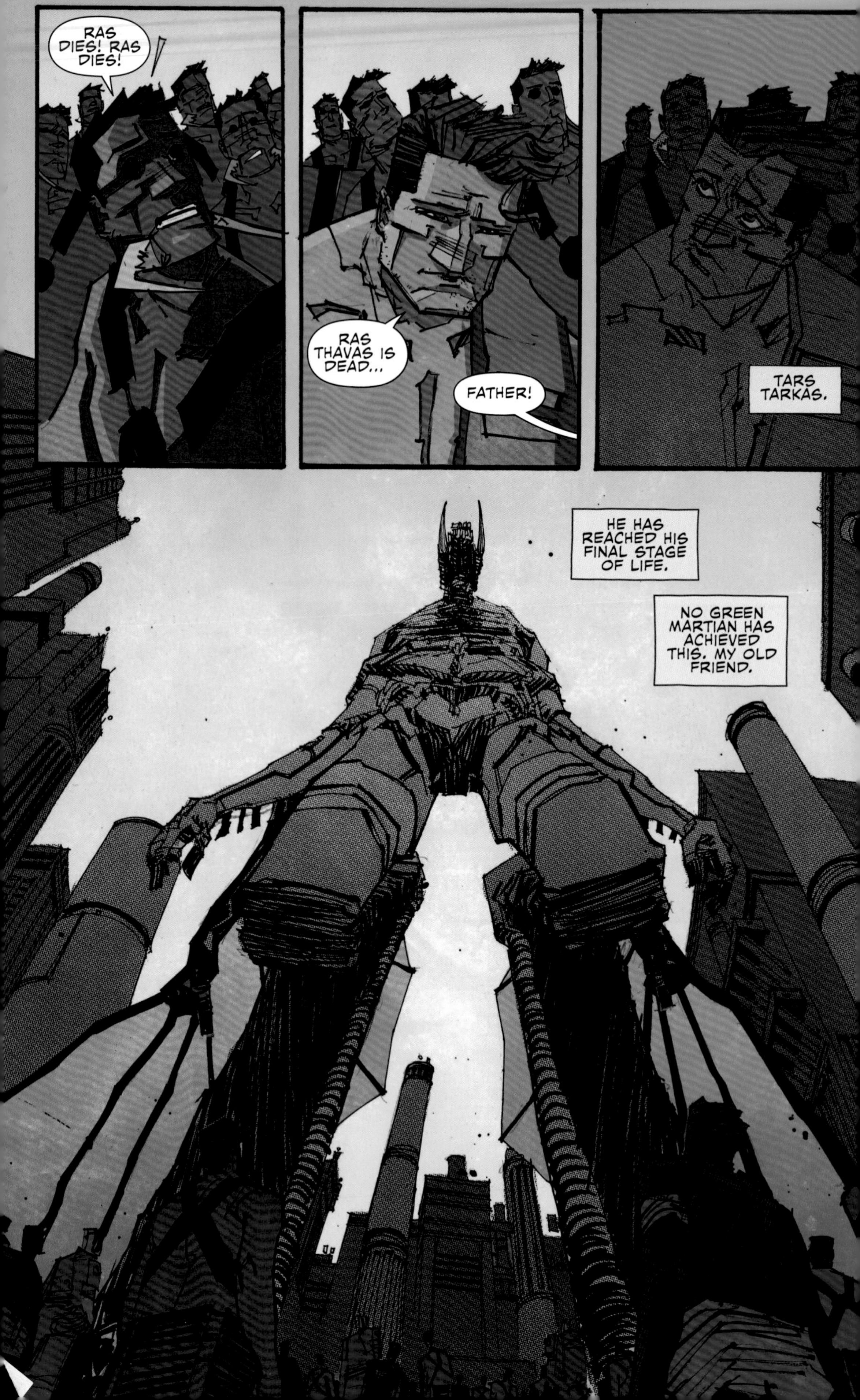
RAS DIES! RAS DIES!
RAS THAVAS IS DEAD...
FATHER!
TARS TARKAS.
HE HAS REACHED HIS FINAL STAGE OF LIFE.
NO GREEN MARTIAN HAS ACHIEVED THIS. MY OLD FRIEND.

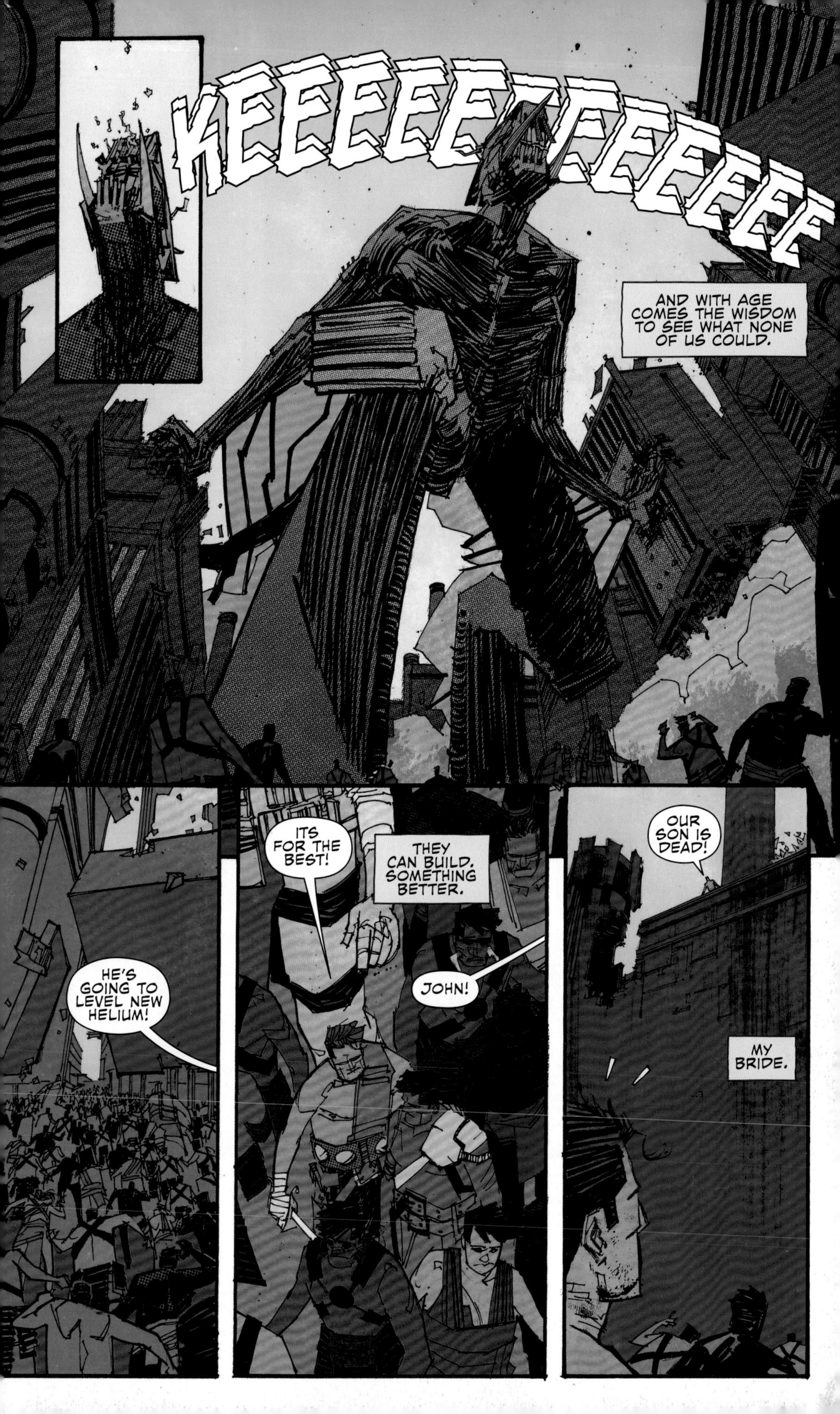
KEEEEEEEEEEEEEEEE
AND WITH AGE COMES THE WISDOM TO SEE WHAT NONE OF US COULD.
HE'S GOING TO LEVEL NEW HELIUM!
ITS FOR THE BEST!
THEY CAN BUILD. SOMETHING BETTER.
JOHN!
OUR SON IS DEAD!
MY BRIDE.

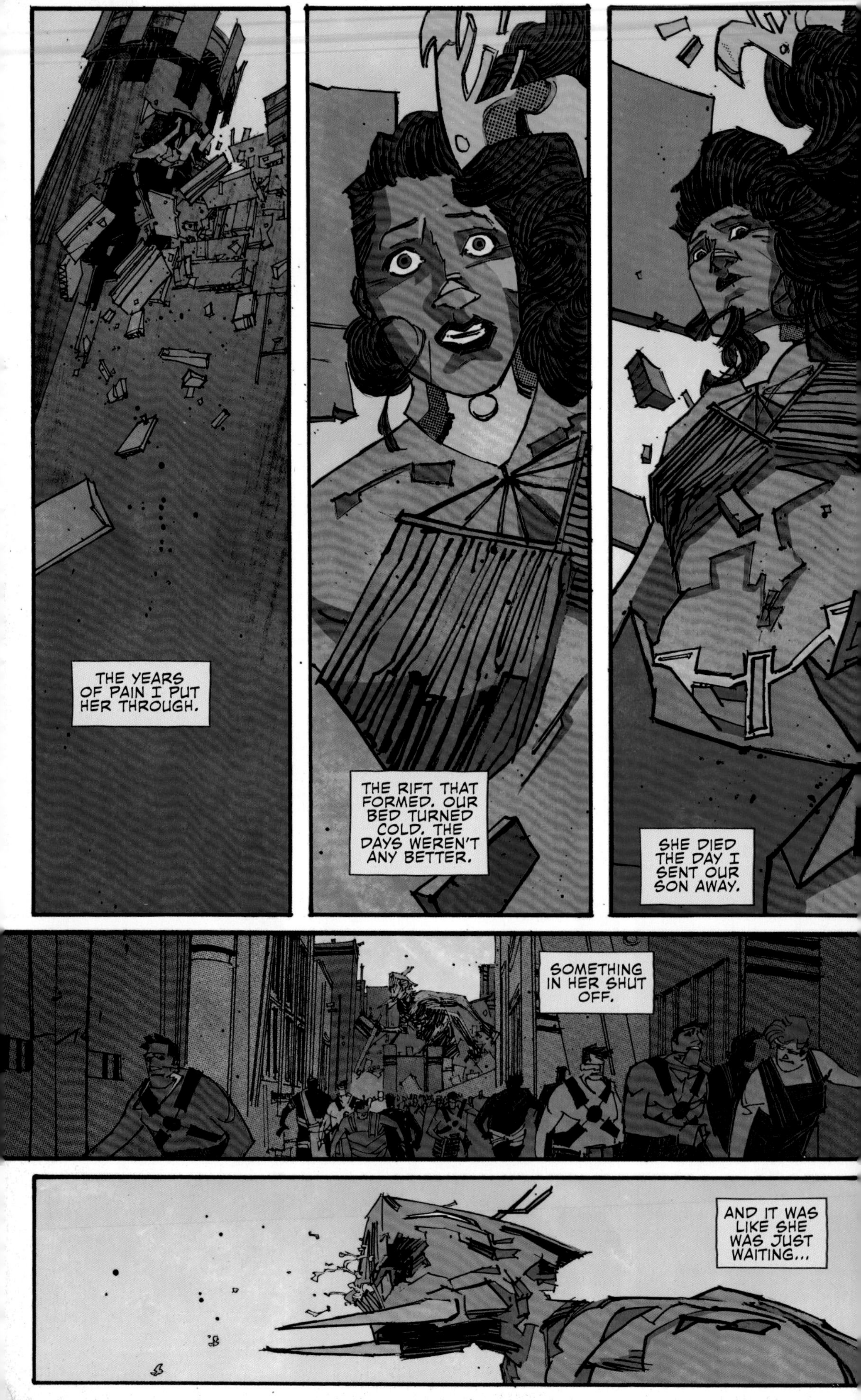
THE YEARS OF PAIN I PUT HER THROUGH.
THE RIFT THAT FORMED. OUR BED TURNED COLD. THE DAYS WEREN'T ANY BETTER.
SHE DIED THE DAY I SENT OUR SON AWAY.
SOMETHING IN HER SHUT OFF.
AND IT WAS LIKE SHE WAS JUST WAITING...

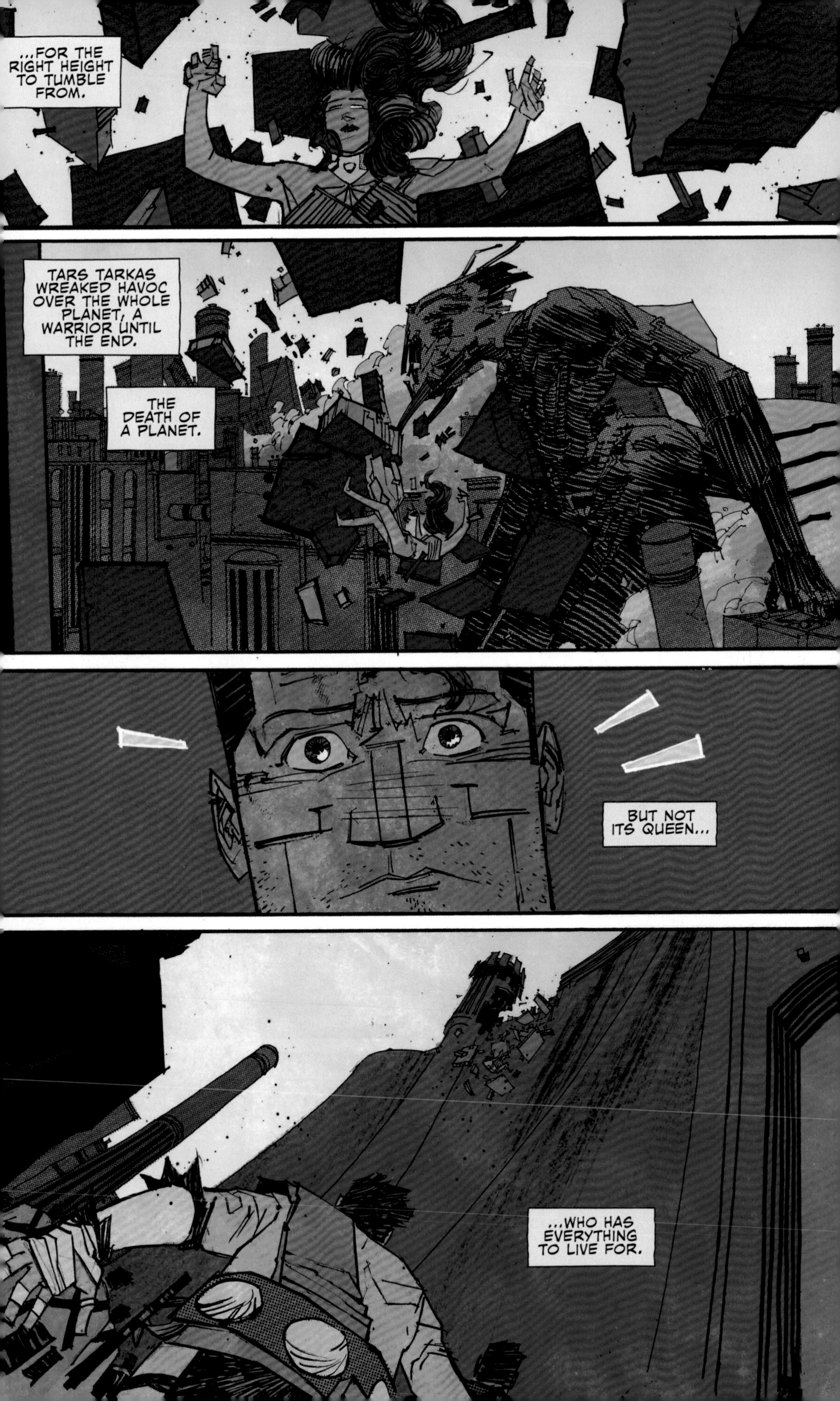
...FOR THE RIGHT HEIGHT TO TUMBLE FROM.
TARS TARKAS WREAKED HAVOC OVER THE WHOLE PLANET, A WARRIOR UNTIL THE END.
THE DEATH OF A PLANET.
BUT NOT ITS QUEEN...
...WHO HAS EVERYTHING TO LIVE FOR.

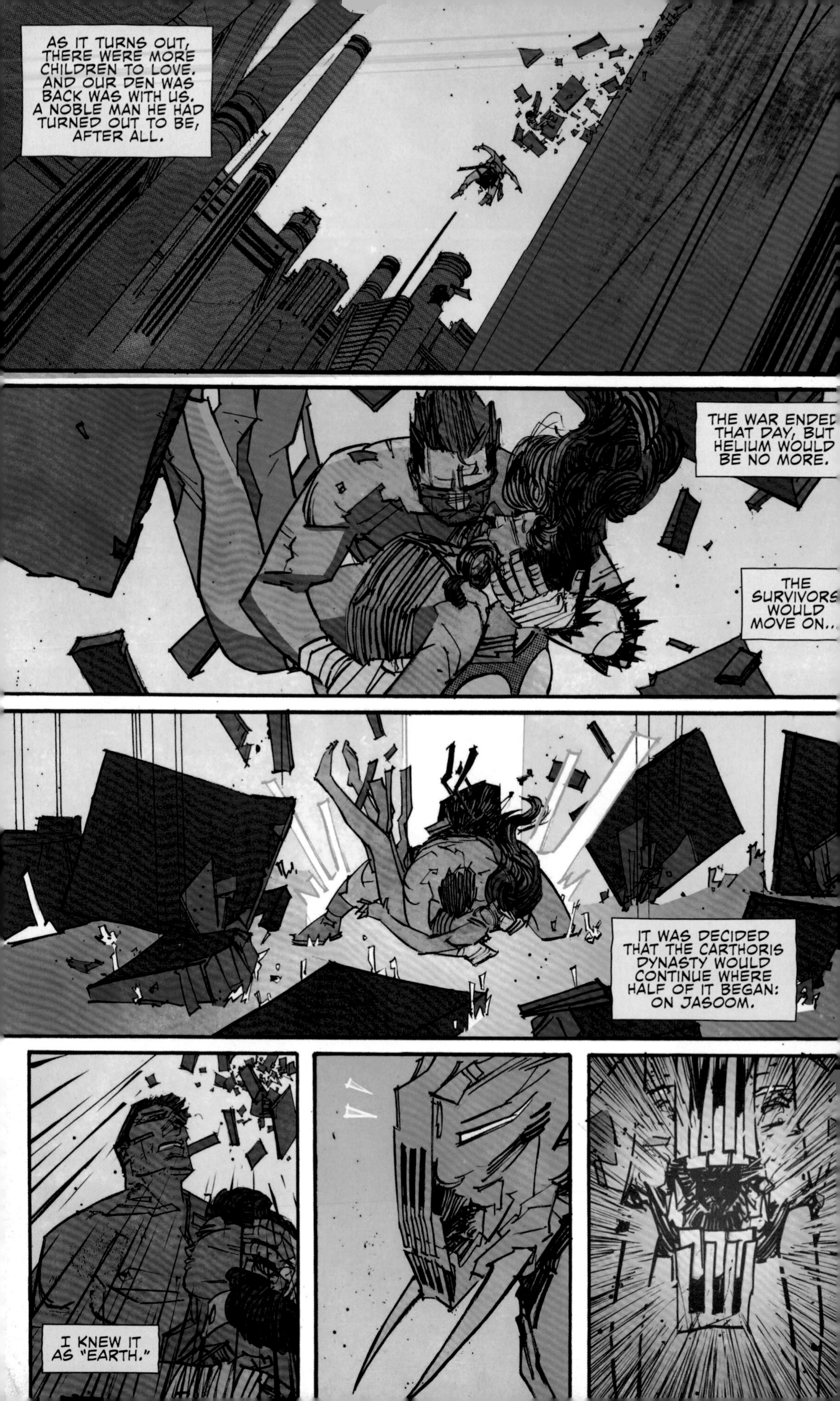
AS IT TURNS OUT, THERE WERE MORE CHILDREN TO LOVE. AND OUR DEN WAS BACK WAS WITH US. A NOBLE MAN HE HAD TURNED OUT TO BE, AFTER ALL.
THE WAR ENDED THAT DAY, BUT HELIUM WOULD BE NO MORE.
THE SURVIVORS WOULD MOVE ON...
IT WAS DECIDED THAT THE CARTHORIS DYNASTY WOULD CONTINUE WHERE HALF OF IT BEGAN: ON JASOOM.
I KNEW IT AS "EARTH."

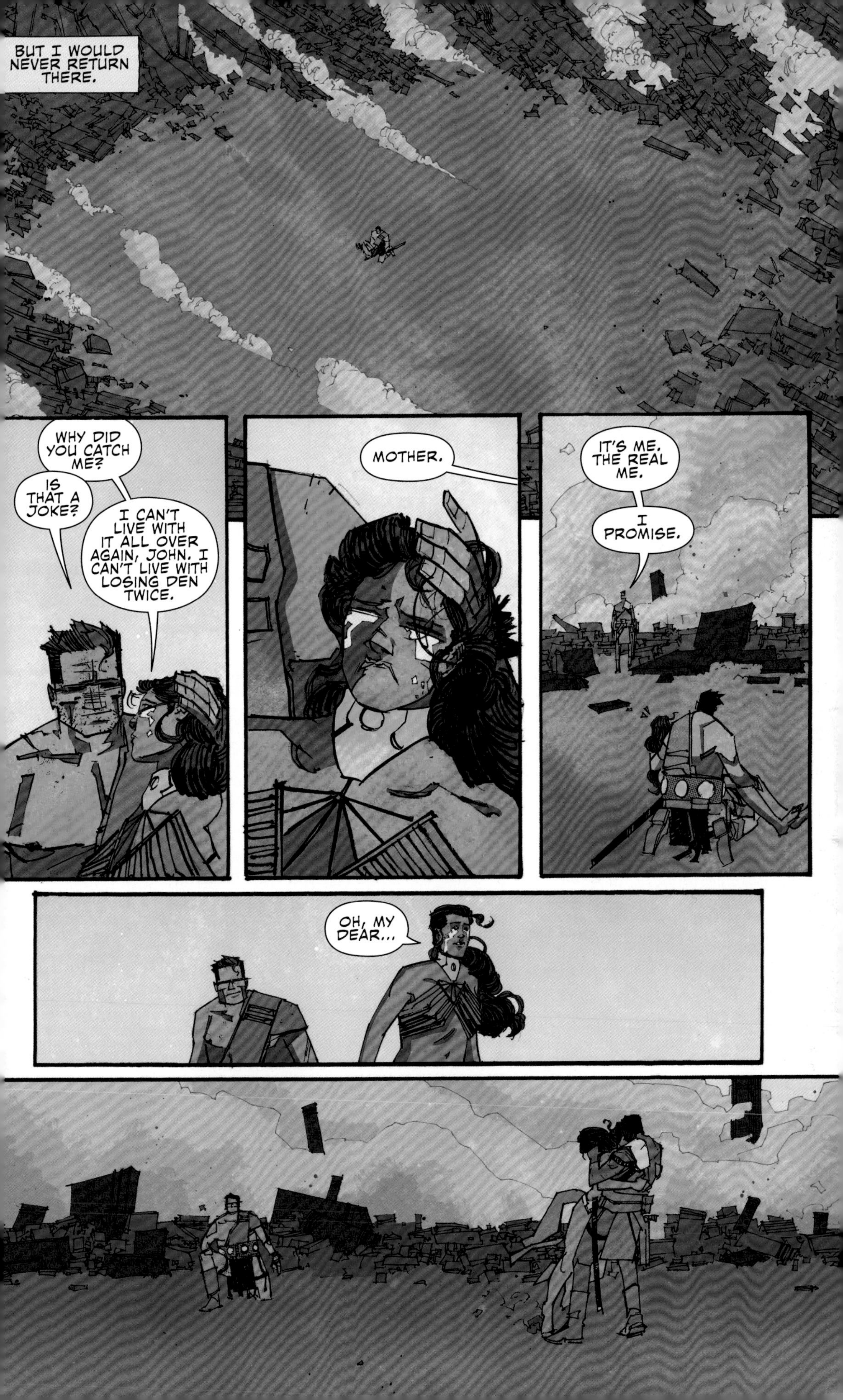

BUT I WOULD NEVER RETURN THERE.
WHY DID YOU CATCH ME?
IS THAT A JOKE?
I CAN'T LIVE WITH IT ALL OVER AGAIN, JOHN. I CAN'T LIVE WITH LOSING DEN TWICE.
MOTHER.
IT'S ME. THE REAL ME.
I PROMISE.
OH, MY DEAR...

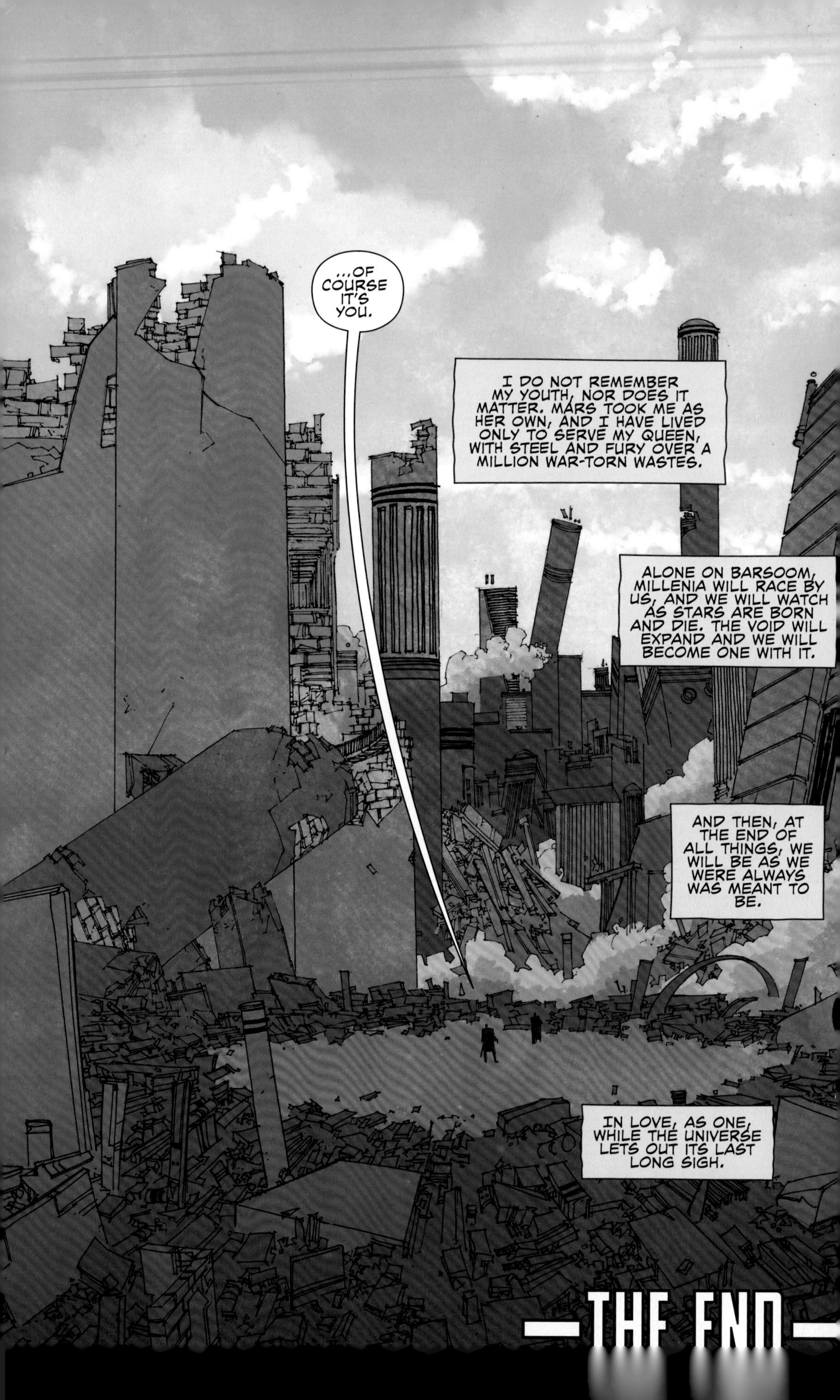

...OF COURSE IT'S YOU.
I DO NOT REMEMBER MY YOUTH, NOR DOES IT MATTER. MARS TOOK ME AS HER OWN, AND I HAVE LIVED ONLY TO SERVE MY QUEEN, WITH STEEL AND FURY OVER A MILLION WAR-TORN WASTES.
ALONE ON BARSOOM, MILLENIA WILL RACE BY US, AND WE WILL WATCH AS STARS ARE BORN AND DIE. THE VOID WILL EXPAND AND WE WILL BECOME ONE WITH IT.
AND THEN, AT THE END OF ALL THINGS, WE WILL BE AS WE WERE ALWAYS WAS MEANT TO BE.
IN LOVE, AS ONE, WHILE THE UNIVERSE LETS OUT ITS LAST LONG SIGH.
THE END

BONUS MATERIAL

ORIGINAL CHARACTER COMPOSITES
& ALTERNATE COVERS BY JUAN DOE,
GABRIEL HARDMAN, AND MORE!

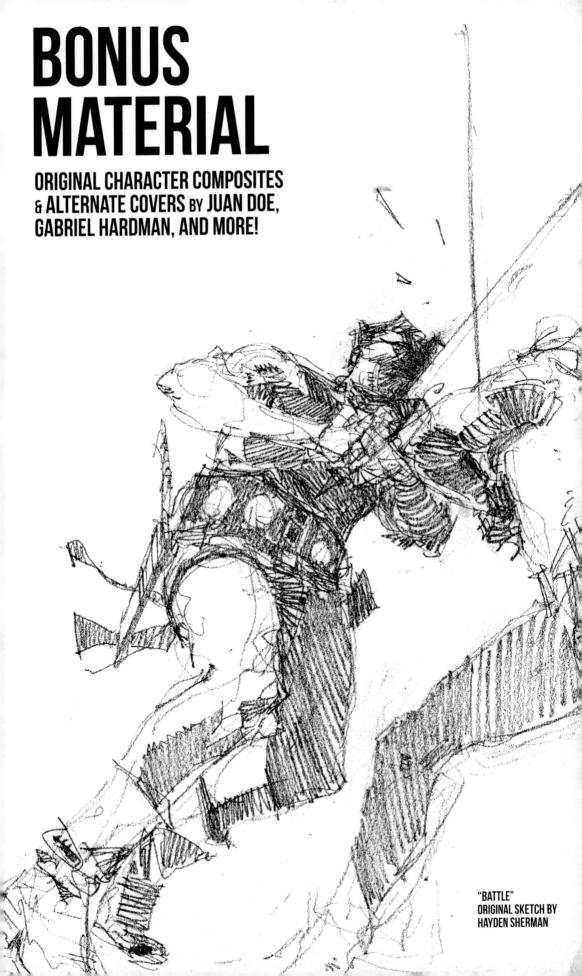

"BATTLE"
ORIGINAL SKETCH BY
HAYDEN SHERMAN

JOHN CARTER

CHARACTER DESCRIPTION FROM SERIES ARTIST HAYDEN SHERMAN

BEFORE (LEFT PAGE)

-LOOK INSPIRED BY AN EARLY "PRINCESS OF MARS" BOOK COVER, BRINGING IN ELEMENTS OF HIS CURRENT LOOK, AND THEN GIVING HIM A STRONG "FRANK FRAZETTA" BODY TYPE.

-CLOTHING IS STILL MINIMAL AS WOULD BE SEEN ON BARSOOM, THE BUCKLES, BELTS, AND STRAPS ALLOW HIM TO CARRY HIS EQUIPMENT WHEREVER HIS ADVENTURE MAY TAKE HIM

NOW (RIGHT PAGE)

-HAVING LEFT FOR THE DESOLATE AND BARREN PLANET WHERE JOHN AND DEJAH NOW LIVE, JOHN IS IN NO NEED OF HIS EQUIPMENT, NOW HE ONLY WEARS A PORTION OF HIS OUTFIT, LEAVING A SERIES OF EMPTY STRAPS HANGING AROUND HIS WAIST.

-TO PROTECT HIMSELF FROM SOME OF TEH HARSH CONDITIONS ON THIS PLANET, JOHN HAS TAKEN TO WEARING A CAPE.

-THE BOOTS ARE GONE AS HE LETS HIMSELF FEEL THE DIRT WHILE HE'S WORKING, WHEN HE TAKES A WRONG STEP HE FEELS IT, AND HIS FEET HAVE BECOME TOUGH FROM IT.

-HOWEVER HE FAVORS HIS HANDS, AND WRAPS THEM TO KEEP THEM IN SHAPE.

-DURING HIS EXILE, JOHN HAS TAKEN TO GROWING OUT HIS BEARD IN A FASHION SIMILAR TO SOMETHING HE'D LIKELY REMEMBER FROM HIS DAYS AS A SOLDIER IN THE CIVIL WAR. IT'S A SMALL COMFORT, AND HELPS HIM HIDE HIS FACE.

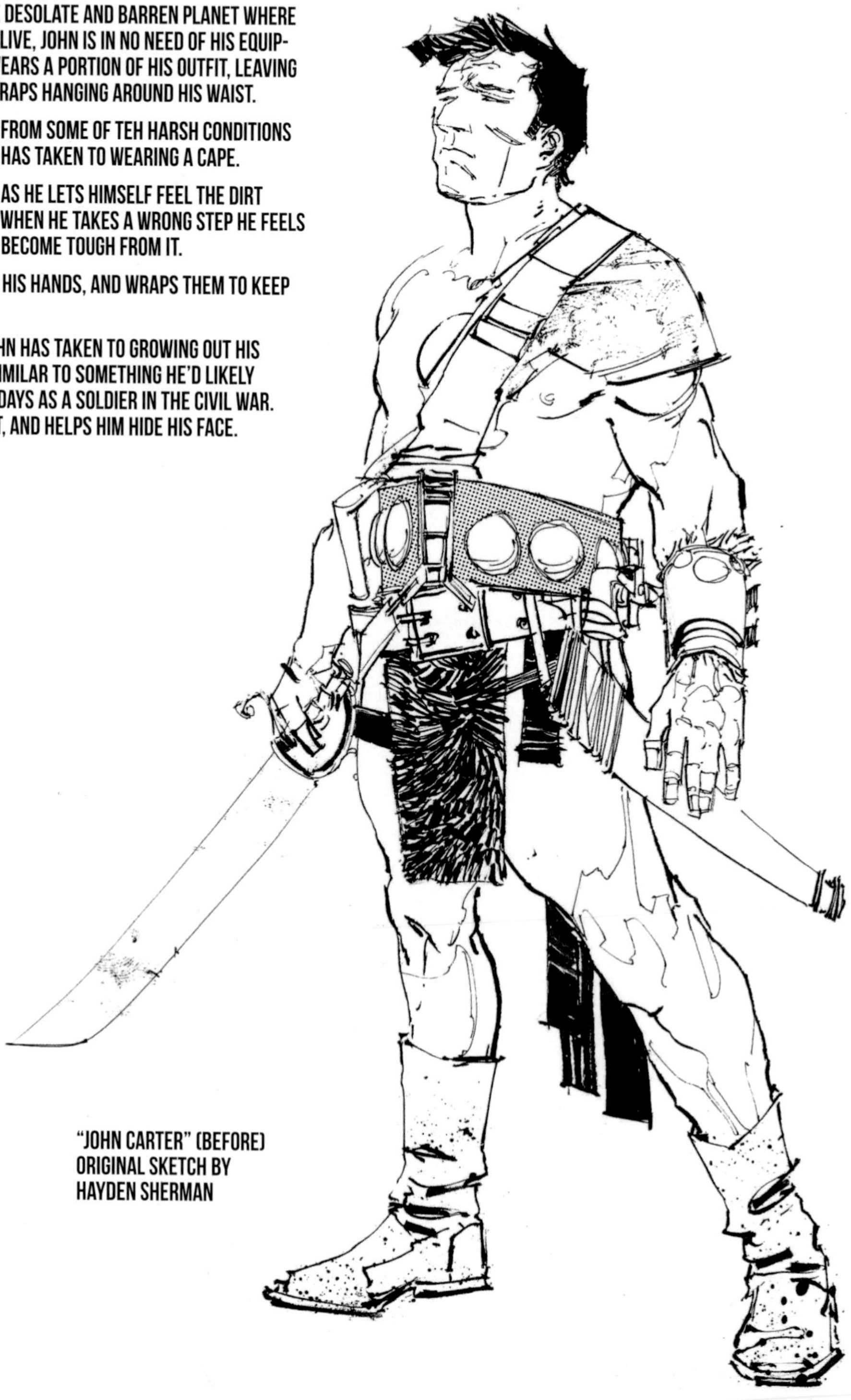

"JOHN CARTER" (BEFORE)
ORIGINAL SKETCH BY
HAYDEN SHERMAN

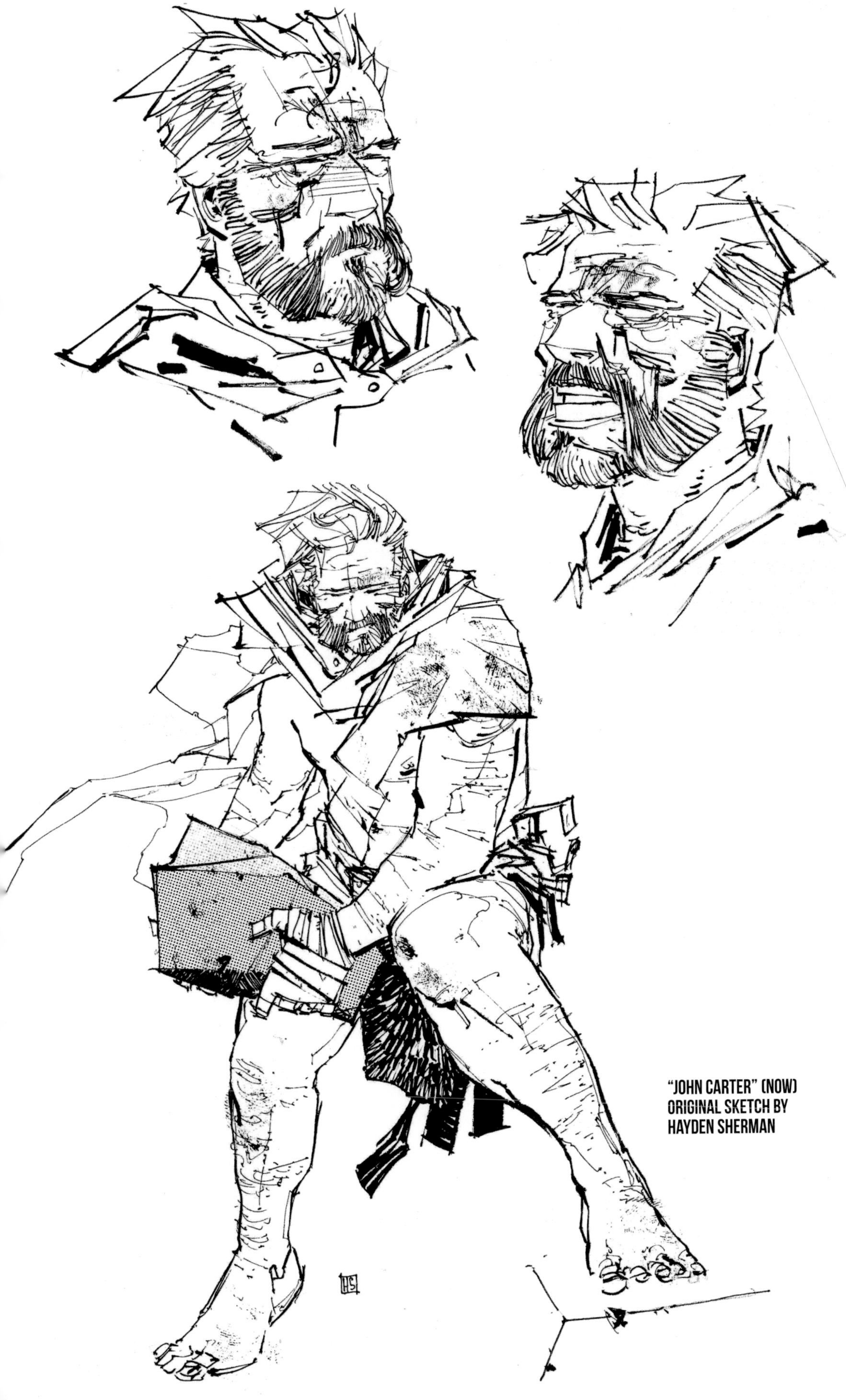

"JOHN CARTER" (NOW)
ORIGINAL SKETCH BY
HAYDEN SHERMAN

DEJAH THORIS

CHARACTER DESCRIPTION FROM SERIES ARTIST HAYDEN SHERMAN

BEFORE (LEFT PAGE)

-AN EXCEPRT FROM THE ORIGINAL BOOK DESCRIBES DEJAH AS BEING ADORNED IN NOTHING BUT JEWELS, SO I ADORNED HER IN MANY MORE JEWELS. THE RED MARTIANS ARE NOT LIKE THE GREEN MARTIANS WHEN IT COMES TO DECORATION, A PRINCESS OF THE RED MARTIANS WOULD LIKELY EXPRESS HER POSITION VISUALLY THROUGH ELABORATE ORNAMENTATION.

-OTHER PIECES OF CLOTH TAKEN FROM PAST BOOK COVER INTERPRETATIONS AND SOME OF HER CURRENT REPRESENTATIONS

NOW (RIGHT PAGE)

-MOURNING THE LOSS OF HER SON, DEJAH REFUSES TO WEAR THE MAJORITY OF HER JEWELRY OR FINE ROYAL CLOTHING. INSTEAD SHE NOW WEARS A SIMPLE BLACK GARMENT WITH A VEIL RUNNING THROUGH IT THAT COMES UP TO COVER HER FACE.

-DUE TO THECONDITION OF THE PLANET SHE WILL QUITE OFTEN BE WEARING A LONG HEAVY BLACK CAPE TO PROTECT HER FROM THE ELEMENTS.

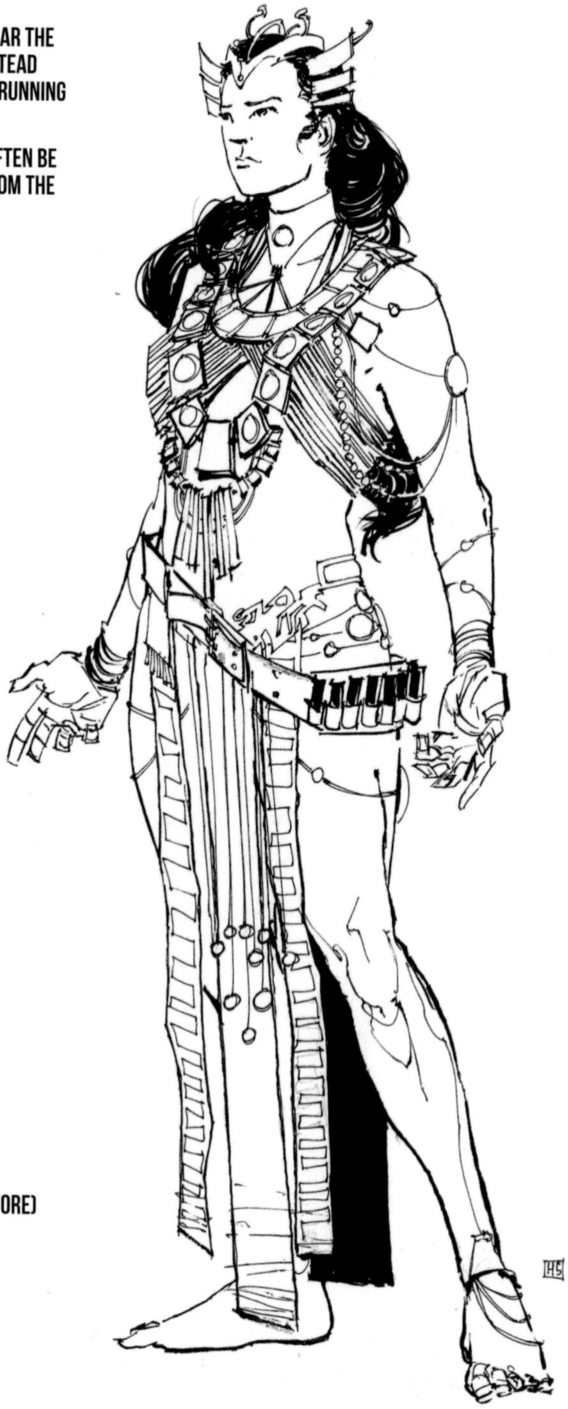

HS

"DEJAH THORIS" (BEFORE)
ORIGINAL SKETCH BY
HAYDEN SHERMAN

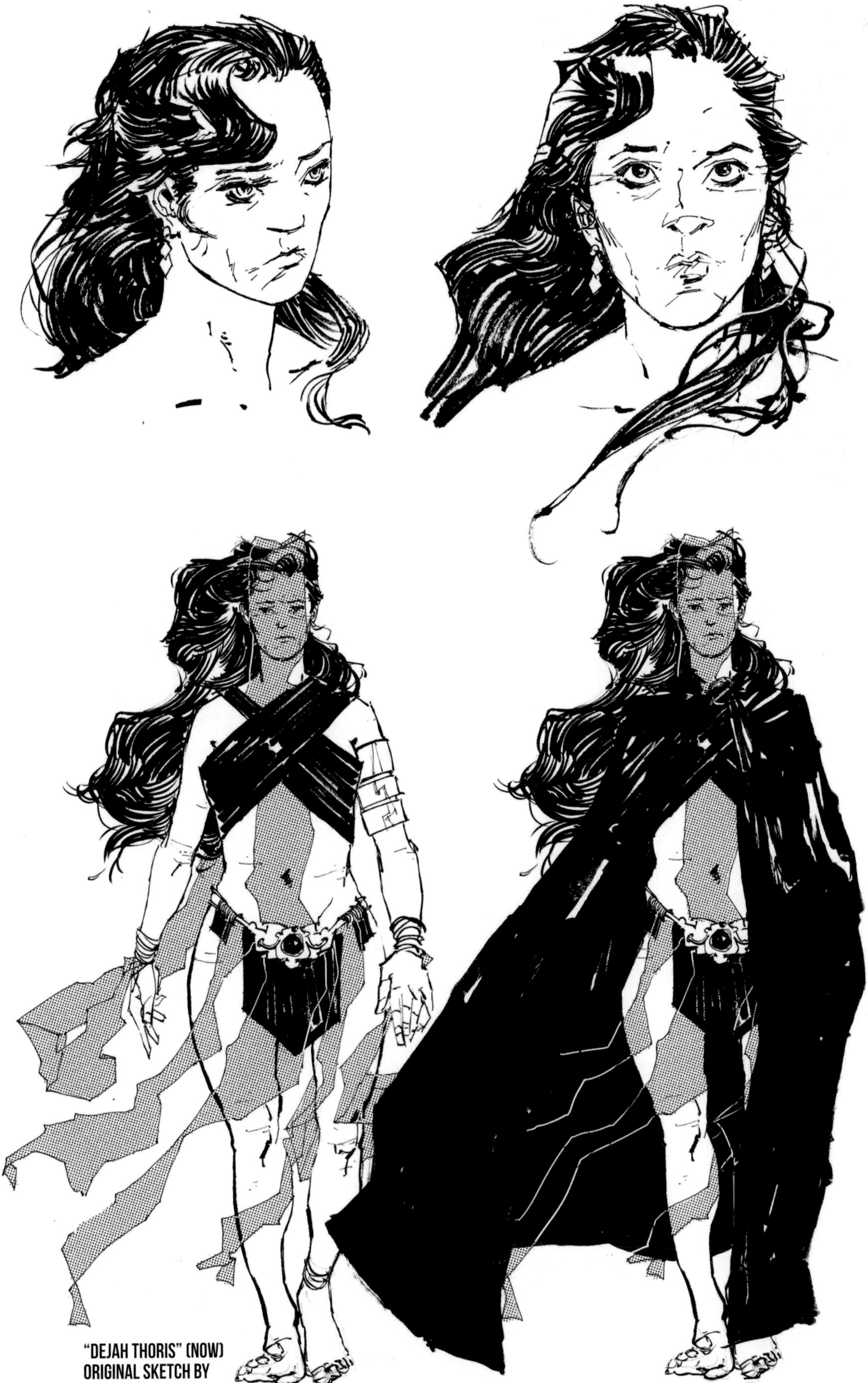

"DEJAH THORIS" (NOW)
ORIGINAL SKETCH BY
HAYDEN SHERMAN

CARTHORIS

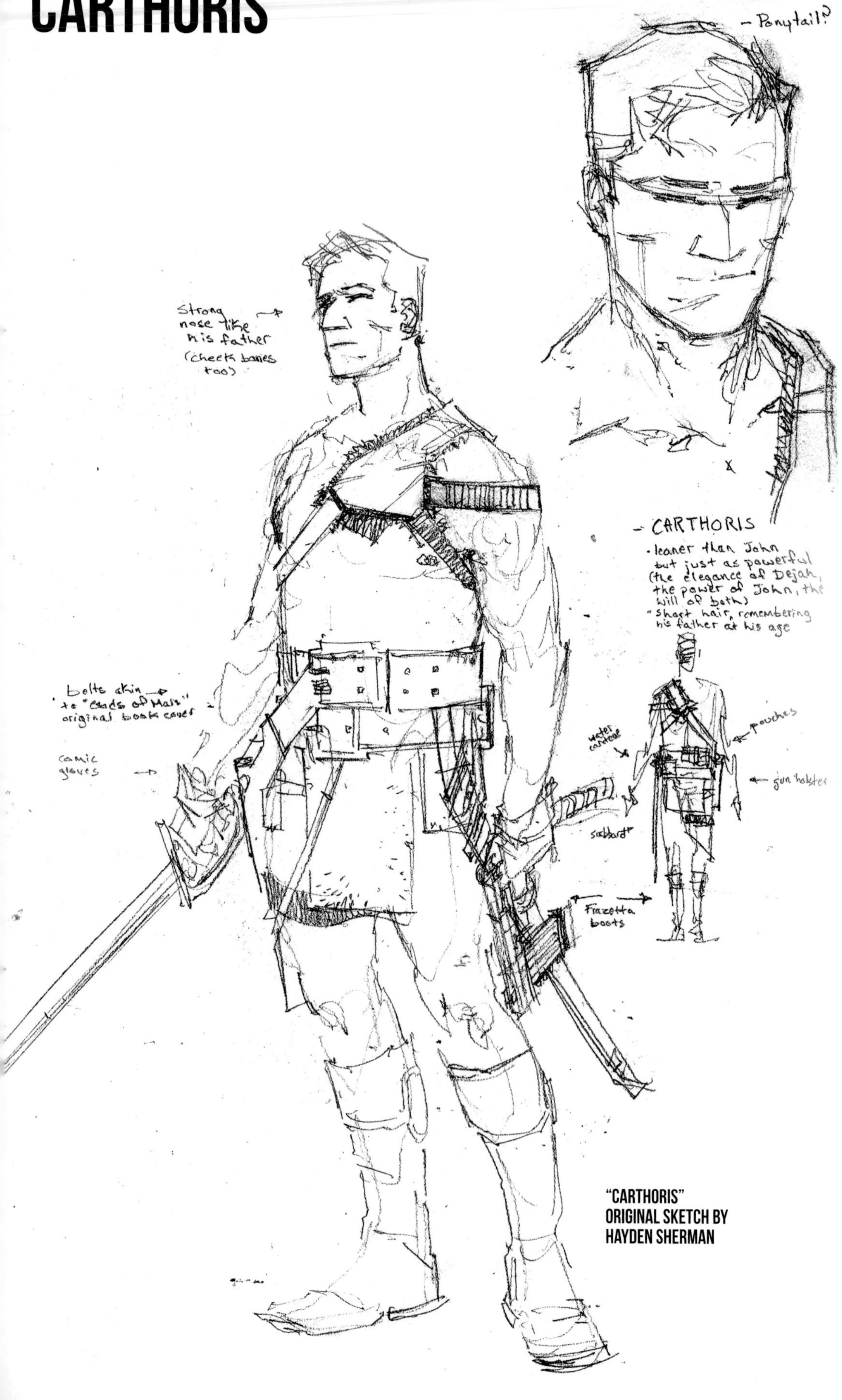

- Ponytail?
Strong nose like his father (cheeks bones too)
- CARTHORIS
• leaner than John but just as powerful (the elegance of Dejah, the power of John, the will of both)
• Short hair, remembering his father at his age
belts akin to "Gods of Mars" original book cover
comic gloves
water canteen
pouches
gun holster
scabbard
Frazetta boots

"CARTHORIS"
ORIGINAL SKETCH BY
HAYDEN SHERMAN

BLACK MARTIAN

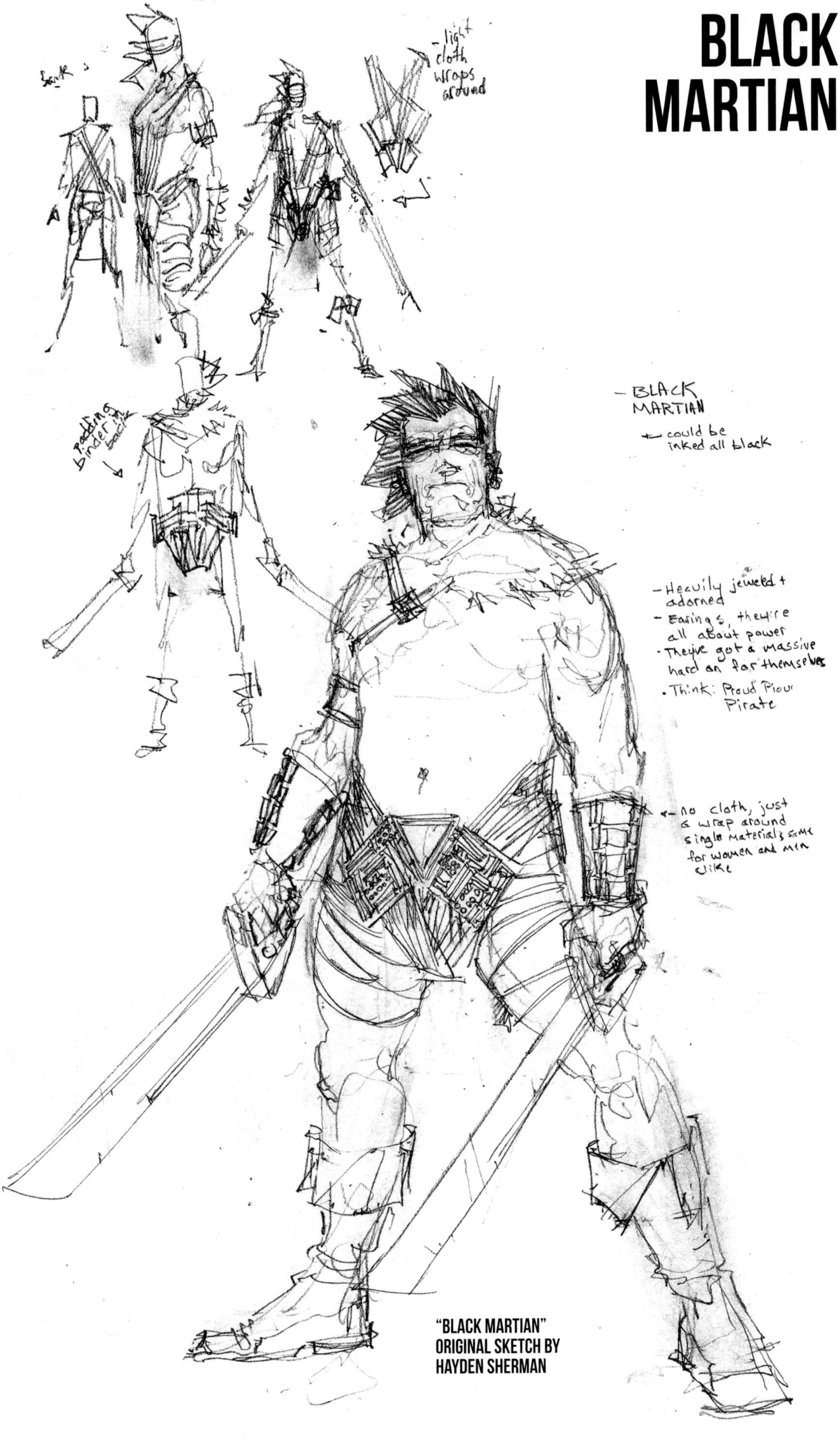

- light cloth wraps around
padding binder in back
- BLACK MARTIAN
could be inked all black
- Heavily jeweled + adorned
- Earings, they're all about power
- They've got a massive hard on for themselves
- Think: Proud Pious Pirate
no cloth, just a wrap around single materials same for women and men alike

"BLACK MARTIAN"
ORIGINAL SKETCH BY
HAYDEN SHERMAN

RAS THAVAS

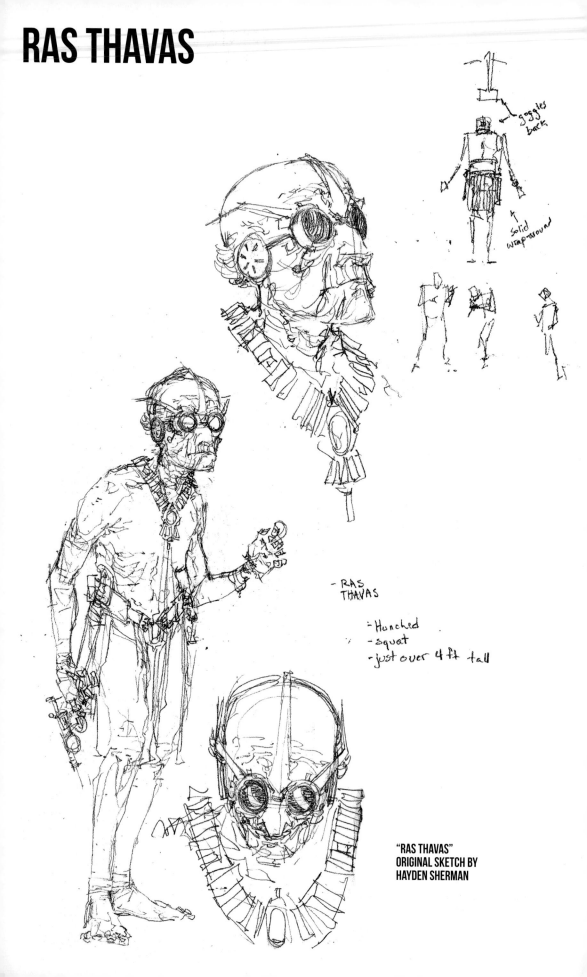

goggles
back

solid
wraparound

- RAS
THAVAS

- Hunched
- squat
- just over 4 ft tall

"RAS THAVAS"
ORIGINAL SKETCH BY
HAYDEN SHERMAN

ULYSSES PAXTON

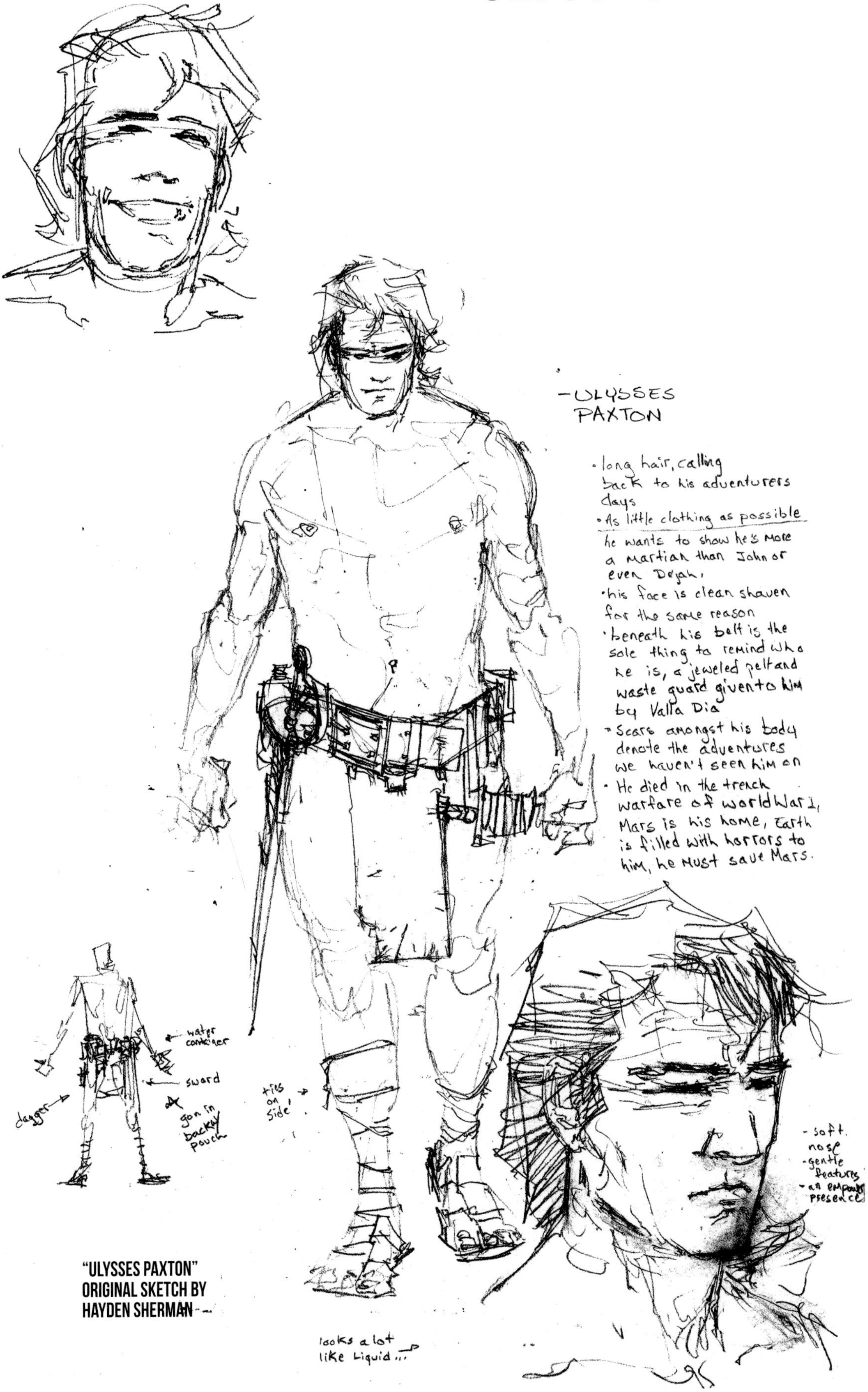

—ULYSSES
PAXTON

- long hair, calling
  back to his adventurers
  days
- As little clothing as possible
  he wants to show he's more
  a martian than John or
  even Dejah,
- his face is clean shaven
  for the same reason
- beneath his belt is the
  sole thing to remind who
  he is, a jeweled pelt and
  waste guard given to him
  by Valla Dia
- Scars amongst his body
  denote the adventures
  we haven't seen him on
- He died in the trench
  warfare of world war I,
  Mars is his home, Earth
  is filled with horrors to
  him, he must save Mars.

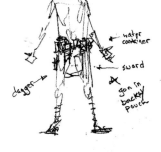

water
container

sword

gun in
backy
pouch

dagger →

ties
on
side

- soft.
  nose
- gentle
  features
- an empowre
  presence

"ULYSSES PAXTON"
ORIGINAL SKETCH BY
HAYDEN SHERMAN ⸳⸳

looks a lot
like Liquid...

TARS TARKAS

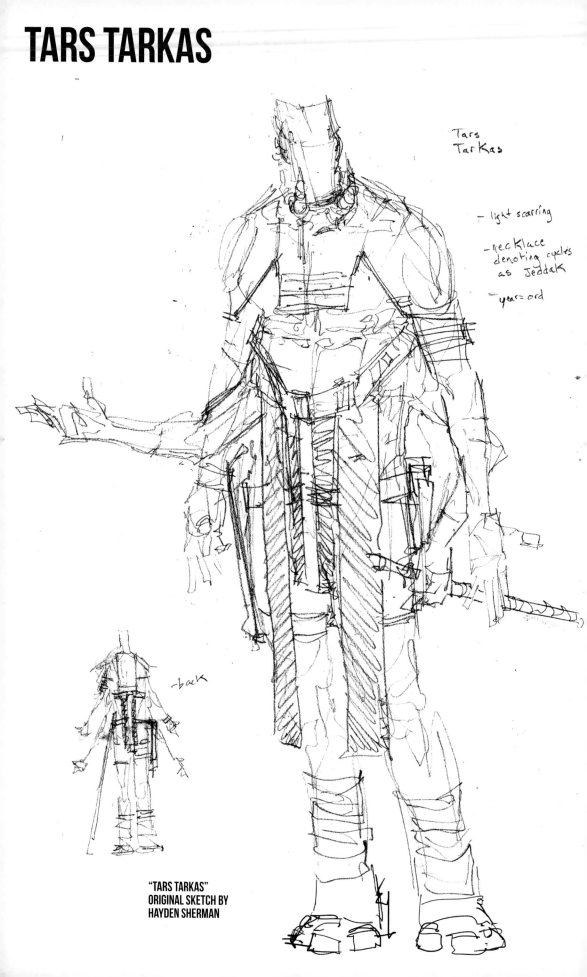

Tars
Tarkas

- light scarring

- necklace
denoting cycles
as Jeddak

- year = ord

-back

"TARS TARKAS"
ORIGINAL SKETCH BY
HAYDEN SHERMAN

MARTIAN WEAPONRY

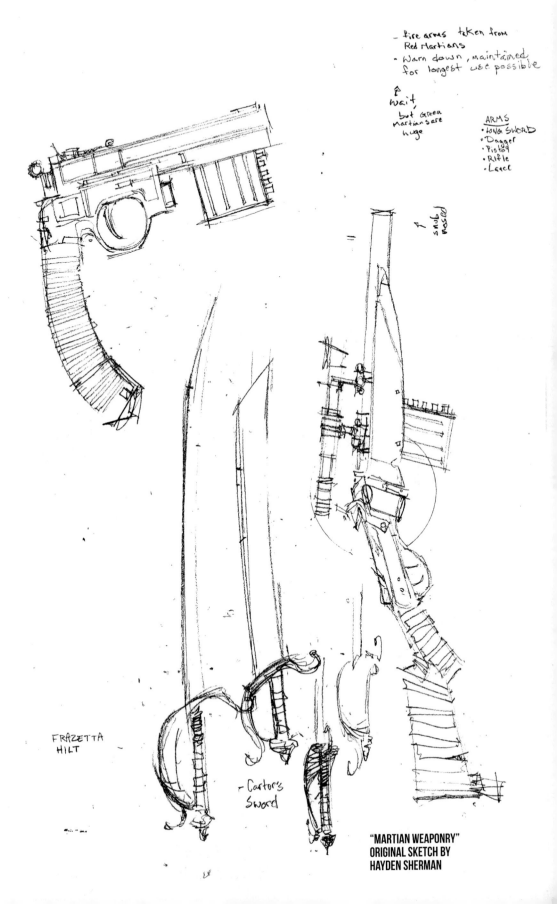

- fire arms taken from
  Red Martians
- Worn down, maintained
  for longest use possible

wait,
but Green
martians are
huge

ARMS
- LONG SWORD
- Dagger
- Pistol
- Rifle
- Lance

snub nosed

FRAZETTA
HILT

- Cartor's
  Sword

"MARTIAN WEAPONRY"
ORIGINAL SKETCH BY
HAYDEN SHERMAN

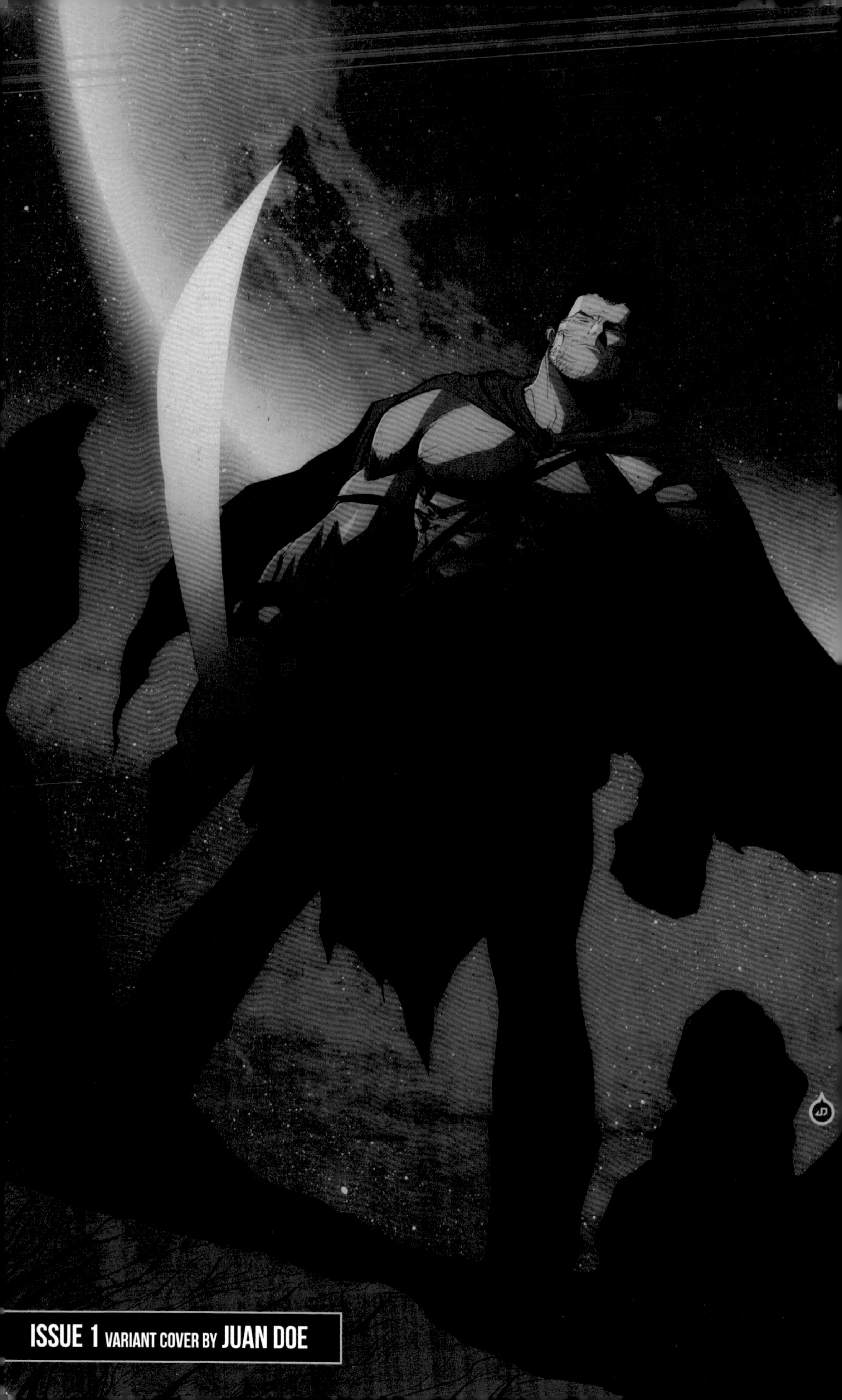

ISSUE 1 VARIANT COVER BY JUAN DOE

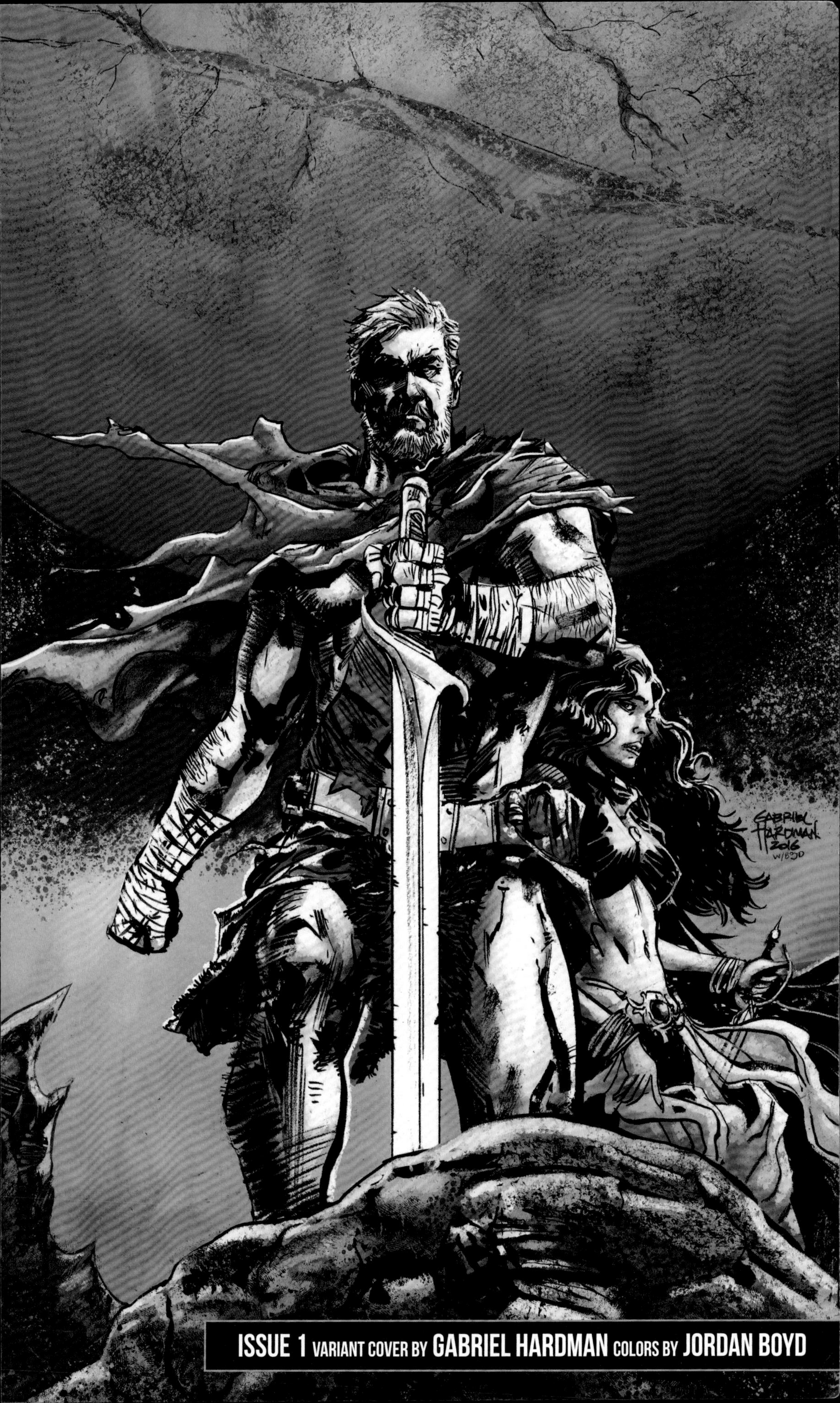
GABRIEL HARDMAN 2016

ISSUE 1 VARIANT COVER BY **GABRIEL HARDMAN** COLORS BY **JORDAN BOYD**

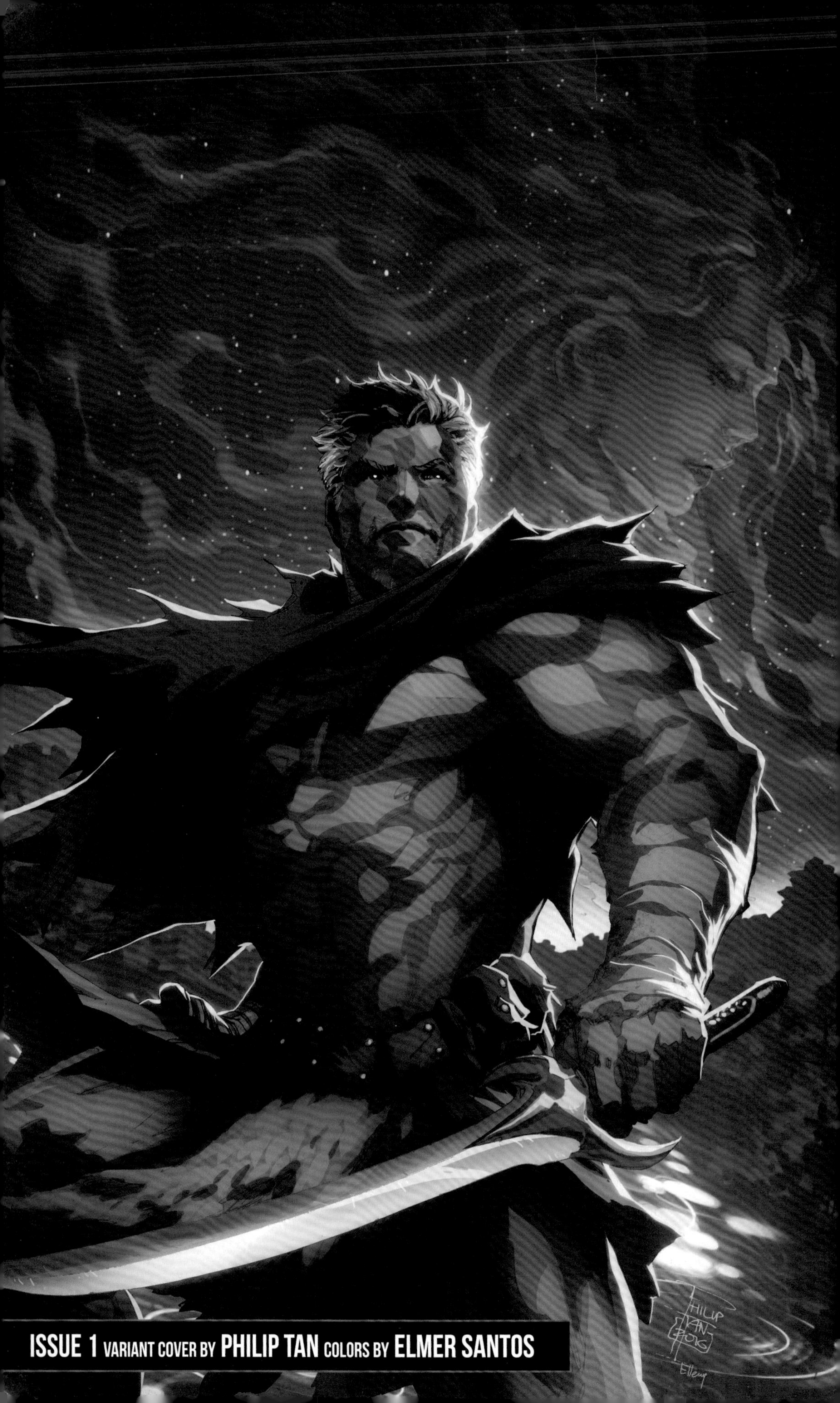

ISSUE 1 VARIANT COVER BY PHILIP TAN COLORS BY ELMER SANTOS

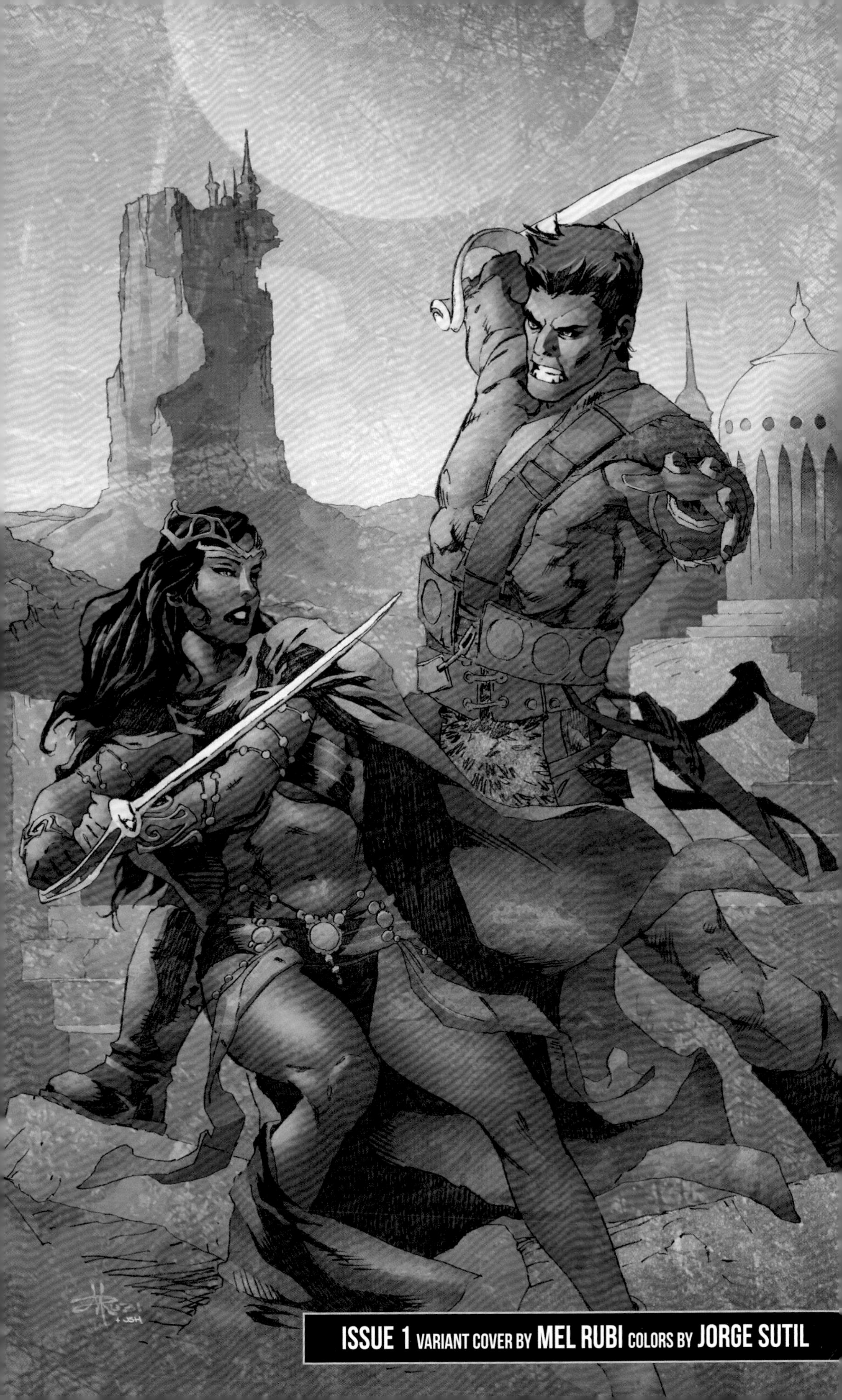

ISSUE 1 VARIANT COVER BY MEL RUBI COLORS BY JORGE SUTIL

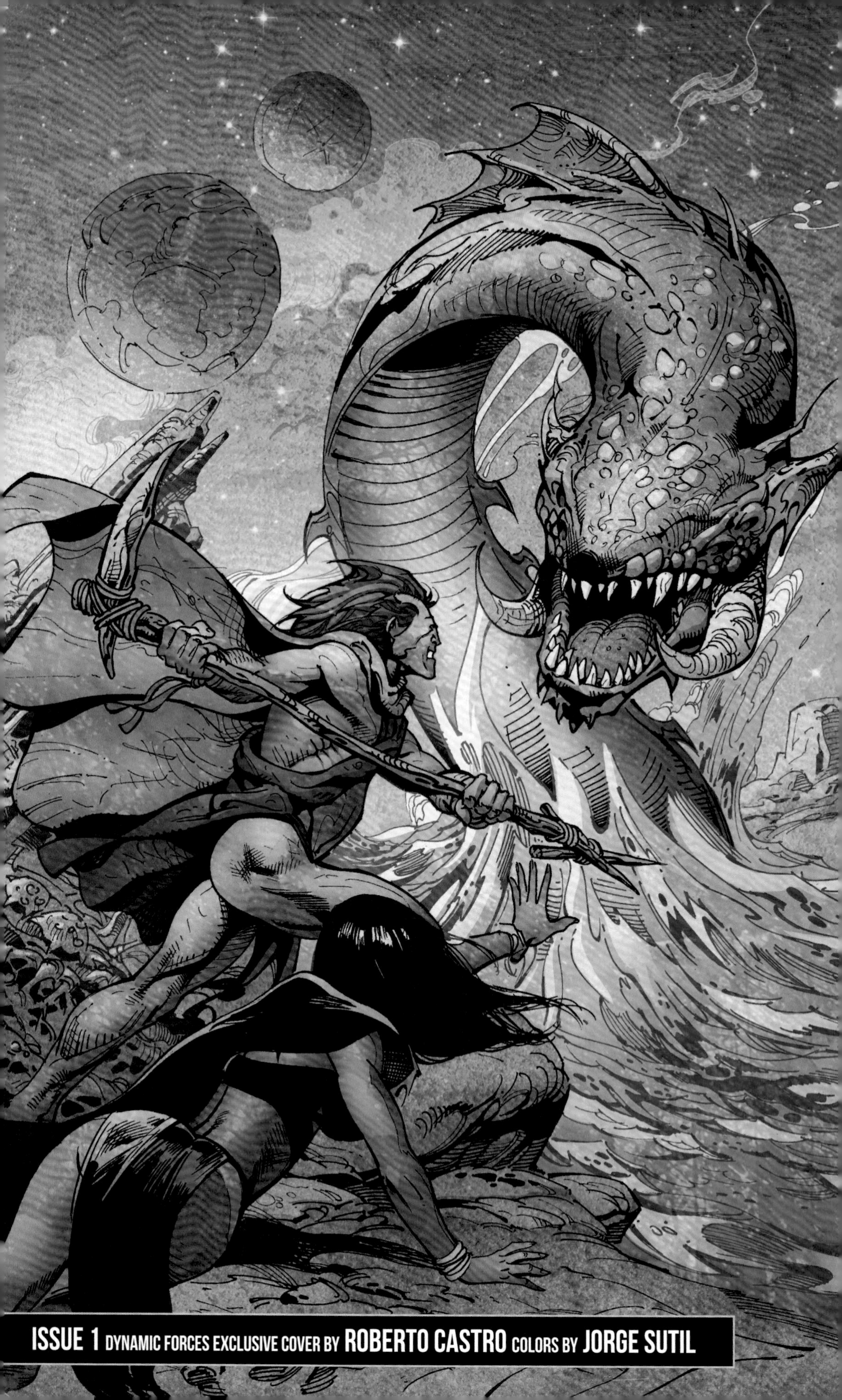

ISSUE 1 DYNAMIC FORCES EXCLUSIVE COVER BY ROBERTO CASTRO COLORS BY JORGE SUTIL

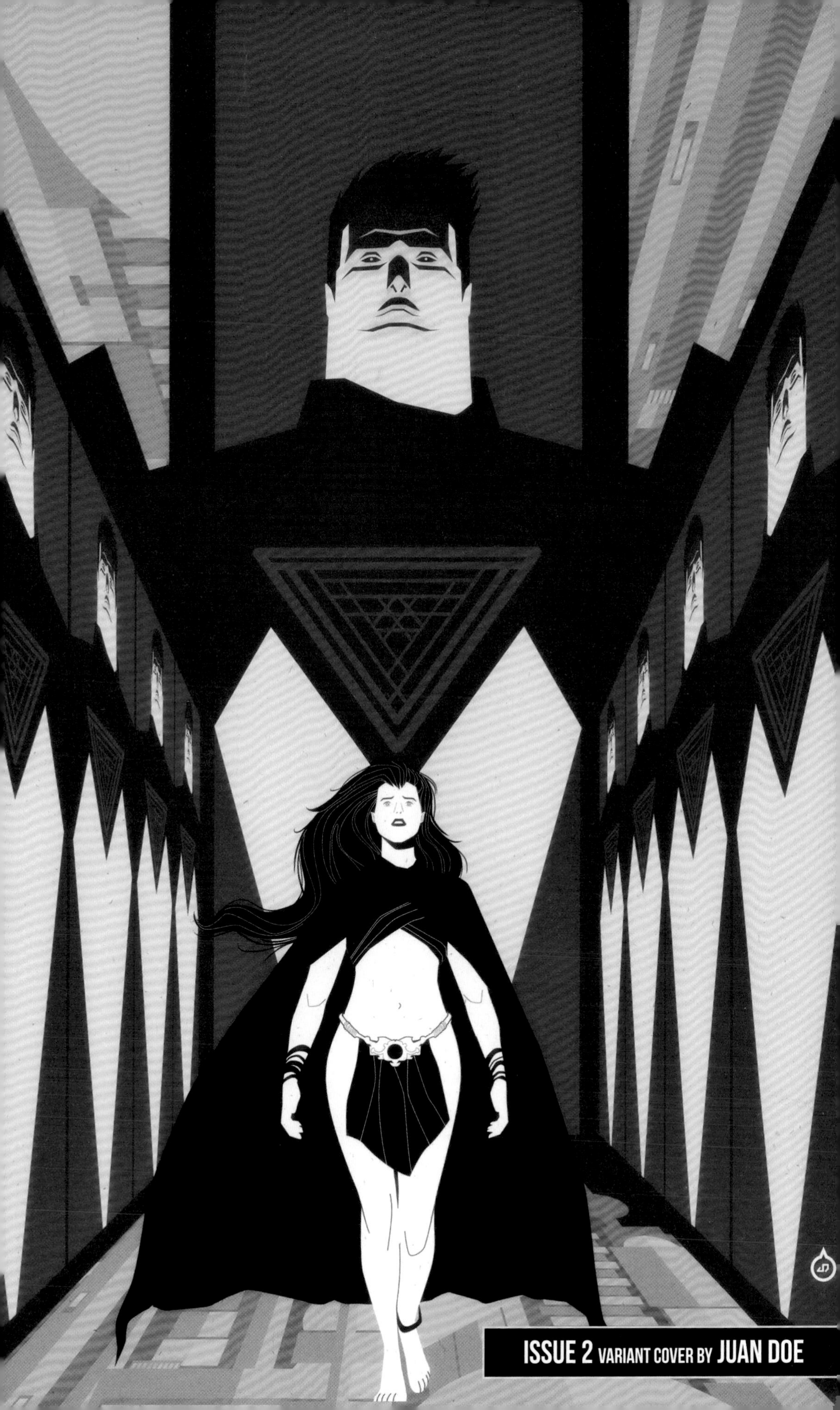

ISSUE 2 VARIANT COVER BY JUAN DOE

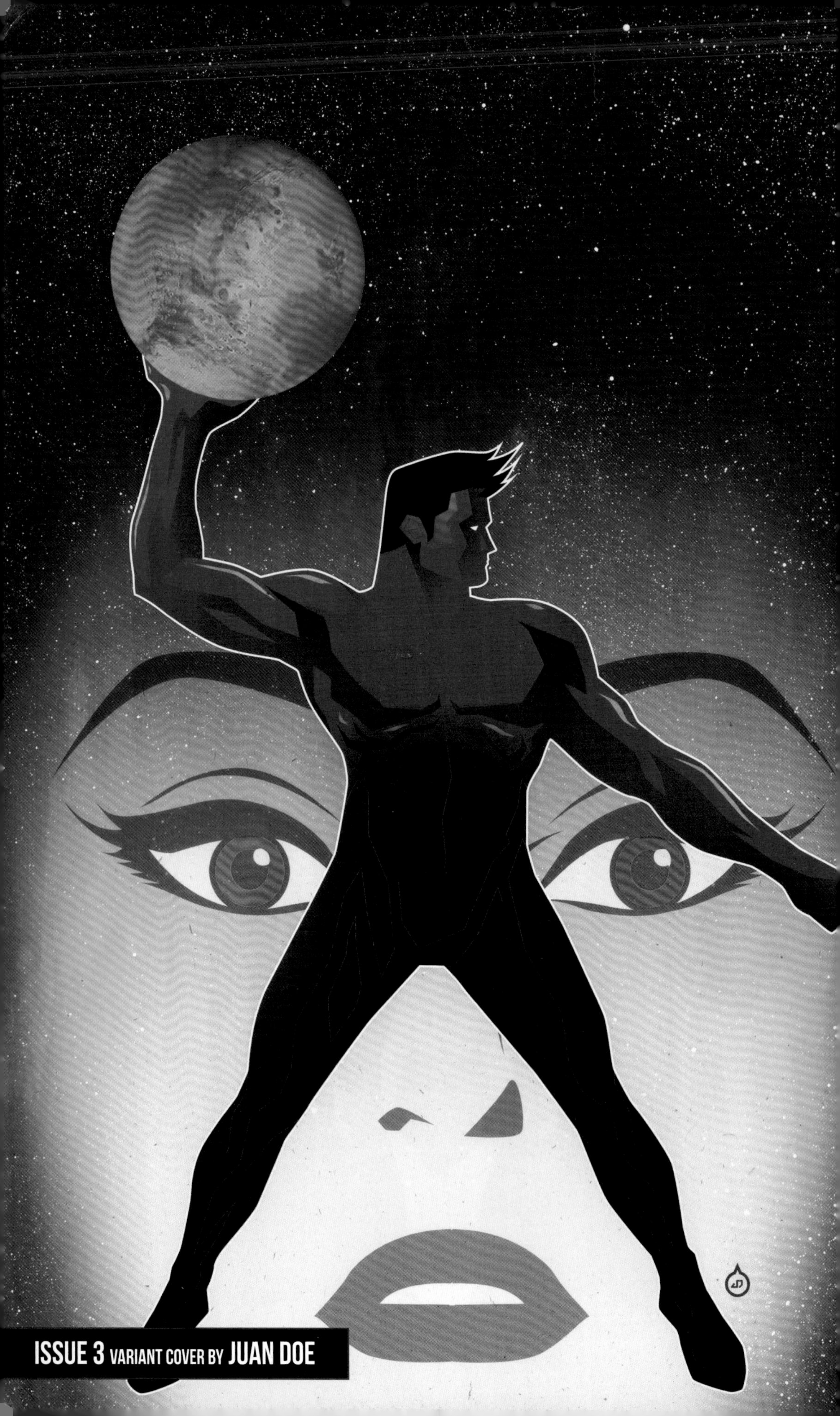

ISSUE 3 VARIANT COVER BY JUAN DOE

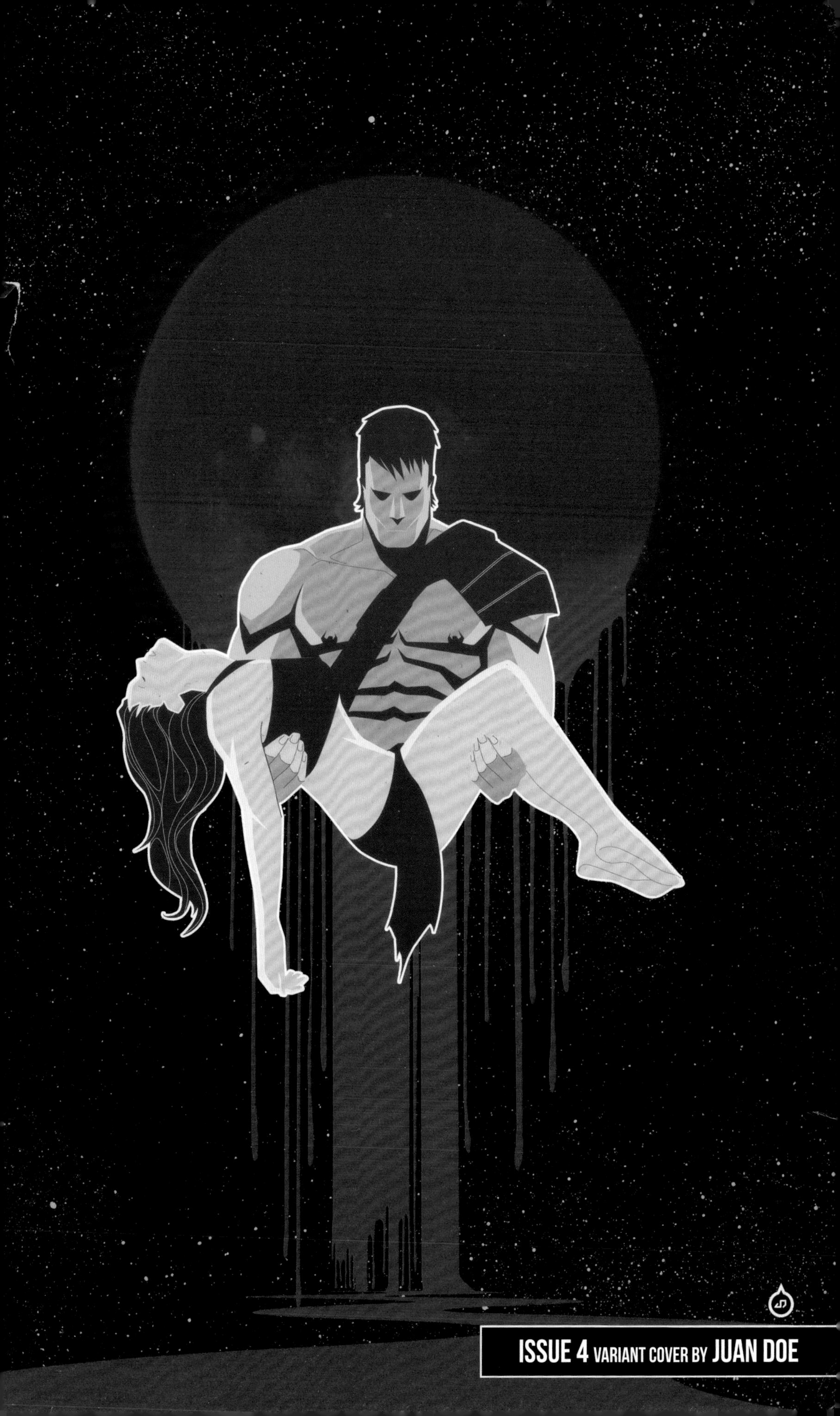

ISSUE 4 VARIANT COVER BY JUAN DOE

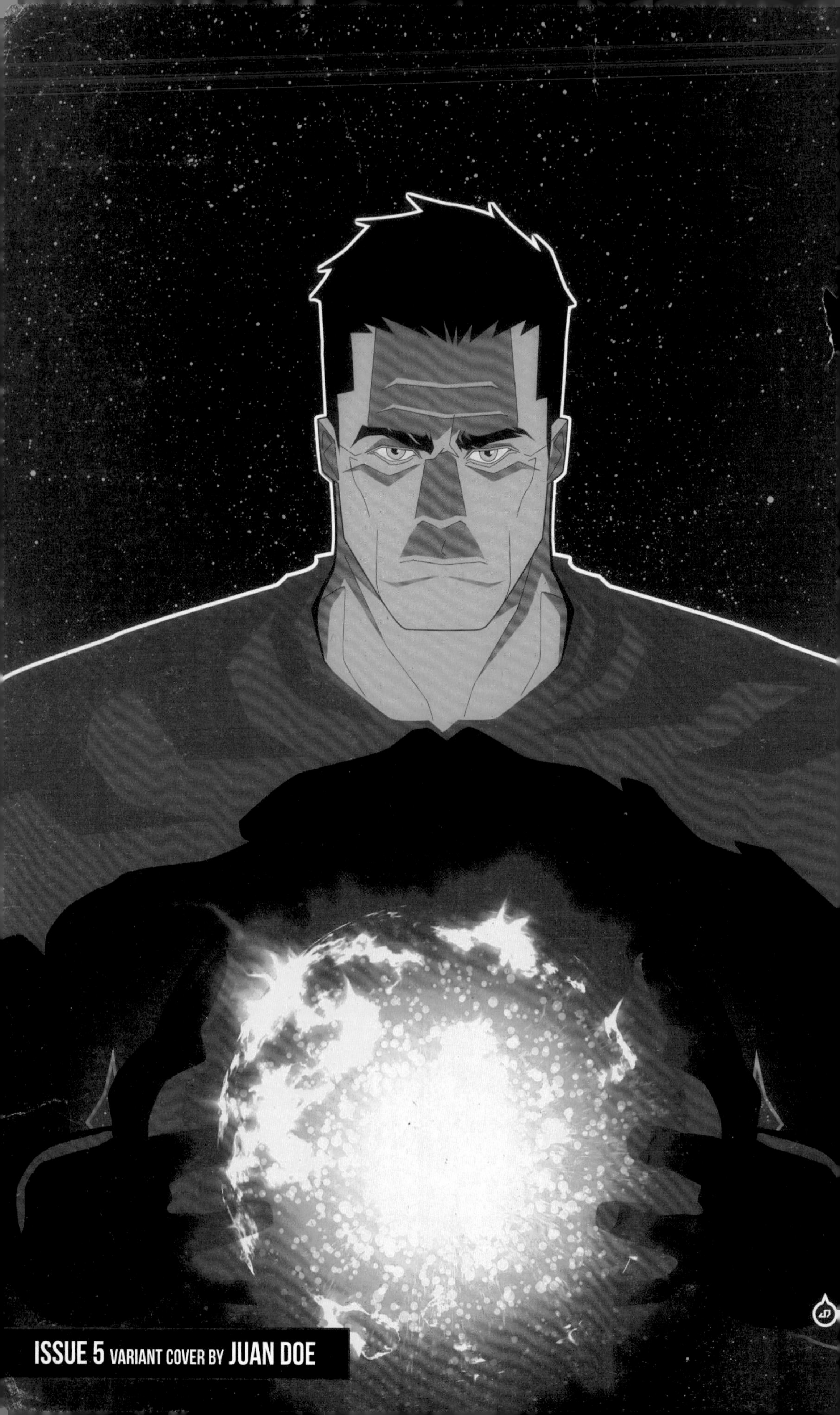

ISSUE 5 VARIANT COVER BY JUAN DOE